BIBLE ANIMALS

BIBLE ANIMALS
AND THE LESSONS
TAUGHT BY THEM
FOR CHILDREN

RICHARD NEWTON
Author of *Bible Promises, Bible Warnings,*
Heroes of the Early Church, Heroes of the Reformation

SOLID GROUND CHRISTIAN BOOKS
BIRMINGHAM, ALABAMA USA

SOLID GROUND CHRISTIAN BOOKS
715 OAK GROVE ROAD
HOMEWOOD AL 35209
205-443-0311
sgcb@charter.net
solid-ground-books.com

BIBLE ANIMALS
And the Lessons Taught by Them for Children

Richard Newton (1812-1887)

From 1894 edition by Oliphant, Anderson & Ferrier, Edinburgh

Cover design by Borgo Design, Tuscaloosa, AL
Contact them at borgogirl@bellsouth.net

Cover image from Ric Ergenbright.
View his excellent work at ricergenbright.com

ISBN 1-59925-102-7

Publisher's Preface to New Edition

In the Memoir of Richard Newton, written by his beloved son, the following is written about the very last sermon in this book called *Bible Animals*:

"One week before he died—on the afternoon of Ascension day—when he had been feeling particularly weak, he suddenly arose from the sofa on which he had been lying, and asked for a paper and glue. He wanted to paste something into this last sermon on 'The Dog.' He got up to his desk, wrote the correction, carefully pasted it upon the neat, clean sheet of paper, and then returned to his bed—having for the last time put his busy pen to his darling sermons."

Thus concluded the remarkable ministry of the man Spurgeon nicknamed "the Prince of Preachers to children." It has been the unspeakable privilege of Solid Ground Christian Books to bring the books of this gifted servant back into print for the first time in more than a century. It is our desire and goal to reprint all the children's titles that ministered to hundreds of thousands of children and adults in nearly 20 languages. May the God of all grace bless these efforts to the salvation of multitudes all over the world.

February 2007

CONTENTS.

——o——

SERMON		PAGE
I. The Lion,		7
II. The Sheep,		18
III. The Camel,		29
IV. The Horse,		42
V. The Deer,		56
VI. The Bee,		68
VII. The Eagle,		77
VIII. The Ant,		91
IX. The Bear,		102
X. The Stork,		113
XI. The Ass,		122
XII. The Elephant,		135
XIII. The Scorpion,		149
XIV. The Dove,		158
XV. The Monkey,		169
XVI. The Dog,		179

I.

THE LION.

'The lion is the strongest among beasts.'—PROVERBS xxx. 30.

WE enter now on a new course of sermons for the young. The subject of these sermons will be *Bible Natural History*. We shall take up one and another of the different beasts and birds mentioned in the Bible, and, in their habits and characters, try to find illustrations of some of the truths taught us in the Bible, and of the duties that spring out of those truths.

The first of the animals mentioned in the Bible that we will take up as our study is the Lion. Solomon tells us in our text that 'a lion is the strongest among beasts.' And this is true. We cannot look at the picture of a lion without seeing that he must be very strong. With a single stroke of his paw the lion can kill a dog, or a sheep, or a wolf. And when he has killed a horse or an ox, he can carry it or drag it away to his den with the greatest ease.

The length of a full-grown lion, from the tip of his nose to the end of his tail, is between seven and eight feet. Its height at its shoulders is about three feet. The male lion has a heavy mass of hair around its neck and head, which is called its mane. And when the lion stands up before us, with its eyes flashing, its mane rising, and its tail waving, it appears to be, as it really is, one of the finest-looking animals that God has made.

The roar of the lion is terrible. The Prophet Amos compares its roar to the voice of God when he says, 'The lion roareth, who will not fear? The Lord hath spoken, who can but prophesy?' (Amos iii. 8). It is not surprising to hear the lion called 'the king of beasts,' or 'the monarch of the forest.' In the Old Testament times there were plenty of lions in the land of Palestine, and nearly all the prophets spoke about them; but none are to be found there now. There are no lions in our country, or in England, except where they are found in menageries. Asia and Africa are the principal countries where lions live and flourish in these days.

7

Our sermon to-day will be about the lion and its lessons. And when we consider the habits and qualities of the lion, we find in them good illustrations of four important lessons which it will be well for us all to learn to practise.

The first of these is—THE LESSON OF MODERATION.

Notwithstanding the great strength of the lion, when he gets enough to eat he is satisfied, and does not go on killing either men or beasts, for the mere love of killing. But it is very different with some other animals. The wolf and the tiger, for example, are unlike the lion in this respect. They have no moderation. When they have had as much as they want to eat they are not satisfied, but will go on killing, just because they love to kill. The lion is satisfied when it has enough to eat, and here we have an illustration of its moderation.

In Wood's *Natural History* we find a story about a lion which shows us how true the point now before us is.

He tells us about a soldier belonging to an English regiment which was stationed at the Cape of Good Hope, in the southern part of Africa. This soldier had been told that up among the Dutch Boers, who lived in the interior of Southern Africa, there were fine opportunities of making money and of getting rich. This was what he very much wanted. So he made up his mind that he would desert from his regiment, and go up among the Dutch Boers, and try to make his fortune there. He watched for a favourable opportunity, and then he deserted and went.

Before going, however, he was careful to get a big bag filled with bread and meat, as his food for the journey, which would last for several days. In that part of Africa lions are very numerous. At night, when this soldier lay down to sleep on the ground, he put the bag which contained his provisions under his head for a pillow. On the second night of his journey he lay down to sleep, with his head on his bag of provisions. During that night, while he was fast asleep, a great lion came prowling around him. When the lion came near him, and smelled the provisions in the bag, he put forth his huge paw, and, pulling the bag from under the soldier's head, carried it off, and made a good supper for himself out of the contents of the bag. And when he had done this he was satisfied. He might have gone back, and sprung upon the sleeping soldier, and torn his body to pieces. But he had gotten something to eat, and that was enough for him. And in acting as he did, that lion was giving a good illustration of the lesson of moderation.

The Bible rule about moderation is given us by the Apostle Paul, in his letter to Timothy, when he says, 'Having food and raiment, let us be therewith content' (1 Timothy vi. 8).

But we often find it hard to learn this lesson; and yet we never can be happy until we do learn it. Here is a good illustration of this. We may call it—

ANNA'S BREAKFAST.

Anna was a little girl about ten years old, who had not learned the lesson of which we are speaking. One morning, on sitting down to breakfast, she said,—

'Mother, won't you tell Jane to bring me some honey?'

'There is none, my dear,' said her mother. 'I sent the last we had to a poor sick girl; but there's some nice syrup.'

'I don't like syrup,' said Anna, 'and if I can't have honey I won't eat my breakfast; I hate buckwheat cakes without honey.'

Mrs. Grey looked sadly at her little girl, and was about to speak to her, when the door opened, and Jane the cook came in, saying,—

'Please, ma'am, here's a poor little girl who wants something to eat.'

'Bring her in, and let me see her,' said Mrs. Grey.

Jane returned directly, leading a little girl about ten years old. She was very pale and thin, and very poorly dressed.

Mrs. Grey kindly led her to the fire, and then gave her some breakfast. In answer to Mrs. Grey's inquiries, she said her name was Mary Willis; that her father had gone to California a year ago; they had become so poor that they were obliged to live in a garret; Nelly the baby was crying for something to eat, and there was nothing to give it. 'So I asked mother to let me go out and beg this morning. It is the first time I ever begged. But I could not bear to see the dear baby crying for something to eat.'

Mrs. Grey left the room, and Anna, who had not spoken a word, helped the little girl to something which she thought she would like. Mrs. Grey soon returned with some warm clothes, in which she dressed Mary. Then she took a basket, and put into it some cold meat and bread, a tin pail full of milk with a tight cover, some tea and sugar, and told her she would go with her and see her mother. Anna, who felt she had done wrong, and had not yet spoken a word, asked if she might go. Her mother said 'Yes.' Then she ran to get her cloak and bonnet. Mary took the basket, feeling very happy to think that she was carrying something for her mother and the dear baby. Mrs. Grey and Anna followed her. They found Mrs. Willis, as Mary had said, living in a garret; but it was as nice and clean as could be. Mrs. Willis was sewing on sailors' shirts, for which she received sixpence each. She could only make two a day, the pay for which would be one shilling. All that this would bring her a week would be six shillings. She had to pay two shillings a week for her rent, and then there was only four shillings a week left for them to live upon.

While hearing all this, Mrs. Grey had given Nelly the baby some bread and milk for breakfast, which made her very happy. Then she arranged with Mrs. Willis to have Willie, Mary's brother, come to her house every morning, and do little jobs for her, and for which she would give him two shillings a week. That would pay for their rent, and she would try and get Mrs. Willis some more profitable work to do.

After tea that evening Anna was alone with her mother. She came and knelt by her side, and, hiding her face in her lap, she said,—

'Oh, mother, I see how very naughty I was this morning. Won't you please forgive me?'

Her mother stooped over her and kissed her. Then she kneeled down with her, and asked God to forgive her, and teach her hereafter to be content with such things as she had.

Anna went to bed that night repeating to herself a hymn her mother had taught her, of which these are the first two verses:

> Whene'er I take my walks abroad,
> How many poor I see!
> What shall I render to the Lord
> For all His gifts to me?

> Not more than others I deserve,
> Yet God has given me more;
> For I have food, while others starve,
> Or beg from door to door.

Anna never forgot the lesson she learned that day. It was the lesson of contentment, or being thankful for such things as we have.

And this is what we are now speaking of in connection with the lion. The first lesson we may learn from the lion is—the lesson of moderation.

The second lesson which the lion teaches us is—THE LESSON OF KINDNESS.

We do not generally take in the idea of kindness in connection with the lion. When we think of the size of the lion, of his great strength, of his huge, bristling mane, of his flashing eye, and of his terrific roar, we think how easy it would be for him to frighten or to kill animals or men; but to look for kindness towards other creatures, on the part of an animal like the lion, is something that we hardly expect to meet with.

And yet we do sometimes meet with very striking acts of

kindness. Here is an illustration of what I mean. The story to which I refer may be called—

THE LION'S PET.

Some years ago, a travelling circus, with a menagerie accompanying it, came to the city of Manchester in England, and remained there for some time.

Great crowds of people came together every day to see the strange sights which were to be seen there. Among those who came one day was a man with a little dog. This dog had just been beaten by another dog with which it had been fighting. The other dog was the larger of the two, and it was no wonder that the little thing should have been beaten. But the owner of the dog was in a perfect rage with it because it did not beat the other dog. He seized the poor creature, and, though it was bleeding and suffering from the effect of the fight, he shook it and beat it most cruelly. Then he hurried into the circus tent, and, going up to the front of the lion's cage, he thrust the dog through the iron bars, expecting to see the lion spring towards him, and devour him in a moment. But he did not do this.

The dog seemed to understand the danger he was in; for he crouched upon the floor, and crept away into a corner of the den, as far from the lion as he could get. The lion fixed his gaze upon him, but did not stir. At last the dog seemed to gather hope, and, crawling slowly towards 'the monarch of the forest,' he looked pleadingly up into his face, as if he meant to say, 'Please, won't you be kind to a poor dog?'

To the surprise of all who were looking on, the king of beasts, who could have crushed the dog to death with one stroke of his huge paw, gently drew the helpless creature to his side, and then raised his lordly head and neck above him, as if he meant to say, 'Don't be afraid, little doggie; I'm your protector now, and no one shall hurt you.'

And now the owner of the dog had gotten over his foolish anger towards him, and felt as if he would like to have him back again. So he went to the keeper of the tent, and asked him to give him his dog.

'You put him in the cage yourself,' said the keeper, 'and you can go and get him out.'

The man went up to the cage and called his dog; but the dog took no notice of him. It was just as if he had said, 'No, I don't want to come. I've got a better master than you, and I would rather stay with him.'

Then the old master called again and again; he whistled and he coaxed, but the dog took no notice of him. At last he got angry, and began to scold and threaten; then the lion looked towards the man with his eyes flashing fire, and gave one of his terrible roars. This frightened the man, who turned and ran away, while all the people in the tent laughed at him. The lion never would let the dog be taken away from him, and so they continued friends together as long as the dog lived.

Now that lion certainly did teach the lesson of kindness; and we ought to learn and practise this lesson, because of the good we can do by kindness.

Here is a good illustration of the power of kindness. This story may be called—

KINDNESS REWARDED.

A number of years ago, an officer of the English Government was stationed on duty in the Highlands of Scotland. In attending to the duties of his office, he had every day to walk a number of miles through the country. One day, in the course of his walk, without exactly knowing why, he felt a desire to look into a cattle-shed, which stood near the side of the road, in a lonely place, far away from any dwelling. On entering it, he found, to his surprise, a poor Irish labourer lying there. This man had been engaged during the summer in doing field-work in that part of the country. As he was on his way home to Ireland, he was taken suddenly sick, and this led him to go into the cattle-shed. He had been there a night and part of a day, and when the officer found out how much he was in want of food, he returned to his lodgings, and got for the poor Irish-man the food that he needed. Then he made him as comfortable as he could, and promised to call and see him again the next day. He kept on doing this for a number of days, till the poor man got well enough to start on his journey to Ireland.

About a year after this had taken place, the officer was removed to Ireland. Before he had been there long, he met in the street one day the very Irishman to whom he had shown so much kindness in Scotland. The poor man became almost wild with delight on seeing the officer, and shouted out at the top of his voice, '*Here's the man that saved my life!*' And in a little while all the people in that part of the country got to know this officer, and what he had done to their countryman. And the kindness of the officer to this man was the means of saving his own life several times; for, during the first year that he was in Ireland, a great famine prevailed there. This led to great suffering, and caused many deaths. On more than one occasion this officer found himself surrounded by men with pistols in their hands, who were about to kill him; but as soon as they saw who it was, they would cry out, '*Sure and you're the man who saved Pat Moony's life: we won't hurt you.*'

And all the time he remained in that district, he was known and spoken of by the people as the man who was kind to a poor sick Irishman, when far away from his home. This was indeed kindness rewarded. And so we see that the second lesson taught us by the lion is—the lesson of kindness.

The third lesson we may learn from the lion is—THE LESSON OF OBEDIENCE.

The one to be obeyed, above all others, is God. He tells us in the Bible what He wants us to do. In the Old Testament we have His ten commandments, and God expects us to show our obedience to Him by keeping these commandments. In the New Testament we are told, 'This is His commandment, that we should believe on His Son Jesus Christ.' And when we learn to love and serve Jesus, we are obeying God in the way in which He wants us to do it. But there is no Bible for the lions, which can tell them what God wants them to do. How then can they obey God? This is a question which may well be asked here. But, without preparing a Bible for the lions, God is able, in other ways, to make them understand what He wants them to do, or not to do. And when they mind what God tells them, in any way, then they obey God themselves, and teach us the lesson of obedience. We have a good illustration of this in what the Bible tells us about Daniel in the lions' den.

At that time Daniel was at the head of all the great princes in the kingdom of Babylon. Some of those wicked princes disliked him, because he was so pious and good. They wanted to find some fault with him, and try and get the king to take away his high office from him. But he was so faithful in the discharge of all his duties, that there was no fault for them to find with him.

Then they made up their minds to find fault with him about his religion. They knew that he was in the habit of praying to God three times a day. And so they got the king to pass a law that no one should offer a prayer to any god for thirty days; and that if any one did so, he should be cast into the den of lions. The king passed this law without thinking about Daniel. When Daniel knew that this law had been passed, he paid no attention to it, but went on praying to God three times a day, as he had been accustomed to do. Then his enemies accused him to the king of breaking the law of the kingdom, and demanded that he should be cast into the den of lions. The king was very fond of Daniel, and when he found how things had turned out, he blamed himself severely for passing such a foolish law, and tried hard to save Daniel from the lions. But he could not do this, for the law had to be executed; and so

Daniel was cast into the den of lions. The thought of this troubled the king so much that he could not sleep any all that night. As soon as it was light in the morning, he rose and dressed himself, and hastened to the lions' den, to see what had become of Daniel. To his surprise, he found him there alive and well. Then he cried out, 'O Daniel, servant of the living God, is thy God, whom thou servest continually, able to deliver thee from the lions?'

And Daniel said, 'O king, live for ever. My God hath sent His angel, and shut the lions' mouths, and they have not hurt me.'

Now the question that comes before us here is this: What did the angel do to the lions, to keep them from devouring Daniel? If he had put muzzles on their jaws, so that they could not open their mouths, we could easily understand it. But he did not do this. We can only think of one other thing which the angel did. He must have made those lions understand, in some way or other, we know not how, that it was the will of God that they must not hurt that man Daniel, who was put in their den. And when the lions knew this, they minded it. They obeyed God; and in doing this they taught you, and me, and all people the important lesson of obedience.

And here is an illustration outside of the Bible, just of the same kind. This story we may call—

THE LION'S SERMON.

A sermon with this singular title has been delivered in the Church of Saint Catherine Cree, Leadenhall Street, London, in the month of October, every year, since the reign of King Charles I., which is more than two hundred years ago. At the time just spoken of, there lived in London a wealthy merchant, whose name was Sir John Gayor.

He was an active member of the church above referred to, and gave large sums of money to help in carrying on the good work in which it was engaged. At one period of his life, he made up his mind, for purposes connected with his business, to undertake a long journey on the continent of Asia. This was then a very dangerous thing to do. In the course of that journey he met with many strange adventures. After his return home, he wrote a history of those adventures, which was printed. But the volume which contained that history was burned in the Great Fire of London. Yet the account of one interesting circumstance connected with that journey has been preserved, and it comes in very well to illustrate the point of our subject now before us.

One day, while travelling through Arabia, Sir John was

separated from his companions, and was obliged to travel by himself alone. As he was doing this, to his great alarm, he saw a huge, fierce-looking lion coming towards him. He had no gun with which to defend himself, and felt sure that the time had come for him to die, unless it should please God to protect and save him.

In a moment he kneeled down and engaged in earnest prayer. He asked the Lord mercifully to spare his life, and deliver him from the jaws of that hungry lion. While he was thus praying, the lion walked close up to him, and went prowling round him several times, and then quietly turned round and went away, without the slightest injury to that man of prayer.

Now, how can we account for this? Just in the same way in which Daniel accounted for his preservation from the lions in that den. God had sent His angel and shut the mouth of that Arabian lion, and made him feel that it was the command of God to him not to hurt that praying man. And this lion obeyed God, just as those lions in Babylon did.

And, on his return to England, Sir John gave £200 to the church above spoken of, on the condition that a sermon should be preached in that church every year in memory of God's goodness in saving him from the jaws of that lion.

And here we see that the third lesson which the lion teaches us is—the lesson of obedience.

This is the most important of all lessons for us to learn. Our happiness, our usefulness, and our salvation all depend upon it. Then let it be our earnest prayer that God may teach us to learn and practise this lesson.

The fourth lesson we may learn from the lion is—THE LESSON OF GRATITUDE.

We find no examples of this part of our subject in what we read in the Bible about lions; but outside of the Bible we do meet with such examples. Here are two which are just to the point. The first may be called—

A LION'S GRATITUDE TO HIS KEEPER.

Some years ago there was a menagerie staying at a town in Ireland, that used to be called Birr, on a river of that name, but which is now called Parsonstown. In this menagerie there was a large cage, in which a lion and a tiger were both kept together. The keeper had always been very kind in his treatment of them. The noble-hearted lion appreciated his kindness, and evidently felt grateful to him for it. But the kindness of the keeper seemed to have no effect upon the tiger. The time came unexpectedly, when the lion had an opportunity of showing his gratitude to the keeper, and he did so in a way that he would never be likely to forget.

One day the keeper had occasion to go into this den, as he was in the habit of doing, for the purpose of cleaning it. While he was thus occupied, the tiger sprang at him, knocked him down, and buried his teeth in the keeper's thigh, as if he intended to tear him in pieces. And he would soon have done this, if it had not been for the lion. But this grateful creature, as soon as he saw the trouble his kind keeper was in, sprang towards the tiger, and, seizing him by the neck, gave him a tremendous shake. This frightened him. In a moment he let go his hold on the keeper; and, as soon as the lion let him off, he sneaked away to the farthest corner of the cave, crouched down on the floor, and hid his head, as if he were ashamed of himself. Now, in acting as he did on this occasion, that noble lion was teaching the lesson of gratitude.

The other illustration of this part of our subject is a well-known story from the pages of Roman history. It dates back as far as the middle of the second century, and may be called—

ANDROCLES AND THE LION.

Androcles was the slave of a wealthy Roman citizen. He was very badly treated by his master, and at last he made up his mind to run away. He did so, and, getting down to the southern part of Italy, he managed in some way or other to get carried over to Africa, which was his native country. In travelling on foot through a forest one day, he saw a cave, and, being tired with his journey, he went into it to sit down and rest. As he was resting there, he saw a huge lion come into the cave. He was hobbling on three feet, and holding up one of his fore-feet, as if it was causing him great pain. Seeing a man in the cave, the lion came limping up to him, and held out his wounded foot as though he wanted to say, 'Please, sir, can you do anything to relieve me of the pain I am suffering from this foot?'

Androcles looked at it, and saw in a moment what was the trouble. There was a thorn in the foot, with a great swelling and inflammation around it. So he gently took away the thorn, and pressed out the clotted blood which had gathered round it. Then he cooled it by bathing it in the water from a spring near the mouth of the cave. This made the lion feel very comfortable, and it kindled in his heart a feeling of gratitude towards the man who had done him the great kindness. He looked at him tenderly, rubbed his head gently against the side of Androcles, leaped joyfully around him, and swung his great tail about, as if he was trying to say, 'I am very much obliged to you for your kindness in relieving my foot of its great pain.'

Then the lion stayed by Androcles, and became his companion in the cave. He used to go out hunting every day, and bring something home for them both to eat. In this way Androcles lived for some time. But at last he had to leave the cave and his friend the lion, and find something to do.

Several years after this he concluded to go back to Italy. But he had not been there long before his old master found him. Then he was put in prison, and was condemned to be thrown to the wild beasts on one of their great public holidays.

The Emperor and thousands of people were there to see the great sight. Androcles was led out into the amphitheatre, and a lion, which had been kept a good while without food, was let loose to devour him. The lion came bounding and roaring towards him, but when he got near to him, instead of springing on him and tearing him to pieces, he crouched at his feet, rubbed his head lovingly against his side, wagged his tail, and looked tenderly into his face. It was the *old lion of the African cave*. He remembered his kind friend, and felt grateful to him still. The Emperor was astonished on seeing this. He sent for Androcles to explain the mystery. He told the story of what had taken place in that cave in Africa. The Emperor was so pleased with what he heard that he pardoned Androcles, and gave him his liberty.

Here we see how well that lion had learned and taught the lesson of gratitude. And when we remember how much more Jesus has done for us than Androcles did for that lion, we should never forget what a debt of gratitude we owe to Him.

Here is a little story which shows us how we should feel on this subject. We may call it—

GRATITUDE FOR SALVATION.

A missionary in India went one Sabbath evening to the dying bed of one of his native converts. 'I understand,' said the dying man, 'that you have been preaching to-day about heaven. To-morrow I expect to be in heaven. The first thing I shall do on arriving there will be to go directly to the blessed Saviour, and thank Him with all my heart for causing you to leave your home in a Christian land, and come to tell us poor darkened heathens about Him, and the way to heaven. Then I shall go and sit down by the pearly gate, and wait till you come. As soon as you arrive, I will take you by the hand and lead you to the Saviour, and say to Him, " Blessed Lord, this is the man that taught me to know and love Thee, and showed me the way to this happy world." '

That man had learned the lesson of gratitude for the great blessing of salvation, and this lesson we should all try to learn.

Now, where is our text to-day? Proverbs xxx. 30. What are the words of the text? 'The lion is the strongest among beasts.' What is the sermon about? The lion and its lessons. How many of these lessons did we speak of? Four. What was the first? *The lesson of moderation.* What was the second? *The lesson of kindness.* What was the third? *The lesson of obedience.* And what was the fourth? *The lesson of gratitude.*

And if we hope to learn and practise these lessons, our constant prayer to God must be, in the language of one of the beautiful Collects, 'that we may both perceive and know what things we ought to do, and also may have grace and power faithfully to fulfil the same, through Jesus Christ our Lord. Amen.'

II.

THE SHEEP.

'I am the Good Shepherd: my sheep hear my voice, and they follow me.'—JOHN x. 14, 27.

THE next of the animals mentioned in the Bible of which we wish to speak, is the sheep. This is a very different animal from the one we considered last, namely, the lion. It is very different in size. It has none of the lion's strength or courage. The lion is a wild animal that has never been of any real use to men. But the sheep is now, and always has been, a tame, domestic animal, and a very useful one. It is useful for its wool, which is employed for making clothing, for its milk, and for its flesh, which forms one of the most wholesome articles of food that God has given to men.

The sheep is the first animal particularly mentioned in the Bible. We find it spoken of in the fourth chapter of Genesis, where we are told that 'Abel was a keeper of sheep.' Sheep are spoken of more frequently in the Bible than any other animal. After a partial examination of this subject, I was going to say that they are spoken of about one hundred and fifty times in the Bible. But just then I was reading what an English clergyman had written on this subject, when I found he said that they are mentioned in the Bible about five hundred times.

In the early times spoken of in the Bible, the sheep which the patriarchs owned formed one of the principal sources of their wealth. We are told of Job, that in the latter part of his life he had fourteen thousand sheep.

We cannot help feeling an interest in a sheep when we look at it. Some of them have horns, and others have none.

The nice soft coat of fleecy wool which the sheep wears, the smoothly-rounded form of its limbs, and the pleasing expression of its patient, quiet-looking face, give it a very attractive appearance. And then there is a kindliness of feeling and a degree of good common sense often found marking the sheep, which are well illustrated by the following little incident :—

Some time ago, a boy about fourteen years old was riding on a pony near the village of Vinsgath, in one of the Shetland Islands. As he was going slowly along the road, he saw a sheep coming out from a field. It came right up to the side of the pony, and then stood still and looked up into his face, and kept bleating mournfully.

It seemed to the boy as if the poor sheep was trying to say, 'Won't you please come and help me?' He felt sure that there was something wrong.

So, getting off from the pony, he fastened it to a tree, and then went along with the sheep. It led him through the field till they came to the bank of a large pond.

On the side of this bank there was a little lamb belonging to the sheep, which had its foot caught fast in a hole. The poor thing was still living, but stiff and cold.

The boy took hold of the lamb, and after some little trouble succeeded in getting its foot loose, and then he laid the lamb down on the grass. As soon as this was done, the mother sheep went and lay down by its side to warm it and give it some milk. But, while doing this, she looked gratefully towards the boy, and kept bleating out her thanks to him, till he mounted his pony and rode off.

But the chief source of our interest in the sheep is that they were used by the Jews as their principal sacrifices to God, and that Jesus is called 'the Lamb of God, that taketh away the sins of the world.'

And then it is a matter of great interest to us to know that Jesus calls His people His sheep, and compares Himself to their Shepherd when He says, 'I am the Good Shepherd, and know my sheep, and am known of mine.'

We cannot consider the sheep here without considering the shepherd too. And so the subject of our sermon to-day will be—

THE GOOD SHEPHERD AND HIS SHEEP.

And in studying this subject there are two questions for us to answer. The first is, WHAT THE GOOD SHEPHERD DOES FOR HIS SHEEP? The other is, WHAT HE EXPECTS HIS SHEEP TO DO FOR HIM?

We are first to consider what the Good Shepherd does for His sheep? He does two things for them.

The first thing that the Good Shepherd does for His sheep is—
TO PROTECT THEM.

Sheep are exposed to many dangers, from which they are not able to protect themselves. When David was a shepherd, he tells us of a lion and a bear, that each came and stole away a lamb from his flock ; and how he went after the wild beasts, and slew them, and saved his lambs. And this is just what Jesus, the Good Shepherd, does for His sheep. He protects them from Satan, their great enemy, 'who goeth about as a roaring lion, seeking whom he may devour.' And in the same way He protects them from all their enemies, and from every danger. Here are some of the precious promises which He gives for His people, in view of the dangers which surround them. In one place He says to each of His people, 'I will never leave thee nor forsake thee.' In another place He says, 'The Lord shall preserve thy going out and thy coming in from this time forth, for evermore.' And there are multitudes of such sweet promises in the Bible. And so we see that under the promised protection of the Good Shepherd, the sheep are always safe.

Here are some illustrations of this part of our subject. Our first story may be called—

RUN OVER.

A Christian mother who lived in the city of New York, in very humble circumstances, had only one child, a little boy about seven years old, whom she had taught to know and love the Saviour. One day, when this good mother was going quietly on with her work at home, she was startled by a loud knock at the door of her humble dwelling.

On opening the door she received this alarming message : 'Hurry away to the police station ; your little boy has been run over.' She was terribly frightened, and, hastening as fast as she could to the station-house, on arriving there she found her little boy surrounded by strangers. The doctor had been sent for, but had not yet arrived. She was told that the wheels of a large carriage had gone over his foot, but, on examining it carefully, she was surprised to find no real injury about the foot.

'Why, Willie darling, how was it possible for the wheel of the carriage to have gone over your foot, and not have crushed it ?' The child looked tenderly up into his mother's face, and said,— 'Mamma dear, I guess God must have put it in a hollow place.'

This shows what faith that little boy had in the protection which Jesus, the Good Shepherd, has promised to exercise over His sheep. He always has 'a hollow place' to put them in when danger is near.

Our next story may be called—

NOT AFRAID OF SATAN.

A little boy came to his father one day, looking very much in earnest, and asked this question : 'Father, is Satan stronger than I am ?'

'Yes, my boy,' said the father.

'Is he stronger than you, father ?'

'Yes, my boy, he is stronger than your father, or any other man.'

'Is he stronger than Jesus, father ?'

'No, my boy,' said the father. 'Jesus is ever so much stronger than he is.'

The little fellow, as he turned away, said, with a smile, 'Then I am not afraid of him.'

That boy felt sure that the Good Shepherd in whom he trusted would protect him from any harm that Satan might try to do him.

Here is another story, which may be called—

A LITTLE GIRL'S FAITH IN THE GOOD SHEPHERD'S LOVE.

This little girl was about nine years old, and lived in Colorado. One afternoon she was trying to bring some calves home. She was led astray by them, and lost her way in the forest.

Night came on, a chilly November night, and, with strange calmness, she kept walking slowly on till morning, not knowing where she was. At last, in God's providence, she reached a farmer's house a long distance away from her home, and there was safe.

Many questions were asked her about how she got through the night. In answer to these she said, 'The wolves kept close to my heels, and snapped at my feet; but I remembered how my mother had taught me always to pray to God for protection when I was in danger. I did so pray, and then I knew that the wolves couldn't hurt me, because God wouldn't let them.'

How sweet that little girl's faith was in that protection which the Good Shepherd exercises over His sheep !

We may close this part of our subject with some sweet lines about trusting God :—

Trust God's wisdom thee to guide,
Trust His goodness to provide;

Trust His saving love and power,
Trust Him every day and hour ;
Trust Him as the only Light,
Trust Him in the darkest night ;
Trust in sickness, trust in health,
Trust in poverty and wealth ;
Trust in joy and trust in grief,
Trust His promise for relief ;
Trust in living, dying, too,
Trust Him all thy journey through !

The first thing that the Good Shepherd does for His sheep is —to protect them.

The second thing which the Good Shepherd does for His sheep is —TO PROVIDE FOR THEM.

This is something which the sheep cannot do for themselves, and unless the shepherd does it for them they must perish. Hence David, when speaking of the Lord as the Shepherd of His sheep, says that 'He leadeth them beside the still waters, and maketh them to lie down in green pastures.'

And when the sheep have still water to drink, and green pastures to lie down in, they have all the provision made for them that they can need. And this is just what Jesus the Good Shepherd does for His sheep. He supplies all their wants according to the riches of His grace. He never leaves them nor forsakes them, till He has done all that He has spoken to them of in His holy Word.

Here are some illustrations of the way in which the Good Shepherd provides for His sheep. Our first story may be called—

GOD DOES HEAR PRAYER.

One bitter cold night, in the winter of 1873, a Christian widow, living in Connecticut, was in great distress. Her money was all gone, and she had nothing with which to get food for her family the next day. She could not sleep any that night. At midnight she arose, and engaged in earnest prayer. She told the Lord about her trouble, and asked Him to provide for her relief. That same night, a cousin of hers, whom she had not seen for several years, found himself so restless that he could not sleep. Then he got up, and, being a Christian man, he engaged in earnest prayer, and especially asked God to bless the suffering poor. While he was praying, the thought of his cousin came into his mind. He felt sure that she was in want, and made up his mind to send her £10 the first thing in the morning.

He did this. And here we see how the Good Shepherd made provision for the wants of one of His needy sheep.

Our next illustration may be called—

GRANNY'S STORY.

'One afternoon,' said a Christian lady to a friend, 'I had taken a long walk, and, feeling tired, I called at a cottage by the roadside, and asked if I might rest there awhile.

' "With pleasure, ma'am," said a clean, plain-looking, middle-aged woman. "We are just having tea, and if you will take a cup with us, we shall be glad."

'I did so, with pleasure ; and found, from conversation with them, that they were a happy Christian family. In the corner, by the fireplace, sat the old grandmother of the family, or "granny," as they called her. She was crippled with rheumatism, and unable to do anything. I spoke a few kind words to her, and this was what she said in reply,—

' "Some folks ask me if I don't find it hard to have to sit here helpless, from morning till night ; but I ain't served the Lord Jesus fifty years without finding out that His grace is sufficient for all the trials of this life. Ah ! I could tell you many a story of His faithfulness. But there is one answer to prayer in particular that I never can forget.

' "My husband hadn't been dead a year, when all my five children were stricken down with scarlet fever. Not a neighbour dare come near us. I nursed them all myself, and no one but the doctor crossed the threshold for seven weeks. Well, one Saturday night, I had eaten the last bit of bread for my supper, and put the last piece of coal on the fire, and I'd not a penny left to buy more.

' "I got my Bible and opened at the 49th chapter of Jeremiah, and read on till I came to the verse which says, 'Leave thy fatherless children, I will preserve them alive ; and let thy widows trust in me.' I stopped there, and knelt down and told the Lord all about my trouble. Then I went to bed. About six o'clock in the morning I heard a knock at the door. I went down and opened it. A strange man stood there with a big basket.

' "Does Mrs. Grant live here ?

' "Yes, said I.

' "My missis has sent this, he answered.

' "Before I could get over my surprise, he'd set the basket down, and walked off as fast as he could.

' "When I opened the basket, there was everything in it that I needed : tea, sugar, bread, butter, candles, and soap. And the strangest thing about it is, that from that day to this I've never found out where it came from, except I know that the Lord sent it.

' "But that wasn't all that happened. Just about nine o'clock on that same Sunday evening, there was another knock at the door. When I opened it, Farmer Griggs, one of the deacons of our chapel, was there.

'"Mrs. Grant, says he, we're all very sorry for you, and if you'll accept it, we made a collection for your benefit to-night; and when this is gone let us know, and there'll be more, for we ain't agoing to let you starve!

'"And there, in the moonlight, he counted into my hand two pounds ten shillings and sixpence."'

Now certainly that good old granny had a very satisfactory, practical proof that Jesus, the Good Shepherd, does provide for His sheep!

And thus we have considered the two things which the Good Shepherd does for His sheep. *He protects them*, and *He provides for them.*

And now we come to consider the other question before us; this is, what the Good Shepherd expects His sheep to do for Him? He expects them to do two things for Him.

The first of these is, He expects them—TO HEAR HIS VOICE. 'My sheep hear my voice,' He says.

In this country, or in England, sheep never know the voice of the shepherd, and cannot tell the difference between his voice and that of any other man. But it was very different in the land where the Bible was written. There the shepherds gave names to their sheep, and when they called them they would answer to the call, and come at once to the shepherd. And Jesus was referring to this when He said that the shepherd 'goeth before his sheep, for they know his voice and follow him; but a stranger will they not follow, for they know not the voice of strangers.' We have a good illustration of this in the following incident:—

Some time ago, in a large village of Palestine, a certain man had a sheep of which he was very fond, and which was a great pet with him. At one time he missed it from the little fold where he used to keep it, in a field adjoining his house. On making inquiries about it, he found that one of his neighbours had it in his field. He asked to have it returned to him, but the man who had it refused to do this; then the owner of the sheep went to the judge who had been appointed to see that the law was properly executed in that part of the country, and brought a charge against his neighbour of stealing his sheep. The judge had the two men brought into court for trial, and the sheep was brought with them. Each of them declared that the sheep belonged to him. But how could it be proved which of those two men was really the owner of the sheep?

After thinking over the matter for a little while, the judge concluded that the best way of settling the question would be by appealing to the sheep itself, and making use of the knowledge which those animals have of the voice of their shepherd or keeper. So he told one of his officers to take the sheep into an adjoining room, and leave it there with the door ajar, so that it could hear when called. Then he told the man who was charged with stealing the sheep to call it.

The man called again and again, but the sheep took no notice of the call.

Then the judge told the other man—the real owner of the sheep—to call it. He called it by the name he had given to it, and which the sheep knew very well. In a moment it pricked up its ears and began to cry—baa ! baa ! as if it wanted to say, 'Here I am.' Then it hastened towards the door of the room in which it was, pushed the door open, and went straight up to him, baaing as it went.

This settled the matter at once. The judge told this man to take the sheep, as it was certainly his ; then he made the other man pay a fine for stealing and lying.

Here we see that the sheep knows the voice of its keeper, or shepherd, when he speaks to it ; so, if we are the sheep of Jesus—the Good Shepherd—we shall hear His voice when He speaks to us. Jesus has many ways of making His sheep hear His voice. Sometimes He does this in ways that seem very wonderful. We have only room for one illustration here. We may call it—

HOW A WANDERING SHEEP WAS MADE TO HEAR THE SHEPHERD'S VOICE.

Some years ago, the captain of an East India vessel was attacked, while cruising in the Indian Ocean, by a piratical vessel. The attack was so sudden and unlooked for that the merchant vessel fell an easy prey into the hands of the pirates. The captain and several of the crew were slain in the conflict, and the rest were bound in chains and put into the pirates' boats to be taken to their vessel. Then the captain of the pirates and some of his men were going down into the cabin to see what treasures they could find before burning the vessel.

On going down the companion-way, a soft, low voice was heard in prayer. The captain motioned to his men to remain on deck, while he went quietly down the stairs to find out where the voice came from. Stooping down, he peeped into a door which was ajar, and there he saw kneeling a fair young mother, with a beautiful boy at her side. One arm was clasped fondly around her child, and the other was lifted up in earnest supplication. And these were the words which the pirate heard her utter in a voice of melting agony, as he saw the tears rolling down her cheeks : 'O God of all mercy, save the life of my dear child, if such be Thy holy will ; but rather let him perish now by the assassin's knife, than fall a living prey into such hands, to be trained to a life of sin and shame. Let him die now, if such be Thy decree ; but oh, let him not live to dishonour Thee, and perish at last eternally !'

The voice ceased, choked with tears of agony. And there stood the pirate, perfectly overwhelmed by the tumult of his own feelings. His thoughts went back to the scenes of his childhood. He had had a pious mother. Her prayers and instructions, for so many years forgotten, rose up before him then, and God's Spirit sent such an arrow of conviction to his heart, that, instead of carrying out his murderous designs, he sank upon his knees, and with heart-breaking agony cried out, 'God be merciful to me, a sinner !'

On rising from his knees, he assured the lady that no harm should be done to her. Then he went on deck, unbound the captive crew, and, restoring them to their ship, returned with his men to their own vessel.

Shortly after this, he surrendered himself to the British East India Government. The Government appointed a trial for him, but, before the time for the trial came, he was taken with fever, from which he died after a few days' sickness. Before his death he made a full confession of the crimes of his past life, with the deepest penitence, and he died humbly trusting in Jesus for the pardon of his sins, and for entrance into heaven.

Now, here is a case in which the Good Shepherd caused His voice to be heard by a sheep that had wandered far, far away from His fold. That was in answer to a mother's prayers. But suppose that pirate had listened to the voice of the Good Shepherd when he was a boy in his mother's home, only think how different a life he would have lived on earth ! Oh, how different a reward he would have in heaven! My dear young friends,—lambs in the fold of Jesus,—oh, listen to the voice of the Good Shepherd now, and His blessing will follow you all your days. You will find it true, in the words of the hymn, that

'T will save you from a thousand snares,
  To mind religion young ;
Grace will preserve your following years,
  And make your virtues strong.

The first thing which the Good Shepherd expects us to do is—to hear His voice. Oh, pray God to help you to do this !

But there is another thing which the Good Shepherd expects His sheep to do, and that is—TO FOLLOW HIM. In our text, Jesus says, 'My sheep hear my voice, and they follow me.' The sheep set us an example here, not only in *hearing* the shepherd, but in *obeying* him. With us, in this country, when a shepherd wants his sheep to go from one place to another, he *drives* them before him. But it is different in the Eastern countries. There, the shepherd calls to his sheep, and goes before them, and they know his voice, and follow him. And here we may learn from the sheep one of the most important of all lessons. It will do us no good to hear the voice of Jesus, the heavenly Shepherd, unless we obey it by following Him. We read in the Bible, 'Blessed are they that hear the Word of God, and keep it,' or do it. Again we read, 'Blessed are they that do His commandments, that they may have a right to the tree of life.'

Here are some examples of following the Good Shepherd, as well as of hearing His voice. The first may be called—

FORGOTTEN, YET NOT LOST.

'What a sermon we had last Sunday!' said a poor woman, who kept a small shop, to a customer, who came in to buy something during the week.

'What was the text?' asked her friend.

'Indeed I can't remember that,' said the woman.

'Well, what was the sermon about?' was the next question.

'I can't exactly tell that,' said the woman; 'but I know this, that the very first thing I did on coming home was to burn up my bad bushel and to throw away my short weights.'

She had been cheating her customers by using false weights and measures. What she had heard in church that day made her see and feel that this was wrong, and she made up her mind not to do so any more. *That* was *following* the voice of the Good Shepherd.

Our next story may be called—

RETURNING GOOD FOR EVIL.

'I'll pay him back again, see if I don't!' said Willie Jackson, with a flushed and angry face, as he came running into the room where his mother sat sewing, one afternoon.

'And who are you going to pay back?' asked his mother.

'Why, Walter Jones, because he took my marbles, and ran away with them,' said Willie.

'Well, I hope you'll pay him back in a good way,' said his mother.

Willie hung down his head, and said nothing; for he was ashamed to let his mother know of the mean way in which he thought of treating Walter.

'I am afraid you intend to act just as badly as Walter has done. Think better of it, my dear boy, and return good for evil. If you don't forgive, you can't ask to be forgiven.'

Before going to bed that night, Willie kneeled down as usual by his mother's side, to say his prayers. In closing with the Lord's Prayer, when he came to the place where it says, 'Forgive us our trespasses as we forgive those who trespass against us,' he stopped.

'Why don't you go on?' asked his mother.

'I can't,' said Willie, 'because I haven't forgiven Walter.'

'Then you had better ask Jesus to help you to forgive him now,' said his mother.

Willie did so. Then he finished the Lord's Prayer, and went to bed, feeling very happy.

And in doing that, Willie was not only hearing the voice of the Good Shepherd, but was following it, and this is what He expects us all to do.

I have just one other story. We may call it—

HOW A SUNDAY SCHOOL BOY FOLLOWED JESUS.

A poor old mother was going to visit her daughter, in the city of London, one evening, just about dark. She was carrying a bundle which was rather heavy for her. As she went on, a little boy came up to her, and said, 'Please, ma'am, may I carry that bundle for a penny? I'm trying to earn a little money, for we have nothing to eat at home.' She let him carry it, and when they reached her daughter's house it was quite dark. All the money she had in her pocket was half a crown and two pennies. An English penny and a half-crown piece are both about the same size. And so, by mistake, the old mother gave the boy the half-crown piece, instead of the penny. On going into the house, she found that her daughter had nothing for themselves or the children to eat. She gave her daughter the two pennies to get some bread for the children, and went to bed herself without any supper, but praying that God would send them something for the morrow.

Early the next morning, there was a knock at the door. The daughter opened the door, and found a little boy standing there, who said,—

'Didn't I bring a bundle here last night, for an old lady?'

'Yes, you did.'

'Where is she?'

'Up-stairs.'

'Please ask her to come down, for I want to see her.'

The old mother soon made her appearance, when the boy said,—

'Please, ma'am, do you know that you gave me a half-crown last night, instead of a penny? Because you did, and here it is.

'Well, my boy, I did just as you say, and I am very much obliged to you for bringing it back. But I would like to know how you came to do this, for I thought you had nothing to eat at home.'

'Yes, we are very bad off,' said the boy, brightening up as he spoke; 'but, you see, I go to Sunday school, and I love Jesus, and am trying to follow Him, so you see I can't be dishonest.'

Yes, that boy was really hearing the voice of the Good Shepherd, and was following Him.

Now, where is our text to-day? John x. 27. What are the words of the text? 'I am the Good Shepherd: my sheep hear my voice, and they follow me.' What is the sermon about? The Good Shepherd and His sheep. How many questions did we have to answer? Two. What was the first? What the Good Shepherd does for His sheep? How many things did we speak of? Two. What are these? *He protects them, and provides for them.*

And what was the other question we considered? What the Good Shepherd expects His sheep to do for Him? *He expects them to hear His voice, and to follow Him.*

And now, in closing this service, let us all lift up our hearts to Jesus, and say, each one for himself or herself, 'O Thou Good Shepherd, teach me to hear Thy voice, and to follow Thee!'

III.

THE CAMEL.

'The camel.'—LEVITICUS xi. 4.

In going on with our study of Bible natural history, the next animal that we take up is the camel. We never hear of the camel in a wild state, but only know of it as a tame and useful animal.

The first mention made of it in the Bible, is in the time of Abraham. We are told that 'Abraham had sheep, and oxen, and asses, and camels.' And camels formed a large part of the wealth of the people who lived in the East, at the time when the Bible was written. This is clear when we are told about Job, that 'he had six thousand camels.' The camels were used by the Eastern people both for bearing burdens, and also for travelling purposes.

There are two kinds of camels spoken of: one is called the

common camel, and has but one hump on its back ; the other is called the Bactrian camel, and this has two humps. The camel stands about six feet high up to its shoulders. Its strength is such that it can carry a burden of from five to six, and even to eight hundred pounds. And its ability to do this is one of the chief things that help to make it so useful to the people of the countries in which it is found. And in studying the history of the camel, we may learn two lessons. One of these is about *an interesting truth ;* the other is about *an important duty.*

The interesting truth that we are taught by the camel is about— THE GOODNESS OF GOD.

We see this illustration in the wonderful way in which the camel has been prepared by God for usefulness among the people who have to travel through the great deserts of Arabia, Egypt, and Africa. In those countries they have been called ' the ships of the desert.' And they may well be so called, because the people of those countries could no more travel over their great deserts without camels, than we could travel over our oceans without ships. And the wonderful way in which God has prepared the camels to bear the hardships they have to meet, in journeying through the deserts, affords us a striking illustration of His goodness.

We see this in several things about the camel. For one thing, we see this in the feet of the camel. If they had hard hoofs, like those of the horse or the cow, they would be unfitted for travelling through the deserts. The hot sand would make their feet sore ; and at every step taken they would sink deep into the sand. But the feet of the camel are covered with hard flesh and a tough skin, which acts like a cushion and keeps it from sinking into the softest sand over which it has to travel ; while neither the heat of the sand, nor the sharp stones often mingled with it, will do them any harm. This is a proof of God's goodness.

And then, the knees of the camel, as well as its feet, show the same thing. The camel stands so high that when the load has to be put on its back, or taken off, it is necessary for it to kneel down. And in doing this so constantly, unless its knees were especially protected, the hot sand on which it kneels, and the sharp stones found among it, would make the camel so lame that it would be unable to walk. But God has furnished the knees of the camel with something just like a tough pad or cushion, so that it can kneel as often as may be desired, without receiving any injury, either from the sand or stones.

And we see the goodness of God again, in the way in which He has arranged the stomach of the camel. It has one stomach, just like that of any other animal, which receives the water it

The Bactrian Camel.

drinks and the food it eats, and digests them. But then, in addition to this, the camel has a second stomach, which is like a water vessel, stowed away behind its other stomach. This will hold from ten to twelve gallons of water. When the camel is about starting on a journey, it will drink as much as it needs, to quench its thirst at the time. Then it will drink on until its other stomach is filled with water. And with this as its supply, it will start on its journey, and travel on for four or five days, over the burning sands of the desert, without ever caring for another drink.

And then there is another thing about the camel, which illustrates the goodness of God, and that is the hump upon its back. This hump is made up of a fatty sort of substance. And in travelling over the desert, when the camel is not able to get the food it needs in any other way, it falls back on what this hump contains, and finds its support in that. How wonderful this is!

And we find similar illustrations of God's goodness in connection with other animals. I will only speak now of one of these, and that is, the surprising way in which God provides for the protection of young deer. The deer have young ones every year. These, in their wild state, are surrounded by dogs, and wolves, and bears, which love to prey upon them. 'And the reason why the deer are not all destroyed while they are young,' says an old Canadian hunter, 'is that no dog, or wolf, or other animal, can smell the track of the deer, while they are too young to take care of themselves. I have often seen this proved,' said the hunter, 'by facts which cannot be denied. I have taken my dogs to the place where I have seen young deer pass by, not more than half an hour before, and they were utterly unable to follow their track, by the scent or smell of the young creatures. But if I take my dogs to the place where I had seen an old deer pass, half a day before, they would instantly smell the track, and follow it.' How strikingly this illustrates the goodness of God! For if the dogs and wolves could follow the track of the young deer as easily as they do that of the older ones, there would soon be an end of the deer, for the young ones would be all destroyed. This is a striking illustration of the goodness of God. And when we think of it, we may take up David's words, and say, 'O praise the Lord for His goodness!'

And I suppose we can all remember something connected with our own experience, which illustrates the goodness of God, in reference to ourselves, personally. I remember one such incident in my own history. I am not in the habit of speaking of myself in these sermons, but I must ask to be excused for doing so now. There is an incident connected with my experience, when I was a little boy, which may come in very well to illustrate the goodness of God.

I was born in Liverpool, England. One day, when I was about six years old, as I was going home from school, there was quite an excitement in the street. It happened that a bull had been taken into a slaughter-house in that neighbourhood, to be killed. They had fastened a rope around his horns, in the usual way. This rope was then put through an iron ring in the floor of the slaughter-house, the bull's head was drawn down to the floor, and a man standing by hit it a heavy blow with an axe which he held in his hands. It generally happened that the blow thus given would cause the animal to fall to the ground, when he would be slaughtered. But in this case it was not so. The blow of the axe, instead of killing the bull, or of knocking him down, only made him angry. He gave a violent jerk, which broke the rope that bound him, and he ran off into the street. Then he went racing along the street as fast as he could go, swinging his tail about, and bellowing as loudly as he could. This made a great excitement. I remembered to have seen men go out into the middle of the street, when a horse was running away, and stop him by standing before him and swinging round their arms. Then I thought I would try and stop that bull in the same way. So I went out into the middle of the street when the bull was coming near, and tried to stop him by swinging round my arms, as I had seen the men do. But the bull never minded me at all. He came bellowing on. When he got quite near to me, I turned and ran away from him. After running a little while, I looked round to see how near he was to me. But just as my head was turned toward him, he struck me on the forehead with one of his horns. This knocked me down on the ground. Then he took hold of my jacket and tore it off, and went on his way. The bull's horn struck my forehead about an inch above my left eye. If the horn had struck me an inch lower, it would have gone through my eye into the brain, and would have killed me. The mark of that wound is here on my forehead now. It has been there all my life. And when in shaving, or brushing my hair, I stand before the looking-glass and see that mark, it makes me think of the goodness of God in preserving my life when I was a little boy.

And then we have illustrations of His goodness all around us. Look at the beautiful green colour of the grass which covers the fields, and of the lovely blue that mantles the sky ; we see the goodness of God in these, for green and blue are the pleasantest colours that we can look upon. Suppose that the trees of the forest and the grass of the fields were always as white as snow, and that the colour of the sky was a blazing red or scarlet, how trying it would be for us to have to gaze on them when the moonday sun was shining! How good it was in God to make the fields green and the sky blue! And as we walk about in the country, everything that we meet with tells us that God is good.

> God is good! Each perfumed flower,
> The smiling field, the dark green wood,
> The insect fluttering for an hour,—
> All things proclaim that God is good.
>
> I hear it in the rushing wind,
> Hills that have for ages stood,
> And clouds, with gold and silver lined,
> Are still repeating, God is good.
>
> Each little rill, that many a year
> Has the same verdant path pursued,
> And every bird, in accents clear,
> Joins in the song that God is good.
>
> The restless sea, with haughty roar,
> Calms each wild wave and billow rude
> Retreats submissive from the shore,
> And swells the chorus, God is good,
>
> The countless hosts of burning stars,
> Sing His praise with light renewed;
> The rising sun each day declares,
> In rays of glory, God is good.
>
> The moon that walks in brightness, says,
> God is good. And man, endued
> With power to speak his Maker's praise,
> Should still repeat that 'God is good.'

And God is so full of goodness, that even when He sends trials upon His people, He sends them for their good. Here is an illustration of this. We may call it—

THE GOODNESS OF GOD IN AFFLICTION.

A Sunday-school teacher had a moveable alphabet, which he used in his class to spell out the most important truth taught in the lesson they were studying. One day, the lesson which he wished them to remember was this: 'The Lord is good to all.' He spelled this out with his letters, and then asked each scholar to repeat it. One little fellow in the class refused to repeat it. The teacher asked him his reason for doing this. He said, 'I don't want to repeat that, because it's not true. God is not good to father or me. He has taken my little brother away, and father is at home crying about it.' The teacher explained to him that God had taken his little brother away not in anger, but in love. He had taken him to that bright

heavenly home, which He was preparing for all His people.
'And now, my dear boy,' said the teacher, 'if you and your
father only learn to love and serve Jesus, He will take you to
meet your brother there, and be happy with him for ever.'
The little boy said, 'Oh, let me go and tell my father about
that !' Then he ran home and told his father what the teacher
had said. And the end of it was that the boy and his father
were both led to seek the Saviour, and became Christians. And
then they saw and felt that even the affliction which had come
upon them in the loss of that dear son and brother, God had
sent in His goodness.

And so we may well feel interested in studying the camel,
because it illustrates for us the important truth of—the goodness
of God.

There is one passage in our Saviour's life in which He speaks
of the camel in a way that is not generally understood, and
which it may therefore be well to speak of here.

One day a man came to Jesus, and asked what he must do
to inherit eternal life. Jesus referred him to the commandments. The man said that he had kept all these from his youth.
Then Jesus, knowing him to be a rich man, said to him, 'Go
and sell that thou hast, and give to the poor, and thou shalt
have treasure in heaven ; and come and follow me. But when
the young man heard that saying, he went away sorrowful :
for he had great possessions. Then Jesus said, How hardly
shall they that have riches enter into the kingdom of heaven.
Again I say unto you, It is easier for a camel to go through the
eye of a needle, than for a rich man to enter into the kingdom
of heaven.' Now if we regard our Saviour as speaking literally
here of an ordinary needle, then we must consider Him as
teaching that it is utterly impossible for a rich man ever to
enter heaven. But this is not so ; for we know that there are
some rich men who are earnest, faithful Christians, and who
are sure to go to heaven. What Jesus meant to teach us when
He used these words was, that riches bring so many temptations
to those who have them as to make it *very hard* for them to get
to heaven. Jesus used the words, 'the eye of a needle,' not in
a literal, but a figurative sense. In the eastern cities, they used
to have in their gates small low openings, which were called
'needles' eyes,' just as we are accustomed to call certain small
windows 'bulls' eyes.' If a camel had to go through one of
those small openings, the load would have to be taken off from
his back ; he would have to get down on his knees, and even
then he would find it very hard work to get through. Still it
would be a possible thing for a camel to do, just as it is possible
for a rich man to enter heaven. This is what Jesus meant when
He spoke about a camel going through the eye of a needle.

And now we come to *the other lesson which the camel illustrates, and that is*—THE LESSON OF PATIENT INDUSTRY.

The life of the camel was a hard and laborious one. It had to carry every day, as we have said before, a burden of from five to six, or even eight hundred pounds' weight. And with this heavy burden on its back, it would have to travel on at the rate of two and a half or three miles an hour. This would be continued every day, from twelve to sixteen, or even twenty hours a day. And to go steadily on, working in this way for twenty or twenty-five years, was certainly to set before us an excellent example of patient industry.

There was one kind of camel called the dromedary, which was used not so much for carrying burdens as for travelling on, just as we use our horses. These camels will journey on at the rate of eight or ten miles an hour. And we are told, on good authority, that sometimes these camels have been known to travel on at this rate for fifty hours at a time, thus making a journey of five hundred miles without stopping. This seems almost impossible, and yet we are assured that it is even so. And if our young people could all be persuaded to practise this lesson of patient industry, so strikingly illustrated by the camel, what a wonderful effect it would have on their success in life! Now let us look at some examples of those who have gone on through life practising this lesson of patient industry, and see what results have followed from it.

Here is a good illustration of this part of our subject. We may call it—

WHAT A BOY DID.

About two hundred and sixty years ago, a poor lad of seventeen was seen travelling on foot in the south of England. He carried over his shoulder at the end of a stick all the clothing he had in the world, and in his pocket he had a few pieces of money, which his mother had given him on parting. This boy's name was John. He was the son of poor but pious parents, and he had six brothers and five sisters, who all had to work hard for a living. He was a Christian boy, and, finding he could not get work near home, with his parents' consent he had set out to seek employment elsewhere.

The first place at which he stopped was the city of Exeter. Here he could not find anything to do, but when he saw the beautiful Exeter Cathedral, and the great library belonging to the Dean of the Cathedral, he made up his mind that he would try to be a scholar. Then he set out for the city of Oxford, which was one of the most famous places of learning in England. This city was two hundred miles from the city of Exeter where he was staying. He had to walk all the way. Sometimes he slept in barns, or on the sheltered side of a haystack. He lived chiefly on bread and water, with an occasional drink of milk.

When he arrived at the splendid city of Oxford, his clothing was nearly worn out and very dusty. His feet were sore ; he was a stranger there, and felt very much discouraged, for he knew not what to do.

He had heard of Exeter College, Oxford, and went there to see if he could get any work to do. To his great delight, they engaged him to carry fuel into the kitchen, to clean pans and kettles, and do that sort of work.

Here, while doing his humble work, he was often seen with a book near him, which he would read and study in his leisure moments.

His fondness for reading and study soon engaged the attention of the gentlemen connected with the college. They admitted him into the institution on a free scholarship, and made provision for his support.

He studied hard, and was soon at the head of his class. He graduated with honour, became a minister of Christ, a great scholar, a bishop, and one of the most useful men in the Church of England. He is well known in history as the Right Rev. John Prideaux, D.D. But it was the blessing of God on his patient industry which raised that poor boy to the high position of honour and usefulness which he occupied.

Our next story may be called—

STICK TO YOUR BUSH.

This story was told by a successful business man, who said that he owed all his success in life to the lesson which this story taught him.

'One day, when I was a lad,' said he, 'a party of boys and girls from our school were going into the country to pick huckleberries. I asked my father if I might go with them, and was delighted when he gave his consent. I got my basket, and was going out of the gate, when my father called me back.

'He took hold of my hand, and said very kindly to me, "Joseph, my boy, what are you going for ? to pick berries or to play ?"

'"To pick berries," I replied.

'"Then, Joseph," said he, "I want to tell you one thing. It is this : when you find a nice good bush, don't leave it to try and find a better one. The other boys and girls will run about, picking one or two berries here, and one or two there, wasting a great deal of time, but getting very few berries. If you do as they do, you will come back with an empty basket. If you want to get berries, the thing for you to do is *to stick to your bush.*"

'I went with the party,' said the gentleman, 'and we had a splendid time. But it was just as my father said. No sooner had one of the boys found a good bush than he called to his companions, and they would leave their places and run off to see what he had found. Not content more than a minute or two in any one place, they would ramble over the whole pasture, getting very tired, and at night they had very few berries. My father's words kept ringing in my ears, and I "stuck to my bush." When I had done with one, I found another and finished that, and then I took another. When night came, I had a large basket full of nice berries, more than all of the others put together, and I was not half as tired as they were.

'I went home very happy that night, and when father looked at my basket full of ripe berries, he said, "Well done, Joseph. You see it was just as I told you. Always stick to your bush."

'Not long after that my father died, and then I had to make my own way in the world as best I could. But my father's words sank deep into my mind, and I never forgot the lesson taught me by that huckleberry party. I always stuck to my bush.

'When I had a fair place, and was doing reasonably well, I was not willing to leave it, and spend days and weeks in trying to find a better place. When other young men would say, "Come with us, and we will find something better to do!" I shook my head and "stuck to my bush."

'After a while my employers took me into partnership with them in their business. I stayed with that firm until the old partners died, and then I took their place. The habit of sticking to my business gave people confidence in me, and led to my success. I owe all I have and am to the lesson my father taught me when he said, "*Stick to your bush.*"'

And the lesson wrapped up in these words is just what we are now considering—the lesson of *patient industry* taught us by the camel.

Now let us glance at the history of some of the Presidents of the United States, and we shall find plenty of illustrations of the lesson we are now studying.

John Adams, our second President, was the son of a farmer of very moderate means. He never would have reached that high office if he had not learned and *practised* the lesson of patient industry.

Andrew Jackson was born in a log hut in North Carolina, and was raised in the pine-woods for which that State is famous. The thing that made him President was the patient industry with which he improved his opportunities.

James K. Polk spent the early part of his life in helping to dig out a living from a farm in North Carolina. He was afterwards a clerk in a country store. It was patient industry which made him President.

Millard Fillmore was the son of a New York farmer, and his home was a very humble one. He learned the business of a clothier. How did he become President? It was by patient industry.

James Buchanan was born in a small town among the Alleghany mountains. His father cut the logs, and built his own house, in what was then a wilderness. What made James Buchanan President? It was patient industry that did it.

Abraham Lincoln was the son of a very poor Kentucky farmer. He lived in a log cabin till he was twenty-one years of age. What led him from that humble log cabin in the woods of Kentucky to the White House at Washington? Patient industry.

Andrew Jackson was apprenticed to a tailor at ten years of age by his widowed mother. He was never able to attend school. All the education he ever had was what he picked up in the evening hours after his day's work was done. How did he ever manage to become President? It was by patient industry.

Ulysses S. Grant was born in humble life. He lived in a poor house on the banks of the Ohio river until he was seventeen years old. What was it, then, which made him one of the greatest generals the world has known, and afterwards President of the United States? Patient industry did it.

James A. Garfield was born in a log cabin. As soon as he was able to do anything, he worked on a farm. Then he learned the trade of a carpenter. After this he worked on the canal. What led that canal boy to become President of the United States? Patient industry did it.

And if we look away from the history of our Presidents, and read the lives of men who have been distinguished in different pursuits of life, all round the world, we shall find among them all illustrations of the important lesson we are now considering. There is Demosthenes, the great orator, and Julius Cæsar, the great warrior, and Henry the Fourth of France, the great ruler, and Lord Bacon and Sir Isaac Newton, the great philosophers, and Benjamin Franklin, and George Washington, and Napoleon Bonaparte. These men were very different from each other in many respects, but yet there was one thing in which they were all alike. They all learned and practised the lesson of patient industry. And it was to this they owed their greatness.

I will finish this part of our subject by quoting some simple, practical lines, which embrace all that I have been trying to say about the lesson which the camel teaches us. They are called —

LITTLE BY LITTLE.

One step, and then another,
  And the longest walk is ended ;
One stitch, and then another,
  And the largest rent is mended
One brick upon another,
  And the highest wall is made ;
One flake upon another,
  And the deepest snow is laid.

So the little coral workers,
  By their slow but constant motion,
Have built those pretty islands
  In the distant dark-blue ocean ;
And the noblest undertakings
  Man's wisdom hath conceived,
By oft-repeated efforts,
  Have been patiently achieved.

Then do not be disheartened
  O'er the work you have to do,
And say that such a mighty task
  You never can get through ;
But just endeavour, day by day,
  Another point to gain,
And soon the mountain that you feared
  Will prove to be a plain.

' Rome was not builded in a day
  The ancient proverb teaches ;
And Nature, by her trees and flowers,
  The same sweet sermon preaches.
Think not of far-off duties,
  But of duties which are near ;
And, having once begun to work,
  Resolve to persevere.

What is our sermon about to-day ? The camel. How many lessons do we learn from the camel ? Two. What is the first ? An interesting truth about *the goodness of God.* What is the second ? An important lesson about *patient industry.*

There are two things this sermon should lead us to do. The first is to thank God for the illustrations of His goodness here furnished. The other is to pray for grace that we may be able to learn and practise the important lesson of patient industry here taught us.

IV.

THE HORSE.

'Hast thou given the horse strength?'—Job xxxix. 19.

THE horse is the next of the Bible animals that we wish to consider. What a noble-looking creature the horse is! With its strong and well-proportioned limbs, its arched neck, its intelligent head, its fine long tail, it presents a very pleasing and graceful appearance. And the horse is a very sensible creature. Here is an incident which illustrates very well this point of the horse's character. We may call it—

THE GOOD SENSE OF A HORSE.

A gentleman named Mr. Andrews, residing in California, had a span of bright little horses to which he was very much attached. He never separated them. In the stable, the field, and the harness, they were always together. This caused a strong attachment to grow between the horses. On one occasion he took some friends in his carriage, drawn by these horses, to a lake not very far from his dwelling, on a fishing excursion. Taking the horses out of the carriage, he led them to the border of the lake, and tied them to two trees, a few rods apart, that they might feed on the grass that grew around them. Then he went into a shanty near by, and sat down to wait for the return of his friends, who were fishing.

He had not been waiting long before he heard the sound of a horse's feet approaching the shanty. The next moment he saw one of his horses standing at the door. The animal put his head in and gave a loud neigh, and then turned round and galloped back towards the spot where his master had left him and his companion fastened safely to the trees.

Surprised at finding his horse loose, and at his singular conduct, Mr. Andrews immediately went after him. On reaching the spot where he had left the horses, he was surprised to see the other horse in the water, entangled in the rope which had fastened him to the tree, and trying hard to keep his head above the water. Mr. Andrews at once took hold of the rope, released the horse from it, and led him out of the water. While he was doing this, the other horse stood by, watching what was going on with the greatest interest. And when he saw that his companion was safe on dry land, he seemed greatly pleased. He went jumping round his master, shaking his head and wagging his tail, as if he was trying to say, 'I am very much obliged to you, sir, for saving my companion from drowning.' Now, there are several things worth noticing in the conduct of this horse. Think of his readiness to notice the trouble his companion was in, the effort he must have made to break the strong rope that bound him to the tree, the good sense he showed in going at once for his master, to come and save the life of his companion ; and then the way in which he tried to show his gratitude to his master for the ready kindness he had shown. All this is very interesting in that horse. And an animal that can act in this way deserves our careful study and our kindest treatment.

Horses are wild in some countries, but they are all tame with us. In the times when the Bible was written, horses were not used for riding on, and for bearing burdens, as we use them now. They were then employed chiefly for warlike purposes. And it is of a war-horse that God is speaking, in the book of Job, when He gives this remarkable description of it :

'Hast thou given the horse strength ? hast thou clothed his neck with thunder ? Canst thou make him afraid as a grasshopper ? the glory of his nostrils is terrible. He paweth in the valley, and rejoiceth in his strength : he goeth on to meet the armed men. He mocketh at fear, and is not affrighted ; neither turneth he back from the sword. The quiver rattleth against him, the glittering spear and the shield. He swalloweth the ground with fierceness and rage : neither believeth he that it is the sound of the trumpet. He saith among the trumpets, Ha, ha! he smelleth the battle afar off, the thunder of the captains, and the shouting.'

The subject of our sermon to-day will be the lessons taught us by the horse. And in studying the natural history of the horse, we can easily find illustrations of four lessons.

The first of these is—THE LESSON OF COURAGE.

We may find horses that have courage about some things, but not about others. At our home on Chestnut Hill, we have a nice gentle horse that we call Dolly. She is not afraid of locomotives. When standing near the railway depot, a train of cars may come thundering along, with the engine snorting and puffing ever so loud, and she will not mind it at all, but will stand perfectly still. Yet, if she is going along the turnpike, and sees a piece of white paper lying on the road, or two or three sheep coming towards her, she will get frightened, and want to run away. But it is in battle, as a war-horse, that this animal shows its courage. God's description of it, in the book of Job, which we have already quoted, refers to the horse in battle. And the lesson of courage which the horse teaches us is a very important one for us to learn. God is helping us to learn this lesson when He says to us, nearly a hundred times in the Bible, 'Fear not.' And over and over again, God tells us 'to be strong, and of a good courage.' Let us look at one or two illustrations of the usefulness of courage. Our first story may be called—

A HERO.

Freddie Jones was a bright, intelligent boy, about ten years old. On coming home from school one afternoon, he went into the sitting-room, where his Aunt Margaret was busy sewing, and began to read a book on history, in which he was very much interested. After reading a while, he laid down the book, and said, 'Auntie, if I were only a general, I think I should be very happy.'

'Are you not happy now?' asked his aunt.

'O yes; but I long to be a hero. It seems like something grand to be a hero. Don't you think so, auntie?'

'Yes,' said Aunt Margaret, 'I admire a hero. Shall I tell you how you may become a hero now—a boy hero—which I think is nobler far even than being a general?'

'Yes,' said Freddie eagerly; 'do tell me!'

'It is by learning to be master of yourself. Do not give way to anger, or any wicked feeling. Never allow yourself to do what you know is wrong. The Bible says, "He that is slow to anger is better than the mighty, and he that ruleth his spirit than he that taketh a city." Think of this, and when tempted to do wrong, have courage to stand up for the right, and you will be a greater hero than Alexander, or Cæsar, or Napoleon.'

Our other story may be called—

A BRAVE BOY.

One morning, when some boys were going to a school in the country, they saw one of their schoolmates driving a cow into a neighbouring field. He opened the gate, saw her safely in, and then, closing it, went into school with the rest of them. After school he let the cow out, and drove her off; and every day for two or three weeks he kept on doing the same. He had never done this before. The boys could not understand what it meant, and they made all sorts of fun of their companion, whose name was James Watson. One of the boys, named Jackson, whose father was the richest man in that part of the country, used to lead off in this sport.

One morning, when they saw him driving the cow, Jackson cried out,—

'Holloa, Jim! what's the price of milk to-day? Is your father going to make a milkman of you?'

'Why not?' asked Jim.

'Oh, nothing. Only don't leave much water in the cans after you rinse them—that's all.'

The boys laughed at Jim; but, without being the least disturbed, he simply said,—

'Never fear. If I should ever rise to be a milkman, I'll give good measure, and good milk too.'

The day after this conversation, there was a public examination in the school to which these boys belonged. A number of ladies and gentlemen from the neighbourhood were present. Prizes were awarded by the Principal of the school, and the two boys spoken of, Watson and Jackson, received the highest prizes for attendance and scholarship. After this was over, the Principal said there was one prize of a gold medal to be awarded, which is not often given, because the conduct which it is intended to reward is not often met with. This medal is a reward for courage. 'And now,' said he, 'I have a story to tell about a brave boy who deserves this medal, and is going to receive it.'

This story will explain about Watson and the cow; listen to it.

'Not long ago,' said the Principal, 'some boys were flying a kite in the street, just as a poor boy rode by on horseback, on his way to the mill. The horse took fright, and threw the boy off, who was so badly hurt that he was carried home, and confined to bed for several weeks. None of the boys who caused the trouble went to inquire about the wounded lad; but another boy, who saw the accident from a distance, not only went to make inquiries, but offered to help.

'He learned that the wounded boy was the grandson of a poor widow, whose only support was the milk of a cow which she owned. This wounded boy had been in the habit of driving her cow to pasture and back.

'"But now he is helpless, what shall I do?" asked the poor widow.

'"Never mind, good woman," said the boy who had called. "I will drive the cow for you till Willie your grandson gets well again."

'But this good boy's kindness did not stop here. When he found that the widow needed money to get medicine for her wounded grandson, he said, "I have some money which my mother gave me to buy a pair of boots with. You can have this, and I will do without the boots for a while."

'"No," said the old woman, "I can't consent to that. But here is a pair of heavy boots that I bought for Willie, who can't wear them now. If you will only buy these, we can get on nicely."

'The boy took the boots, clumsy as they were, and has worn them ever since.

'Well, when the other boys in the school found out that one

of their companions was driving a cow every day, they laughed, and jeered, and made all sorts of fun of him. His great, clumsy cowhide boots were a special object of their mirth. But, never minding what his schoolmates did or said, the noble boy went bravely cn and kept his promise, till the wounded grandson of the poor widow was well again.

'Now, ladies and gentlemen, I appeal to you, if there was not true courage in that boy's conduct? It was only yesterday, by mere accident, that I found out about the kindness and the courage of this boy. James Watson, the boy of whom I am speaking, will please come forward.'

Covered with blushes, James stepped modestly forward. The Principal put the gold medal round his neck; and then loud cheers burst forth from all present, that made the schoolhouse ring again.

When the exercises were over, the scholars who had made fun of James came forward and begged his pardon, and felt proud to have him as their friend.

That boy was a real hero. And if we learn to follow his example, we shall all be heroes too. The first lesson illustrated by the horse is— the lesson of courage.

The second lesson we may learn from the horse is—THE LESSON OF DOCILITY.

This is a harder word than I like to use. I tried to find a simpler word for it, but did not succeed. Yet it can easily be explained, so that any member of the infant school can understand it. Docility means a readiness to learn. Horses are very ready to learn, and in this they teach us the lesson of docility. God has sent us into this world that we may learn to know and do His will. And He has given us the Bible with its great truths; the Church, with its ministers and services, and the Sunday school, with teachers to help us in learning this lesson, which it is so important for us to know. And the horse sets us a good example here in its docility or readiness to learn. Here are some illustrations of this. The first may be called—

PROF. BARTHOLOMEW'S HORSES, AND WHAT THEY LEARNED.

These horses were on exhibition in Boston some time ago. And the lessons of which I am now to tell were taught the horses by kindness, and the performance of them was witnessed by thousands of people. Here are some of the lessons which these horses would go through at the word of their teacher.

A number of horses are brought on the stage. Each of them, when his name is called, goes to the front of the stage, makes his bow to the audience, and then retires.

Next a horse is brought on the stage, and stands there. The Professor says to him, 'Get me my pocket-handkerchief.' He goes directly to a desk, opens it, and brings the Professor his handkerchief.

Another horse comes on the stage, and when told what to do, he takes a sponge, goes up to a blackboard, and rubs out the figures on it.

Another horse is brought on the stage, and there, just as he is told, marches slowly, trots or runs, and then walks off.

Another horse comes out, and walks round so as to make the figure 8, by turning to the right hand or to the left, just as he is told to do.

Then four horses are brought out for a game of leap-frog. They stand in a line one behind the other. Another horse comes out, he stands still for a moment, and at the word of command he leaps over the first horse from right to left, then over the second from left to right, and over the others in the same way.

Then two horses appeared, and when told to do so, they mounted a plank and played see-saw as nicely as any two boys could have done.

Then a set of twelve horses came out and went through drill, just as a company of soldiers would do. These different commands were given them and were instantly obeyed : march, countermarch, to the right, to the left, form a hollow square, attack the fort, fire a cannon (this they pretended to do by snapping with their teeth), and finally, capture the enemy's flag, and pass it round to each other. All this was done. But their last performance was the most curious of all. This was a scene in court which they had been taught to imitate.

A horse, charged with murder, was brought in as a prisoner in chains. A jury of twelve horses was formed to try the prisoner. A donkey was brought out to act as judge. Professor B. made a charge to the jury, telling them what the evidence had been for, and against the prisoner. Then the jury retired to another room. Presently they returned. One of them had a piece of paper in his mouth, on which some person in the other room had written the words, 'Not guilty.' This was passed from one to the other. The last juryman handed it to the donkey judge. He handed it to Professor B., who took it and read out the verdict, 'Not guilty.' Then he told one of the horses that was acting as sheriff to take off the prisoner's chains and let him go free, which was done at once.

This hardly seems possible ; yet it is true. These things were done over and over again in the city of Boston, as thousands of people there can testify.

Now surely these horses illustrate the lesson of docility.

They were ready to learn. And this is one of the most important lessons for us to learn.

I have just one other story here. We may call it—

WHAT DOCILITY, OR READINESS TO LEARN, DID FOR A BOY.

This story of himself was told by a New York merchant to a friend.

'My father died,' said he, 'when I was a little boy about ten years old. He had failed in business a little while before his death, and left his family poor. There were five children, of whom I was the oldest. Mother had to struggle very hard for our support, and I made up my mind to do what I could to help her. I first tried to get a situation in a store, but did not succeed in that. Then I tried selling newspapers. One evening I jumped on a car, and called out my papers in the best way I could. A gentleman, who was just going to get out, called to me, "Here, my boy, I want a paper." I gave him one. He put the pay for it into my hand, and stepped out of the car. As soon as he was gone, I looked at what he had given me, and found that instead of a two cent piece, it was a two dollar and a half gold piece. I had never had so much money in my hand at one time before, and it made me feel very strange. As soon as the car stopped, I jumped off, and ran home as fast as I could, and showed the gold piece to my mother, telling her at the same time how I got it.

'I wanted her to let me go out at once and buy some things that we needed very much. But my mother would not let me do that. She said the gentleman had given it to me by mistake; that I had no right to any more of the money than the two cents, which was the price of the paper; that, if I used the rest of it, it would be like stealing, and God's blessing would not rest upon me, and I never should prosper. Then she asked me to promise that I would keep the money, and try to find out the gentleman who gave it to me, and return it to him. I was very unwilling at first to do this; but, knowing that it was right for a boy to practise docility, or learn to obey his mother, I made up my mind to do what she wanted me, and so I gave her the promise.

'The next evening I began my work of selling papers as usual. After going through several cars, I saw the gentleman who had given me the gold piece. Going up to him, I said, "Sir, you bought a paper of me last evening."

'"Well," said he, "perhaps I did. I know I bought one of some boy. But what's the matter? Didn't I pay you?"

'"Yes, you did, sir. But instead of two cents, you gave me a gold piece, and here it is, sir." He looked surprised, and said, "Thank you, my boy. You are an honest fellow. Where do you live?"

'I told him. Then he said, "I want another paper, and here's half a dollar for it."

'All the gentlemen near us in the car, who heard what was said, bought papers of me, and they each gave me four or five times the usual price. Pretty soon my papers were all gone, and I ran home, feeling very rich, and told mother all about it.

'The next day that gentleman called to see my mother, and asked her to send me down to his office in the morning. After that I sold no more papers. The gentleman gave me a situation in his store. It was a low place at first; but I rose by degrees, and now I am a partner in that firm.'

Here we see how that boy had learned the lesson of docility. He was ready to do what his mother taught him. That brought God's blessing upon him, and it will do the same for us, if we learn this second lesson which the horse teaches us—the lesson of docility.

The third lesson we may learn from the horse is—THE LESSON OF KINDNESS.

We had this lesson in our sermon about the lion. But we find better illustrations of it in the horse than in the lion. And this lesson is so important that we cannot have it brought before us too often. The best kindness that we know anything about is that which God shows to us. It is interesting to notice how God's kindness is spoken of in the Bible. It is called '*merciful* kindness,' '*everlasting* kindness;' it is '*excellent* loving kindness,' '*marvellous* loving kindness,' 'loving kindness that is better than life,' and 'loving kindness with which God *crowns* His people.' And as God Himself is so ready to show loving kindness to us, He expects us to do the same among ourselves. One of the great commands of the Bible is, 'Be ye kind one to another.'

And in studying the history of the horse, we find two things about kindness illustrated. One of these is, *How easily the horse is governed by kindness.* The other is, *How ready the horse is to return kindness that has been shown to it.*

Let us look for a moment at the first of these lessons, *How easily the horse is governed by kindness.* We do not find any illustrations of this in the Bible, but there are plenty outside of the Bible. Here are two that come in nicely. The first may be called—

THE POWER OF KINDNESS.

A gentleman who was travelling through the country stopped at a farmer's house one night. He noticed that there

was a gentle little girl, named Nellie, who by her kind ways had
great influence over the other members of the family, and over the
animals on the farm, too, as may be seen from this incident:

The farmer was going to town next morning, and agreed to
take the stranger with him. The family came out to see them
start. The farmer picked up the reins, and, with a jerk, said,
'Dick, go 'long!' But Dick didn't go 'long. The farmer
cracked the whip about the pony's ears, and shouted, 'Dick,
you rascal, get up!' It was no use. Dick stood still. Then
the whip came down with a heavy hand, but the stubborn
horse only shook his head, as much as to say, 'No, I won't!'
A stout lad came out, and seized the bridle, and pulled and
jerked it, and kicked the rebellious pony, but he wouldn't
move a step. Just then little Nellie came out, and her gentle
voice was heard saying, 'Oh, Jimmy, don't do so.' The pony
knew Nellie's voice. Her loving hand was laid on the horse,
and a low, simple word was spoken. In a moment his stiff
muscles were relaxed, and the air of stubbornness about him
all passed away. 'Poor Dick,' she said in her gentle voice,
and at the same time stroking and softly patting his neck with
her childlike hand. 'Now, go along, you naughty fellow,' she
said, in a half chiding but tender voice, as she drew slightly
on the bridle. The pony turned, and rubbed his head against
her arm for a moment, and then started off in a cheerful trot,
and there was no more trouble that day.

The stranger turned to the farmer, and said,—

'What wonderful power that little girl has in her hand
and voice!'

'O yes,' said the farmer; 'she's good. Everybody and
everything loves her.'

Here is another story, which may be called—

CURED BY KINDNESS.

Willie Davis was a little boy about ten years old, who lived
in the country. He was a member of 'The Band of Mercy,'
which had been formed in their Sunday school. The pledge
which each of the members of that Band repeated at their
meetings was this: 'I will try to be kind to all living
creatures, and to protect them from cruelty.' Willie was
faithful in carrying out that pledge. One day, when walking
along the road, he saw their butcher whipping most unmerci-
fully his poor half-starved horse. On seeing this, Willie cried
out, 'Oh, Mr. Smith, you oughtn't to do so.' But the next
moment the horse started and galloped away. He ran for
more than a mile. The waggon was broken to pieces, and the
butcher was thrown out and badly bruised.

The next day, 'the vicious beast,' as the neighbours called that horse, was offered for sale. But nobody cared to buy him at any price. They all said he was good for nothing. But Willie persuaded his father, Mr. Ely, to buy him for use on the farm. He wanted to try and see if that horse could not be cured of his bad ways, and be made a good horse by being kindly treated. The people said it was foolish to buy such a horse, for he never would be of any use. Even the butcher, who sold him, said he would bite, and rear, and kick, and run away. But Mr. Ely bought the horse to please Willie, whose tender heart was full of pity for the poor animal. 'We will be so kind to him,' said Willie to his papa, 'that he won't want to be bad any more.' So they agreed to try Willie's plan.

And that plan soon began to tell upon him. Not long after that, when Mr. Ely and Willie were seen driving the horse, their neighbours would look with surprise at the change which had taken place in him. He would go along just as slowly as was desired ; he would stop the moment they said 'whoa' to him ; he would come when called, would start, or run, when told, and always loved to rub his head against the shoulder of Willie or his father. And what had made the change? It was not force. The poor creature had been beaten and kicked and starved before, and he grew worse and worse under that treatment. But now he was differently treated. He had a nice bed in the stable, he was well fed, well watered, not over-driven or over-loaded, never whipped, or kicked, or scolded. Kind words were spoken to him, and now and then an apple or a lump of sugar was given to him. There was no gentler, safer, or more faithful horse than he was to be found in all that country. And kindness had made this great change in him.

Here we see—how easily the horse can be governed by kindness. But while the horse is easily governed by kindness, *He is ready to return the kindness showed to him.*

Our first illustration of this may be called—

A LADY RESCUED FROM DROWNING BY A HORSE.

This story was published in an English paper, which is devoted principally to considering the wonders of nature, and the habits and characteristics of animals.

A lady, the wife of a wealthy farmer, living near Toronto, in Canada, was walking about the farm one day. In the course of her walk, she was crossing a plank bridge, which crossed a deep and rapid stream that ran through the farm.

In crossing this, she missed her footing, and fell into the water. Now she was in the greatest possible danger. She was encumbered with her clothing; she could not swim, and there was no one within hearing to render her any help. But, in the field through which that stream flowed, her favourite horse was grazing. This horse had always been treated by his mistress with the greatest kindness, and always seemed to be grateful for it.

But we should hardly have expected that in this state of things a horse would be able to understand the danger to which his mistress was exposed. But this horse did. On looking around and seeing his mistress struggling in the water, he started, and, galloping to the edge of the stream, plunged in, and swam towards her. Then he took hold of her dress, and brought her safely to the dry land. And in doing this he was only returning to his mistress the kindness she had showed to him.

I have one other illustration of this part of our subject; we may call it—

THE STORY OF THE ARAB HORSE.

We know how fond the Arabs are of their horses, and how kindly they treat them.

There was an Arab chief once who had a horse that was a great favourite with him, and was treated like one of his family. On one occasion this chief was engaged in war with the Turks. He was defeated in battle, and was taken prisoner with a number of his tribe. On the night after the battle, the prisoners had their hands and feet bound with strong cords, and were left in the field outside the Turkish camp to spend the night. The horses were tied to stakes driven into the ground, not far from where their masters were.

This chief could not sleep any that night for thinking of his defeat, and that he should probably never see his family again. As he lay there awake, he could hear the horses neighing, and recognised the voice of his own horse. He wanted very much to get near him, but he could not walk; yet, after trying a while, he managed, by rolling over the grass, to get close to where his horse was. Then he called him by name, and spoke to him kindly, as he was accustomed to do.

On hearing his master's voice, the horse gave a spring, and broke the cord which bound him to the stake. Then he came up to his master, and rubbed his head against him, and neighed joyfully over him. After this, he took hold with his teeth of the cord with which his master was bound, and, lifting him from the ground, started off to carry him home. He kept on all that night, and the greater part of the following day, stopping occasionally to rest, till finally, arriving at his master's tent, he laid him down before his family, and then fell to the earth and died.

How noble that was! Surely that horse did return the kindness that had been showed to him.

And so the third lesson we learn from the horse is—the lesson of kindness.

The fourth lesson we may learn from the horse is—THE LESSON OF USEFULNESS.

When we look around in this busy world, among all the animals that God has made, we find no one that is so useful to us as the horse. In how many different ways does he help us? Along our canals the horses draw the boats that are loaded with merchandise of various kinds ; on our farms the horse is used for ploughing and for reaping ; on our turnpike roads we see them carrying loads of hay and straw, and other products of the farm, for sale in our great towns and cities. And then, returning, they draw the waggons back, filled with manure for the fields, or with goods of various kinds for the use of our farmers and their families. In our large cities the ways are endless in which the horse makes himself useful. And if we go out to the Park, in an afternoon, we see countless numbers and varieties of beautiful carriages, filled with ladies and gentlemen, whose health and comfort and real enjoyment are promoted by this useful animal.

And then, after death, as well as during his life, there is no more useful animal than the horse. Almost every part of the horse, after his death, is made use of in some way. His hair is used for making cloth ; his skin for making gloves ; his bones for making buttons, or else they are ground into powder which is used to fertilize our fields. In France, and other parts of Europe, the flesh of the horse is used for food ; and the physicians there declare that it is quite equal to our beef. And even the very hoofs of the horse are used for making glue. Certainly we have the lesson of usefulness well illustrated in the horse. And when we think of this it should lead us all to try and make ourselves as useful as possible to those about us.

Let us look at some examples of the way in which we may do this.

Our first example may be called—

SYDNEY SMITH'S RULE FOR USEFULNESS.

Sydney Smith was a well-known and useful minister in the Church of England. One day, a member of his congregation asked him how he could make himself useful. 'My friend,' said Mr. Smith, 'I will give you this short rule for usefulness. Try to make one person happy every day ; and then, at the end of ten years, you will have the pleasure of thinking that you have been useful to three thousand six hundred and fifty people.'

Our next story may be called—

HOW JOHNNY SAVED THE TRAIN.

Johnny Tompkins was a little fellow about eight years old. His father was a conductor on one of our great railroads. Johnny was trying to be a Christian, and make himself useful.

In talking with his mother one day, he said,—

'I don't suppose, mother, that little folks like me can ever be of any use.'

'Why, yes,' said his mother; 'if little folks only *try* to be useful, and *ask God to help them*, they may do a great deal of good.'

That evening, Johnny was sent to meet his father at the station, near which they lived.

The train in which Mr. Tompkins had arrived was at the end of its journey, and was to stay there all night.

As soon as he saw Johnny, he took him by the hand, and led him into the last car of the train which had just arrived, and, giving him a seat near the stove, told him to wait there a few moments, and then he would come and take him home.

Now it happened that, by some mistake, one of the brakemen had unfastened the car in which Johnny was sitting from the train to which it belonged. Just beyond the station where that train was standing there was a down grade on the railroad. As Johnny's father was leaving the train, a locomotive struck the other end of that train. This pushed the car that Johnny was in off the level ground where it had been standing, and started it down the descending grade.

When Johnny found that the car was in motion, and no one in it but himself, he was very much frightened. And, as he looked out of the front door of the car, he saw a red light far down along the road. He knew at once that it was an express train, coming along in the opposite direction to that in which his car was going. Something must be done at once, or there would be a smash-up, in which he would be killed, and numbers of people in the approaching train.

What should he do? He thought of his mother's words. Then he dropped on his knees, and asked God to help a little boy in a runaway car.

As soon as he rose from his knees, he saw his father's red signal lantern, lighted, and standing near the stove. In a moment he picked it up, and went out and stood on the front platform, swinging the red lantern up and down. The fireman on the express train saw it, and shouted to the conductor, 'Danger ahead!' Then the steam was shut off, the engine was reversed, the air brakes were put on, and the train stopped. As Johnny's car came near, it was switched off on a side track, and all danger was over.

When the passengers came out of the express train, and saw a little fellow with a red light on the platform of the runaway car, and heard how he had saved their train from destruction, they raised cheer after cheer for him in the stillness of the night.

A purse of money was quickly made up for him, but that was little to Johnny compared with the happiness he found in thinking that God had made him useful in saving perhaps a hundred lives, which would have been lost if that express train had dashed into the runaway car.

I have only one other story to illustrate this part of our subject ; we may call it—

THE RIGHT PLACE, AFTER ALL.

Some time ago, there was an earnest Christian man, who was connected with the police department in the city of Birmingham, England. In discharging his daily duties, he saw so many sad forms of sin and wickedness, that it made him feel uncomfortable, and he wished very much to get another situation. He asked his wife to unite with him in daily prayer, that it might please God to get him something else to do. They kept on praying in this way for some time, but no change came. At last the policeman came home one evening, looking very thoughtful. He said to his wife, 'Do you know, my dear, we have been making a mistake in asking God to take me out of my present situation. I think now that God has put me where I am *to work for Him.* And I am going to pray that He will help me to make myself useful where I am.'

Then he began a new life, and was all the time watching for opportunities of doing good. He became so useful in his work, that he was soon made the head of the detective police department. He had a wonderful memory for faces, and when he once knew a person's name, he never forgot it. Here is an illustration of one of the ways in which he made himself useful. One day a man called to see him, and was shown into his private office. Looking at the detective, the stranger said, 'Do you know me, sir ?' The detective replied, 'Wait a moment, and I'll tell you. Yes, I recollect you. Fourteen years ago I arrested you. You were tried, and sentenced to fourteen years' imprisonment. Your name is so and so.' 'All right,' replied the man, 'but that is not all. After my sentence, when you had me conducted to the cell, you waited a moment, and then spoke some kind words to me, which I have never forgotten. This is what you said, "My friend, this is a bad job for you. You've been serving a hard master, and now you're in for the wages. You will have plenty of time to think. Won't you come to the Lord and ask Him to make a new man of you? Read your Bible, and pray, and give your heart to Jesus. It is not too late for a change; only turn now, and you'll come out a changed man, to lead an honest and honourable life." Then you shook hands with me, and pleaded so earnestly, that I made up my mind to follow your advice, *and I have done it.* The Lord has forgiven me. I went into that prison a poor, wretched sinner; I have come out of it a new creature in Christ Jesus. My time is just up, and the first thing I wanted to do, on getting out of prison, was to come and thank you for the kind words you spoke to me, and the good you have done me, both for body and for soul, for time and for eternity.'

This shows us that wherever we are placed we can work for God, and make ourselves useful to those about us.

And so we see that the fourth lesson we may learn from the horse is—the lesson of usefulness.

Now, where is our text to-day? Job xxxix. 19. What are the words of the text? 'Hast Thou given the horse strength?' What is the sermon about? The lessons taught us by the horse. How many of these lessons did we have? Four. What is the first? *The lesson of courage.* What is the second? *The lesson of docility.* And what does docility mean? It means a readiness to learn. What is the third lesson we learn from the horse? *The lesson of kindness.* And what is the fourth? *The lesson of usefulness.*

These are all valuable lessons for us to learn. Let us try to carry these four words away with us—*courage—docility—kindness*—and *usefulness.* And let us ask God to help us in learning and practising these lessons, and then, like our blessed Saviour, we shall be able to '*go about doing good.*'

V.

THE DEER.

'As the hart panteth after the water brooks, so panteth my soul after Thee, O God.'—PSALM xlii. 1.

OUR subject to-day is the lessons which we learn from the deer.

The deer is an animal which is frequently mentioned in the Bible, though it is often called in the Word of God a hind, or a hart. There are many kinds of deer, such as the red deer, the fallow deer, the wild deer, and the domesticated deer.

Nearly all these different kinds of deer were formerly found in Palestine, so that the allusions in the Scriptures to the deer are very frequent, and refer to the same kind of deer with which we are familiar. One of the first allusions that we have to the deer in the Bible is in Genesis xlix. 21, where Jacob, in blessing his sons, prophesies their future. Speaking of Naphtali, he says, 'Naphtali is a hind let loose ; he giveth goodly words.' That deer's flesh was used at the table, is shown by 1 Kings iv. 22, 23, where we read the account of King Solomon's provisions : 'And Solomon's provision for one day was thirty measures of fine flour, and threescore measures of meal, ten fat oxen, and twenty oxen out of the pastures, and an hundred sheep, beside harts, and roebucks, and fallow deer, and fatted fowl.'

An allusion is made to the speed and quickness of the deer in several passages in the Bible. In Isaiah xxxv. 6, we read : 'Then shall the lame man leap as an hart, and the tongue of the dumb sing : for in the wilderness shall waters break out, and streams in the desert. And a passage in 2 Samuel xxii. 33, 34, reads : 'God is my strength and power : and He maketh my way perfect. He maketh my feet like hinds' feet ; and setteth me upon my high places.'

Nearly four hundred years after these words of King David, we find Habakkuk using the same image (iii. 18, 19): 'Yet I will rejoice in the Lord, I will joy in the God of my salvation. The Lord God is my strength, and He will make my feet like hinds' feet, and He will make me to walk upon mine high places. To the chief singer on my stringed instruments.'

There is another passage in Solomon's Song, ii. 8, 9, which is an allusion to the deer ; it reads as follows : 'The voice of my beloved ! behold, he cometh leaping upon the mountains, skipping upon the hills. My beloved is like a roe or a young hart : behold, he standeth behind our wall, he looketh forth at the windows, showing himself through the lattice.'

'There is one passage in the Bible which is familiar to us in many ways,' says the Rev. J. G. Wood in his work on natural history, 'and not the least in that it has been chosen as the text of so many well-known anthems. Psalm xlii. 1, 2 : "As the hart panteth after the water brooks, so panteth my soul after Thee, O God. My soul thirsteth for God, for the living God : when shall I come and appear before God ?" Beautiful as this passage is, it cannot be fully understood without the context.'

David wrote this psalm before he had risen to royal power, and while he was fleeing from his enemies from place to place, and seeking uncertain shelter in the rock caves. In verse 6 he enumerates some of the spots in which he has been forced to reside, far away from the altar, the priests, and the sacrifice, for he has been hunted about from place to place by his enemies, as a stag is hunted by the hounds; and his very soul thirsted for the distant Tabernacle in which the Shekinah—the visible presence of God—rested on the mercy-seat between the golden cherubim.

Wild and unsettled as was the early life of David, this was the ever-reigning thought in his mind; and there is scarcely a psalm that he wrote in which we do not find some allusion to the visible presence of God among men. No matter what might be the trouble through which he had to pass, even though he trod the valley of the shadow of death, the thought of his God was soothing as water to the hunted stag, and in that thought he ever found repose. Through all his many trials and adversities, through his deep remorse for his sins, through his wounded paternal affection, and through his success and prosperity, that one thought was the ruling power.

He begins his career with it when he faced Goliath: 'Thou comest to me with a sword, and with a spear, and with a shield; but I come to thee in the name of the Lord of Hosts, the God of the armies of Israel.' He closes his career with the same thought, and in the 'last words' that are recorded he charged his son to 'keep the commandments of the Lord, that he might do wisely all that he had to do.'

It was evidently this passage from the Psalms of the 'hart at the water brooks,' which Sir Walter Scott had in mind when he began his famous poem of *The Lady of the Lake*, Canto I.:

> The stag at eve had drunk his fill,
> Where danced the moon on Monan's rill,
> And deep his midnight lair had made
> In lone Glenartney's hazel shade;
> But when the sun a beacon red
> Had twinkled on Benvoirlich's head,
> The deep-mouthed bloodhounds' heavy bay
> Resounded up the rocky way,
> And faint, from farther distance borne,
> Were heard the clanging hoof and horn.

The deer has some very remarkable traits. The gentle and affectionate disposition of the deer is well known by all who study out its habits.

Its timidity, its grace, its activity, and the lightness and elegance of its motion, its swiftness, its maternal affection, its quickness and alertness in hearing sounds which tell of approaching danger, its defence of its young when put to bay, its instinct in taking to the water to elude its pursuers, and in this way of throwing the dogs off the scent, its playfulness and grace, its beautiful walk and bounding steps, are some of the

many traits of this animal, which gives it a prominent place
among the animals of the Bible. One of the most wonderful
things about the deer, after considering its grace and quickness
of motion, is the peculiar formation and shape of its horns.
The horns of oxen and cows are hollow, permanent, and formed
around a muscular centre ; moreover, they are composed of a
peculiar substance similar to the material of which hoofs and
talons are composed. But the horns of the deer are formed on
a very different principle : in the first place, they are solid
deposits of bone ; in the second place, they are deciduous, that
is, they are only retained during a part of the year ; and in the
third place, they are deposits from the external instead of the
internal.

The process of formation, says a writer on natural history, is
so singular, that I shall give a short account of the progress of
the 'horn' during its short-lived existence. 'We will suppose
that a full-grown stag is hiding in the depths of the forests in
the month of March. He has no horns of any kind, and is
hardly to be distinguished from a doe but for his superior size.
On his head are two slight prominences covered with a kind of
velvety skin. In a few days the prominences become much
larger, and in a week or so begin to assume a horn-like shape.
Now, grasp these budding horns with your hand, and you will
find them quite hot, considerably hotter than those of the young
ox. They are hot because this velvety substance, with which
they are covered, is little else than a thick mass of arteries and
veins, through which the blood is pouring almost with the
rapidity of inflammation, depositing with every touch a minute
portion of bony matter. More and more rapidly increases the
growth. The external arteries become enlarged to supply a
sufficient tide of blood to the horns through their arteries, whose
size can be imagined from the grooves that they leave on the horn.
At this period of their growth, the horn can be easily broken
off, and if they are wounded in any way, the blood pours out with
astonishing rapidity. At length the process is complete, and
the noble animal walks decorated proudly with his enormous
mass of horns. But the horns are at present useless or worse
than useless to him, for not only does he not use them, but he
fears the slightest touch, because the blood still pours round
them. How is this to be stopped, and how is the velvety
covering to be got rid of ? In a manner no less simple than
wonderful.

'The arteries, having completed their work in depositing
sufficient matter for the substance of the horn, now turn their
attention to the base. It will be seen that all the arteries that
supply blood to the horns must necessarily pass up its base.
As the bony substance is deposited, each artery leaves for itself

a groove, very deep at the base, and becoming shallower towards the tip. The entire horn being furnished, the base now becomes enlarged ; the grooves in which the arteries lie are covered by a bony deposit that compresses the artery within ; the deposit becomes gradually thicker, and the arteries are in consequence gradually reduced in size, until at last they are completely obliterated, and the supply of blood cut off entirely. The velvet, being thus deprived of its nutriment, soon dies, and in a few days dries up, when the deer rubs off the shrivelled fragments against the trees, and is ready for combat.

'Sometimes the deer is so impatient that he rubs off the velvet before the arteries are entirely obliterated, and consequently loses some blood. I have seen a reindeer busily engaged in rubbing off the velvet while the blood was trickling down the horns, and the velvet hanging in crimson rags dripping with blood. The animal presented the most ferocious appearance at the time.'

So much, then, for the history of this Bible animal—the deer. Let us now learn the lessons which this noble animal teaches us.

We learn four lessons from the deer.

First of all, we learn A LESSON OF QUICKNESS IN FLEEING FROM DANGER.

The moment a deer hears the report of a gun, or the baying of a dog in the forest, immediately it takes to flight to escape the danger. Its promptness and quickness in taking to the water secures its deliverance from the approaching danger.

Some time ago, a whole family were sitting together around the fireside, when the oldest girl in the family suddenly broke the silence by saying,—

'Why is Fred like the cat's tail ?'

The whole family—father, mother, brother, and sisters, all except Fred—were waiting, muffled and gloved, for him to be ready to go with them to the lecture. Tardy Fred had been loitering about doing nothing in particular in a dreamy, aimless fashion, and had yet to brush his hair, don his boots, overcoat, cap, muffler, and mittens, when roguish sister Mary propounded this conundrum as the sedate old family cat walked across the floor and took possession of the cushioned chair.

'Don't you see ? Because he's always behind.'

Fred turned from the glass with cheeks a little flushed by the laugh which Mary had raised, hurried into his outer clothes, and by the time the rest had waited for him full five minutes he was ready.

'Always behind.' Yes, that is his great failing. He is as quick-motioned as other boys ; can run as fast, jump as far, and can skate as well ; but he is always the late one. He is seldom ever ready to sit down at meals when the rest are ; perhaps will get absorbed in a book, and forget to wash, or brush his hair, till the rest are taking their seats. I should be sorry to tell you how often tardy-marks stand against his name on the school register, such a bad habit he has fallen into of waiting till the last minute before he starts. And on Sunday morning he will sit reading or dreaming over something, and never seem to think of getting ready for church till it is almost time to go. Then he is in a great flutter, and can't find this, that, or the other ; the whole family have to help him, and he generally brings up in the rear after all.

Well, it is only a habit, but it is a very bad one. Fred must leave off dreaming, and fall to doing instead. Promptness in action has done untold good, and saved multitudes of lives, while tardiness has destroyed myriads. In temporal things as well as spiritual, 'Now is the accepted time.'

The devil has a great many servants, and they are all busy and active ones. They ride in the railroad trains, they sail on the steamboats, they swarm along the highways of the country and the thoroughfares of the city ; they do business in the busy marts ; they are everywhere and in all places. Some are so vile-looking that one instinctively turns from them in disgust ; but some are so sociable, insinuating, and plausible, that they almost deceive at times the very elect. Among the latter class are to be found the devil's four chief servants. Here are their names :

'There is no danger ;' that is one.
'Only this once ;' that is another.
'Everybody does so ;' this is the third.
'By and by ;' that is the fourth.

When tempted from the path of strict rectitude, and 'There is no danger' urges you on, say, 'Get thee behind me, Satan !'

When tempted to give the Sabbath up to pleasure, or to do a little labour in the workshop or counting-room, and 'Only this once,' or 'Everybody does so,' whispers at your elbow, do not listen for a moment to the dangerous counsel.

All four are cheats and liars. They mean to deceive and cheat you out of heaven.

'Behold,' says God, 'now is the accepted time, *now is the day of salvation.*'

The deer teaches us to be prompt in avoiding temptation ; so that the first lesson which we learn from the deer is—the lesson of quickness in fleeing from danger.

The second lesson which we learn from the deer is—THE LESSON OF SELF-RELIANCE.

The deer is the most timid, and, in a certain way, the most

defenceless of all animals. Yet it is one of the hardest and most difficult creatures to capture. The reason why it escapes so surely is not only that it is quick in heeding the approach of danger, but it is self-reliant in getting out of the reach of danger.

Many boys and girls make a failure in life because they do not learn to help themselves. They depend on father and mother even to hang up their hats and to find their playthings. When they become men and women, they will depend upon husbands and wives to do the same thing.

'A nail to hang a hat on,' said an old man of eighty years, 'is worth everything to a boy.' He had been 'through the mill,' as people say, so that he knew. His mother had a nail for him when he was a boy—a nail to hang his hat on, and nothing else. It was 'Henry's nail' from January to January, year in and year out, and no other member of the family was allowed to appropriate it for any purpose whatever. If the broom by chance was hung thereon, or an apron or coat, it was soon removed, because that nail was 'to hang Henry's hat on,' and that nail did much for Henry: it helped to make him what he was in manhood—a careful, systematic, orderly man at home and abroad, on his farm, and in his house. He never wanted another to do what he could do for himself.

Young folks are apt to think that certain things, good in themselves, are not honourable. To be a blacksmith or a boot-maker, to work on a farm or drive a team, is beneath their dignity as compared with being a merchant, or practising medicine or law.

This is pride, an enemy to success and happiness. No necessary labour is discreditable. It is never dishonourable to be useful. It is beneath no one's dignity to earn bread by the sweat of the brow. When boys who have such false notions of dignity become men, they are ashamed to help themselves as they ought, and for want of this quality they live and die unhonoured. Trying to save their dignity, they lose it.

Here is a story I have from a very successful merchant. When he began business for himself, he carried his wares from shop to shop. At length his business increased to such an extent that he hired a room in the Marlborough Hotel in Boston, during the business season, and thither the merchants, having been duly notified, would repair to make purchases. Among all his customers there was only one man who would carry to his store the goods which he had purchased. But there was one merchant, and the largest buyer of the whole number, who was not ashamed to be seen carrying a case of goods through the streets. Sometimes he would purchase four cases, and would say, 'Now I will take two and you take two, and we will carry them right over to the store.'

So the manufacturer and the merchant often went through
the streets of Boston quite heavily loaded. This merchant, of
all the number who went to the Marlborough Hotel for their
purchases, succeeded in business. He became a wealthy man,
when all the others failed. The manufacturer who was not
ashamed to help himself is now living—one of the wealthy men
of Massachusetts, ready to aid by his generous gifts every good
object that comes along, and honoured by all who know
him.

We are all architects, or labourers, together with God as the
great Architect, in building up our character ; day by day we
are building up the soul into strength or into weakness. The
building which we construct is not visible, for it is the soul ; it
is not formless, however, because it is invisible ; but real and
substantial, only with a finer substance than the senses can
perceive.

And a wondrous pile it is, with many parts, and eternal uses.
Like Solomon's temple, it goes up without sign of hammer or
toil ; no solid granite, no glistening marble, but thoughts, feelings, purposes, are its materials ; out of these thin and fleeting
things we are building a structure which shall outlive the
mountains, the globe, and time itself.

> ' Little by little,' an acorn said,
> As it slowly sank in its mossy bed :
> ' I am improving every day,
> Hidden deep in the earth away.'
> Little by little each day it grew,
> Little by little it sipped the dew :
> Downward it sent out a thread-like root,
> Up in the air sprang a tiny shoot.
> Day after day, and year after year,
> Little by little the leaves appear ;
> And the slender branches spread far and wide,
> Till the mighty oak is the forest's pride.
>
> ' Little by little,' said a thoughtful boy,
> ' Moment by moment I'll well employ,
> Learning a little every day,
> And not spending all my time in play ;
> And still this rule in my mind shall dwell—
> Whatever I do, I'll do it well.
> Little by little I'll learn to know
> The treasured wisdom of long ago ;
> And one of these days perhaps we'll see
> The world will be the better for me.'
> And do you not think that this simple plan
> Made him a wise and useful man ?

The second lesson that we learn from the deer is—the lesson
of self-reliance.

The third lesson which we learn from the deer is—THE LESSON OF KINDNESS TO OUR FELLOWS. All that the deer asks is to be let alone by dogs and hunters. The mother deer with her young is as gentle and tender as any human mother could be.

There is a story told by a naturalist, that a newly-born deer, hardly an hour old, crouched low to the earth, in obedience to a light tap on its shoulder from its mother's hoof; she, with the intense watchfulness of her kind, had scented a possible danger, and so warned her young one to hide itself. That there is no animal so watchful and tender and kind as is the female deer, all hunters know by experience. It is easy work to deceive the stag who leads the herd; but to evade the eyes and ears of the hind is a very different business, and taxes well the resources of a practised hunter. I think we can learn a great lesson from the kindness and tenderness of the deer family to one another.

The power of the religion of Jesus Christ consists in this: that it makes us kind.

'Bear ye one another's burdens,' says the apostle, 'and so fulfil the law of Christ.' The American poet, Joaquin Miller, writes as follows, a little piece which he has called, 'Is it Worth While?'—

Is it worth while that we jostle a brother,
  Bearing his load on the rough road of life?
Is it worth while that we jeer at each other,
  In blackness of heart, that we war to the knife?
  God pity us all in our pitiful strife.

God pity us all, as we jostle each other,
  God pardon us all for the triumphs we feel,
When a fellow goes down 'neath his load on the heather,
  Pierced to the heart: Words are keener than steel,
  And mightier far for woe than for weal.

Were it not well, in this brief little journey,
  On over the isthmus, down into the tide,
We give him a fish, instead of a serpent,
  Ere folding the hands to be and abide
  For ever and aye in dust at his side?

Look at the roses saluting each other;
  Look at the herds all at peace on the plain:
Man, and man only, makes war on his brother,
  And laughs in his heart at his peril and pain,
  Shamed by the beasts that go down on the plain.

Is it worth while that we battle to humble
  Some poor fellow down into the dust?
God pity us all! Time too soon will tumble
  All of us together, like leaves in a gust,
  Humbled, indeed, down into the dust.

Here is a story about the effect of kindness, which we may
call—

THE POWER OF SYMPATHY.

It is told by one who was a soldier in a Wisconsin regiment.
He says:

'When I was in the army, I was in a Wisconsin regiment.
There was a man who came into our lines through the Southern
lines, who wanted to join our regiment. He was brought
before the officers and questioned pretty closely, and finally he
was sworn into our ranks. He said he had been on a long
march, and hadn't got any letters for about two weeks. One
beautiful summer night, when all through the camp the
Wisconsin soldiers had got their letters and were reading them,
this man came up to me, and said,—

'"Jim, I wish I was dead!"

'"Dead! what for?"

'"Well, I haven't got any mother to write to me; my
mother's dead. My father is in the Southern army, and would
shoot me at sight for joining the Union forces. I've got no one
to take an interest in me. I've got no home to go to after the
war is over. I'd rather die than live."'

Well, this Wisconsin man wrote home to his mother and told
her all about the case; and it wasn't long before the chaplain
said,—

'"Here's a letter for you."

'"For me? No, you are mistaken. I've got no one to write
me letters. My folks are in the South, and they couldn't get a
letter through the lines. I don't know any one in the North."

'Says the chaplain, "You open that letter, and if it isn't for
you I will take it and be responsible for it."

'He took that letter, opened it, and read it—that letter from
a Christian mother, stating how she loved him, how she took
an interest in him, and that, when the war was over, he was
to make Wisconsin his own home. Oh, how the tears flowed
down his cheeks! how he wept for joy as he thought of that!
He sat down and answered that letter, and in a few days an
answer came back. It read like this:

'"My dear son;" and just as soon as he saw that, away he
went down the lines, shouting, "Boys, I've got a mother!
Glory!" And there wasn't a man in the whole regiment so
anxious for the war to close, and to get home to see his
"mother," as that man was.'

My dear children, let us remember that cruelty and harshness
are relics of the beast nature within us. Let us try and imitate
the kindness and gentleness of the loveable animals about us, as
the deer, who is kind and gentle to its fellows. Let us try and

E

take a kind and pleasant view of our fellow-men, and when we come to a hard place, or a hard nature in life, let us learn to—

'LET IT PASS!'

Be not swift to take offence ;
  Let it pass !
Anger is a foe to sense ;
  Let it pass !
Brood not darkly o'er a wrong,
Which will disappear ere long,
Rather sing this cheery song,—
  Let it pass !
  Let it pass !

If for good they've render'd ill,
  Let it pass !
Oh, be kind and gentle still ;
  Let it pass !
Time at last makes all things straight,
Let us not resent, but wait,
And our triumph shall be great.
  Let it pass !
  Let it pass !

The fourth and last lesson which we learn from the deer is—THE LESSON OF DEPENDING UPON PRESENT SUPPLIES. There is one wonderful Psalm (cx.), which is supposed to have been written by David. It describes the triumphs of the great Messiah, and begins as follows :

'The Lord said unto my Lord, Sit Thou at my right hand, until I make Thine enemies Thy footstool.

'The Lord shall send the rod of Thy strength out of Zion ; rule Thou in the midst of Thine enemies.'

It ends with the following words (verses 5, 6, and 7) :—

'The Lord at thy right hand shall strike through kings in the day of His wrath. He shall judge among the heathen, He shall fill the places with the dead bodies, He shall wound the heads over many countries.

'He shall drink of the brook in the way, therefore shall He lift up the head.'

This idea, in the last verse, of drinking of the brook in the way, has evident reference to the stag or doe in its march through the wilderness, supplying itself with the sustenance which it finds in its way. We sometimes worry ourselves about what we are to do next week, or next month, or next year. It is a great deal better for us to learn a lesson from the stag, and 'drink of the brook in the way ;' by which I mean, do the present duty, and leave the future to take care of itself.

Here are some beautiful verses which illustrate this lesson of our subject, and the lesson of dependency upon our present supplies. This poem is called—

'DOE YE NEXTE THYNGE.'

From an old English parsonage,
   Down by the sea,
There came, in the twilight,
   A message to me;
Its quaint Saxon legend,
   Deeply engraven,
Hath, as it seems to me,
   Teaching from heaven;
And through the hours
   The quiet words ring,
Like a low inspiration,
   'Doe ye nexte thynge.'

Many a questioning,
   Many a fear,
Many a doubt,
   Hath its quieting here.
Moment by moment,
   Let down from heaven,
Time, opportunity,
   Guidance are given;
Fear not to-morrows,
   Child of the King;
Trust them with Jesus,
   'Doe ye nexte thynge.'

Oh, He would have thee
   Daily more free,
Knowing the might
   Of thy Royal degree;
Ever in waiting,
   Glad for His call;
Tranquil in chastening,
   Trusting through all.
Comings and goings
   No turmoil need bring;
His all thy future—
   'Doe ye nexte thynge.'

Do it immediately,
   Do it with prayer,
Do it reliantly,
   Casting off care;
Do it with reverence,
   Tracing His hand,
Who hath placed it before thee
   With earnest command.
Stayed on Omnipotence,
   Safe 'neath His wing,
Leave all resultings—
   'Doe ye nexte thynge.'

Looking to Jesus ;
  Ever serener,
Working or suffering,
  Be thy demeanour !
In the shade of His presence,
  The rest of His calm,
The light of His countenance,
  Live out thy psalm.
Strong in His faithfulness,
  Praise Him and sing ;
Then, as He beckons thee,
  ' Doe ye nexte thynge.'

These, then, are the four lessons which we learn from the deer : First, we learn *the lesson of quickness in fleeing from danger;* secondly, we learn *the lesson of self-reliance;* thirdly, we learn *the lesson of kindness to our fellows;* and fourthly, we learn *the lesson of depending on present supplies.*

Let us all try in life, my dear children, to be as thirsty after God and our duty as the hart is when it panteth after the water brooks.

VI.

THE BEE.

'They compassed me about like bees.'—PSALM cxviii. 12.

THE bee and honey are very often mentioned in the Bible.

Bees, from a very early time, have lived in hives which they have formed among rocks.

The hiving bee of Syria is very much like the American bee, but smaller. Most of the references to the bees in the Bible refer to their fearful sting. In Deut. xiv. 4, we read : 'And the Amorites, which dwelt in that mountain, came out against you, and chased you, as bees do, and destroyed you in Seir, even unto Hormah.' In the words of our text we read : 'They compassed me about like bees.'

In the seventh chapter of Isaiah, eighteenth verse, we read : 'And it shall come to pass in that day, that the Lord shall hiss for the fly that is in the uttermost part of the rivers of Egypt, and for the bee that is in the land of Assyria.' This idea of 'hissing' for the bee is the same as that which bee-keepers have to-day, when they want to have a colony of bees swarm. They jingle bells, blow horns and other utensils, beat on tin pans, and call out, hello ! hi-oh ! and hist ! or heigh-oh ! when they want a colony of bees to swarm.

We remember in the book of Deuteronomy that the land of

promise was always spoken of 'as a land flowing with milk and honey.'

David speaks of honey falling out of a rock in Psalm lxxxi. 16 : 'He should have fed them also with the finest of the wheat, and with honey out of the rock should I have satisfied thee.' Again, in 1 Samuel xiv. 25, 26, we read : 'And all they of the land came to a wood, and there was honey upon the ground.

'And when the people were come into the wood, behold the honey dropped, but no man put his hand to his mouth, for the people feared the oath.'

In Judges xiv. 18, we read : 'And the men of the city said unto him on the seventh day, before the sun went down, What is sweeter than honey ? and what is stronger than a lion ? And he said unto them, If ye had not plowed with my heifer, ye had not found out my riddle.'

In the wilderness of Judea bees were more numerous than in other parts of Syria, and this honey was a part of the diet of John the Baptist when he preached in the wilderness.

To-day the Bedouin Arabs seek honey from the comb, and bottle it in skins. Honey has been from a very early date an article of commerce in the East. Old Jacob sent down to his son Joseph, the governor of Egypt, and to his other sons, honey. Honey was considered by the Jews as a valuable article of trade. When Ishmael had killed Gedaliah and others, ten men tried to please him by bribing him. They said, 'Slay us not, for we have treasures in the field, a barrel of oil and of honey.' That honey was held to be very valuable is shown in 1 Samuel xiv. Saul the king issued an order that nobody should eat anything during the day of the battle, until evening. His son Jonathan, who had not heard his father's order, being very hungry, came across honey oozing on the ground from a niche in the rock where it had been stored. He held forth the end of his rod, and ate from it, and was satisfied. There is a very curious passage in the book of Proverbs xxv. 16, which was evidently written for the bee-keepers of that day : 'Hast thou found honey ? Eat so much as is sufficient for thee, lest thou be filled therewith, and vomit it.'

Another warning is given in verse 27 : 'It is not good to eat much honey : so for men to search their own glory is not glory.' These, then, are the allusions which we find in the Bible to honey and the honey-bee.

Let us now study out for some of the ways and habits of this wonderful little worker. Bees only flourish when associated in large numbers, as a colony. In a solitary state a single bee is almost as lifeless as a new-born child. It is not able to endure the ordinary chill of a summer night.

Mr. Langstroth, an authority on bees, says :

'If a certain colony of bees is examined a short time before it swarms, three different kinds of bees will be found in the hive. The first is the big bee, commonly called the queen bee. The second, some hundreds of large bees called "drones." The third among these are of a smaller kind, called "workers," or common bees, and are those seen on the blossoms. The queen bee is the ruler of the hive. All the eggs are laid by her. The large bees are called the drones, and are a sort of nobility who keep near the queen. The thousands of smaller bees are called the workers; they are the ones who go after the honey. The queen bee, or mother bee, is the common mother of the whole colony. She is necessary to the welfare of the hive, and a colony without a queen must surely depreciate, as a body would without a spirit.

'The queen bee is treated by the bees as every mother should be by her children—with the most unbounded respect and affection. The circle of her hive is her home, and the bees are constantly surrounding her, displaying in many ways their dutiful regard; offering her honey from time to time, always getting out of her way, and making her a clear path when she wishes to move on the combs. If she is taken from them, as soon as they have ascertained their loss, the whole colony is thrown into a state of the most intense excitement. All the labours of the hive are at once abandoned, and the bees run over the combs, and the whole of them run out of the hive, and look, as in anxious search, after their beloved mother. Not being able to find her, they return to their desolate home, and by their actions, and in many other ways, reveal their deep sense of loss. Their moans sound like a succession of wails on the minor key, and cannot any more be mistaken, by the experienced bee-keeper, for their ordinary happy hum, than the piteous moaning of a sick child can be confounded by the mother with its happy laughter in its days of health.'

The 'drones' are a very curious insect; they are a sort of nobility who hang around the court during the days of summer. They will not work, and are merely ornaments, but they have a terrible day of reckoning when the fall comes.

The ten thousand workers, or common bees, who have been toiling all summer, going back and forth, bringing honey into the hive, turn upon the drones when the first frost comes, and kill them right and left. It is something frightful to witness this massacre of the drones. It is like the massacre of the Sicilian vespers, or the massacre of St. Bartholomew's Day.

The workers go for the drones with their stings, trample them under foot, and pierce them through and through with their sharp probosces. The poor drones seem to have no way to defend themselves, and, not having been workers, and having no share in the labour of the hive, they are turned out into the dreary winter, or are massacred in cold blood by the working bees. In many ways they seem to form a band of union, as the Knights of Labour do.

The building of the honeycomb is carried on with the greatest activity in the hive. The cells are built in the night, while the honey is gathered during the day, and in this way no time is lost. If the weather is too wet to allow the bees to go abroad, the comb is rapidly constructed by day and by night. 'On the return of a fair day, the bees gather an unusual quantity of honey,' says Mr. Langstroth, as they have plenty of room for storage. Thus it often happens that by their wise economy of time they lose nothing, even if confined for several days to their hive.

When the poet says,

> How doth the little busy bee
> Improve each shining hour,

he might with equal truth have described her as utilizing the dark nights in her bountiful labours.

The number of workers in a hive varies very much ; a good swarm ought to contain from fifteen to twenty thousand bees.

The honey-bee is capable of being tamed and domesticated to a most surprising degree. The honey-bee never volunteers an attack on any one ; he gets on the defensive when crowded, but he only fights in self-defence.

In the spring of the year, as soon as the hive is well filled with comb, the new swarm begins to crowd. It is time the population of bees began to make preparations for migration. Says an authority on this subject,—

'About the time of the young queen's arrival at maturity, the drones are always found in the greatest abundance. The swarm is led off by the old queen, unless she has previously died, or some accident has befallen her, in which case the swarm is led by one of the young ones, reared to supply her loss. The old mother leaves soon after the cells are ceiled over. There are no indications, from which one can judge with certainty, when the bees are first going to swarm. Sometimes the weather will be unfavourable, or the blossoms fail to yield an abundant supply of honey, so it is very uncertain just when they are ready to swarm.

'On the day fixed for their departure, the queen bee appears very restless, and, instead of depositing her eggs in the cells, she climbs over the combs, and imparts her agitation to the whole colony. The bees fill themselves with honey before they start. A short time before the swarm rises, a few bees may be seen sporting in the air, and looking towards the doorway ; occasionally flitting in and out, as though they were impatient for the important event to take place. At length a very violent agitation commences in the hives. The bees appear almost frantic, whirling around in a certain way, like the circles made by a stone thrown into the still water, until at last the whole hive is in a state of great commotion, and the bees rush impatiently to the entrance, and pour forth in one steady stream. Not a bee lags behind, but each one pushes straight ahead, as though fleeing for dear life. They fly in direct course ; hence the expression, "to make a bee-line" to the desired spot.'

It used to be considered necessary, at swarming and hiving time, for people to ring bells, beat kettles, and fire guns in order to make a noise, and encourage the bees in flying. This is so yet. It is the old queen who generally leads the swarm, and some new queen bee takes the place she left in the old hive, and carries on the business—with a 'new sign,' as it were.

It is very difficult, in the short space of time given us in this sermon, my dear children, to tell you minutely more about the wonderful habits of the bees : how they ventilate their hives, how they make pollen or bee-bread, how they protect the hive against the extremes of heat and cold and dampness, how they make their comb, in which the wax is formed, how they rob one another, like the barons of old, — one hive of bees robbing another,—how they are broken up by the death of their queen, how they fight their great enemy the bee-moth, and how they seem to have anger among themselves when there are those in the hive who do not work up to the standard of the hive.

All these wonderful points in the nature of this most remarkable insect we must pass over, and come to the lessons which we learn from the bee.

'They compass me about like bees.'

We may carry from the hive to our homes several important lessons.

During work, the bees are so intensely absorbed in their duties, that they can think of nothing else.

The first lesson we learn from the bee is—THE LESSON OF LOYALTY. They all love their queen. She is their ruler and their mother, and they are her subjects and her children. Without her, home would be nothing. She makes the home what it is. She is queen, and must be obeyed.

History informs us of an old Roman soldier who had served forty years in the interests of his country—thirty years as an officer ; he had been present at one hundred and twenty battles ; had been wounded forty-five times ; received fourteen crowns for saving Roman citizens, three mural crowns for having been first to mount the breach, and eight golden crowns for having snatched the Roman Legion from the enemy. All this bravery was performed by one noble warrior.

Such a life as this is indeed a life of loyalty to one's country.

The second lesson we learn from the bee is—THE LESSON OF LOVING THE HOME. Bees are keepers at home. They are very much attached to their hive. No mother of a family loves her home more than a queen bee; and all the true worker bees take after their mother in this respect. Some people have a genius for helping; there are others who seem to have a genius for hindering.

'There goes a man,' said his neighbour, speaking of a village carpenter, 'who has done more good, I really believe, in this community than any other person who ever lived in it. He cannot talk very well in prayer meeting, and he doesn't often try. He isn't very rich in this world's goods, and it's very little that he can put down on subscription papers for any other object; but a new family never moves into the village that he does not find them out, give them a neighbourly welcome, and offer any little service he can render. He is usually on the look-out to give strangers a seat in his pew at church. He is always ready to watch with a sick neighbour, and look after his affairs for him; and I have sometimes thought he and his wife keep house-plants in winter just for the sake of being able to send little bouquets to invalids. He finds time for a pleasant word for every child he meets; and you will always see them climbing into his one-horse waggon when he has no other load. He really seems to have a genius for helping folks in all sorts of common ways, and it does me good every day just to meet him on the streets.'

The second lesson we learn from the bee is—the lesson of loving our home, and of having the power of helping one another.

The third lesson we learn from the bee is—THE LESSON OF CLEANLINESS.

The care with which they remove dirt of all kinds is something remarkable.

They seem to believe what many Christians believe, that 'cleanliness is next to godliness.'

Every boy and girl may well follow the example of these wise little philosophers, the bees, and keep everything clean in their homes.

The fourth lesson we learn from the bee is—A LESSON OF SYMPATHY.

I have seen a wounded bee carried at length, and laid on the bee-board in the warm sunshine. One bee would lick the sufferer from head to foot with his tongue, another would roll him over and over in the sunshine. After they had succeeded in doing this, they would carry him to his sick-bed. This shows us the sympathy of the bee, and sympathy is the most divine thing in the world.

Here is a story which illustrates this point, which we may call—

THE DYING BOY'S BORROWED SHILLING.

On December 28th, Dean Stanley addressed a number of children in Westminster Abbey, and in the course of his remarks he told the following story :—'Not long ago, in Edinburgh, two gentlemen were standing at the door of an hotel, one very cold day, when a little boy, with a poor, thin, blue face, his feet bare and red with the cold, and with nothing to cover him but a bundle of rags, came and said, "Please, sir, buy some matches." "No ; I don't want any," the gentleman said. "But they are only a penny a box," the poor little fellow pleaded. "Yes ; but you see we don't want a box," the gentleman said again. "Then I will gie ye twa boxes for a penny," the boy said at last, and so, to get rid of him, the gentleman who tells the story says,—

' " I bought a box, but then I found I had no change, so I said, 'I will buy a box to-morrow.' 'Oh, do buy them to-night, if you please !' the boy pleaded again ; 'I will run and get ye the change, for I am verra hungry.' So I gave him the shilling, and he started away. I waited for him, but no boy came. Then I thought I had lost my shilling : still there was that in the boy's face I trusted, and I did not like to think bad of him. Late in the evening I was told a little boy wanted to see me ; when he was brought in, I found it was a smaller brother of the boy that got my shilling, but, if possible, still more ragged, and poor, and thin.

' " He stood a moment, diving into his rags, as if he was seeking something, and then said, 'Are you the gentleman that bought the matches frae Sandy ?' 'Yes.' 'Weel, then, here's fourpence out o' yer shilling. Sandy cannot come ; he's very ill ; a cart run over him and knocked him down, and he lost his bonnet and his matches and your sevenpence, and both his legs are broken, and the doctor says he'll die ; and that's a'.' And then, putting the fourpence on the table, the child broke down into great sobs. So I fed the little man, and I went with him to see Sandy. I found that the two little things lived alone, their father and mother being dead.

' " Poor Sandy was lying on a bundle of shavings ; he knew me as soon as I came in, and said, 'I got the change, sir, and was coming back ; and then the horse knocked me down, and

both my legs were broken ; and oh, Reuby ! little Reuby ! I
am sure I am dying ; and who will take care of you when I am
gone ? What will ye do, Reuby ?' Then I took his hand, and
said I would always take care of Reuby. He understood me,
and had just strength to look up at me as if to thank me. The
light went out of his blue eyes. In a moment

> He lay within the light of God,
>   Like a babe upon the breast,
> Where the wicked cease from troubling,
>   And the weary are at rest."'

The fifth and last lesson which we learn from the bee is—THE
LESSON OF BEING HAPPY IN ONE'S WORK. ' Place yourselves,' says
one who has written on this subject, ' before a hive, and see the
indefatigable industry of its busy toilers. Let the bee's hum
inspire you with the honourable resolution to do all things
cheerfully in the active duties of life. We ought to be happy
and cheerful in our work.'

' Are you not wearying for our heavenly rest ?' said White-
field one day to an old clergyman.

' No, certainly not ! ' he replied.

' Why not ?' was the surprised rejoinder.

' Why, my good friend,' said the old minister, ' if you were
to send your servant into the fields to do a certain portion of
work for you, and promised to give him rest and refreshment
in the evening, what would you say if you found him languid
and discontented in the middle of the day, and murmuring,
" Would to God it were evening ! " Would you not bid him be
up and doing, and finish his work, and then go home and get
the promised rest ? Just so does God say to you and me.'

Here is the way in which an old coloured preacher described
the lessons which we learn from the bee.

' There's a bee humming in that clover-head yonder,' said
Uncle True ; ' you can't hear it when you're talkin', but if
you jest keep still a minute, you can hear it as plain as a
church-bell, and I think it's jest as pooty a noise—leastways, it
tells me more.'

' Indeed ! ' said I. ' I should like to know what it tells
you.'

' Well, in the first place, it shows me that honey's to be got
out o' all the flowers, even the leetlest and homeliest. The bee
gets it in the onlikeliest places, you see. He don't turn up his
nose at a mullein-stalk, no more'n he does at a garden pink ;
and I shouldn't wonder if the Lord had put jest as much honey
in one as t' other. But if he was a bee with an aristocratic turn
o' mind, and wouldn't look for honey anywheres but in garden
pinks and damask roses, it's my opinion that he'd go home to

his hive empty-handed the biggest part o' the time. And I suppose the Lord has put about as much honey in one man's road as another's; if he only knew how to look for it, and didn't despise mullein-stalks.

'Then the bee shows me it's a man's business to hive up honey; not jest to go around amusin' himself with the flowers, and takin' only what tastes good, and what he can eat at the time, but to store it up against the winter of old age and trouble. I mean the honey of wisdom, and that begins in the fear of God. And, besides all that, the bee shows me that a man should go to his honest day's work with a joyful spirit, singin' and makin' melody in his heart, and not to be agoin' round with a sour face, and a grumblin' tongue, and a cross-grained temper, jest as if he thought the Lord who made him didn't know what was good for him.'

These, then, are the lessons which we learn from the bee. We might learn a great many more than these, for we might learn the lesson of being fond of fresh air, which the bees teach us by the way in which they ventilate their houses. We might learn the lesson of early rising from the bees, for they are up with the first ray of sunshine in the morning. They always go to bed when the sun goes down. Even the drones, or lazy idlers in the hives, are not allowed to go to balls and parties after seven o'clock, and dance with the wasps and grasshoppers, and then come home by the light of the moon. Though they do no work, they have got to go to bed when the others go. There is no outside club-house for the drones. Still another lesson which we may learn from the bee is the lesson of being peace-makers. They will not attack unless they are first attacked, and their stings they use merely in the defence of their queen or their homestead. But those lessons which we have marked off to-day are important; let us therefore go back and learn what they are.

First of all, they teach us *the lesson of loyalty.*

Second, they teach us *a lesson of loving one's home.*

Third, they teach us *the lesson of cleanliness.*

Fourth, they teach us *the lesson of sympathy.*

Fifth, they teach us *the lesson of cheerfulness in work.*

In conclusion, my dear children, how wonderful are the marvellous works of God!

Well might we say with the Psalmist (Psalm civ. 24–32): 'O Lord, how manifold are Thy works! in wisdom hast Thou made them all: the earth is full of Thy riches. So is the great and wide sea also, wherein are things creeping innumerable, both small and great beasts.

'There go the ships: and there is that leviathan, whom Thou hast made to take his pastime therein.

'These wait all upon thee ; that Thou mayest give them meat in due season.

'When Thou givest it them, they gather it, and when Thou openest Thy hand, they are filled with good.

'When Thou hidest Thy face, they are troubled : when Thou takest away their breath, they die, and are turned again to their dust.

'When Thou lettest Thy breath go forth, they shall be made : and Thou shalt renew the face of the earth.

'The glorious majesty of the Lord shall endure for ever : the Lord shall rejoice in His works.'

VII.

THE EAGLE.

'The way of the eagle in the air—is wonderful.'—PROV. xxx. 19.

WE have spoken of five of the beasts mentioned in the Bible. And now we take up one of the Bible birds, namely, the eagle. Some birds are larger than the eagle, and others are more beautiful ; but, when we come to consider the natural history of this noble bird, we find it very interesting and instructive. As the lion is called 'the king of beasts,' so the eagle is called 'the king of birds.' Eagles are of different kinds and sizes. What is called the Golden Eagle is of the largest size. It measures three feet and a half from the tip of its beak down to its feet ; and when its wings are spread out they measure about ten feet. There is another kind, known as the Imperial Eagle, the spread of whose wings is about six feet. And there is another kind, known as the Marine Eagle, whose wings when spread out measure a little over four feet.

On their national coat of arms the Americans have this noble bird to represent their country, and they call it 'The American Eagle.' During the late war, a soldier in a regiment from Wisconsin had a fine-looking eagle, which he had tamed and kept as a pet. It was called 'old Abe,' in honour of President Lincoln. The soldier took this eagle with him all through the war. It was present in more than thirty battles. It was wounded twice, but would never leave its master. And when the soldiers of that regiment shouted 'hurrah !' over any victory gained, 'old Abe' would flap his wings, and utter loud cries with them.

In our text Solomon says, 'The way of the eagle in the air is wonderful.'

And our sermon to-day will be about—

THE EAGLE AND ITS WONDERS.

There are four wonderful things about the eagle, of which we wish to speak.

In the first place, the eagle is wonderful for ITS STRENGTH.

We see the strength of the eagle in the way it flies. The swiftness of its flight shows its strength. We are told by those who have made a study of natural history, that the eagle is often known to fly at the rate of between forty and fifty miles an hour. And then, the great height to which it flies, as well as its speed, shows its strength. If you and I were standing in sight of an eagle's nest on the peak of a high mountain, we might see it leave its nest, and fly up, and up, toward the sun, till it was quite out of sight. It must have very great strength to enable it to do this. And then, in the food which it carries to its nest, for its young ones to eat, we see the strength of the eagle. It carries geese, and turkeys, and kids, and lambs, and even little children for its young ones to feed on.

In one of the cantons of Switzerland, two little girls were playing together in a meadow; one of them was about three years old, and the other five. While they were busy in their play, an eagle came and swooped down upon them. He seized hold of the oldest child, and carried it away to his nest, which was about the distance of a mile and a half from where he found the child. And there the remains of the poor child were found by a hunter some time afterwards. How great the strength of that eagle must have been to enable it to carry that child so far!

Now it is God who gives the eagle its great strength. And what God does for the eagle, in this way, He can do for all His servants. He says to each of His people, 'I will strengthen thee' (Isaiah xli. 10).

The Apostle Paul was feeling the truth and preciousness of this promise when he said, 'I can do all things through Christ, who strengtheneth me' (Philippians iv. 13). And what Jesus did for Paul, He is ready to do for you, and me, and for all His people. No matter how hard the duty is that we have to perform, if we only seek from God the strength He has promised us, we shall be able to do it with ease and comfort.

Here are some illustrations of the way in which Jesus gives His people strength.

The first may be called—

THE SOLDIER'S STRENGTH.

A young soldier came to the chaplain of his regiment, and told him that the first night he was in the barracks, before going

The Eagle.

to bed, he kneeled down to say his prayers, as he was accustomed to do. But the other soldiers all laughed, and made fun of him, and threw their boots at him. 'And now,' he asked, 'what would you advise me to do?'

The chaplain advised him to say his prayers in bed, without kneeling down.

The next time the chaplain met the soldier, he asked him if he had tried his plan, and how it succeeded.

'I tried it for a night or two,' said the soldier; 'but then I thought it seemed like being ashamed of Jesus, who is my Captain. So I asked Him to give me strength to do what was right. Since then, I have kneeled down every night to say my prayers. And now the men don't laugh at me any more; but a good many of them kneel down themselves and say their own prayers.'

Now, here we see how God gave that brave soldier strength to do his duty, and what a blessing his example was to his comrades, in leading them to do their duty too.

The only other story here may be called—

HELP IN TROUBLE.

This is a story which my dear mother, now in heaven, used to tell me and my brothers and sisters when we were little children. My mother, when a girl, lived in the town of Bridgenorth, Shropshire, in England. 'Near my father's house,' she used to say, 'there lived a man who was a baker, and who supplied our family with bread. He and his wife were not religious people, and never went to church. But after a while the baker's wife took to going to the Methodist church in their neighbourhood. Before long she was converted, and joined the church. This made her husband very angry. He told her not to go to church, but she went. Then, when she came home at night, he would beat her severely, and drag her round the room by the hair of her head. But still she kept on going to church.

'One Sunday evening he said to her, "Wife, I have told you not to go to church, and yet you go. I have beaten you over and over again, but still you will go. Now, I want to say to you that, if you go to-night, as sure as I am a living man, the moment you are gone I'll start the fire in the big oven, and make it as hot as I can, and when you come home I'll put you into the oven, and roast you alive." His wife knew he was a very determined man, and that he would be sure to do what he had threatened. Then she went up to her chamber, and, kneeling down, told the Lord all about it. She asked Him to give her strength to do her duty; and to have mercy on her husband, and make him a Christian.

'Then she put on her bonnet and shawl, and went to church. As soon as she was gone, her husband went into the bakery, and

F

started a fire in the oven. He kept on throwing in the wood for an hour or so, till the oven was hotter than ever it had been before. Then, fearing that perhaps his wife would not come home that night, but might go and stay with some of their neighbours, he put on his hat, and started to go to the church and bring his wife home. When he got there he found that the service was not over. He gently opened the door of the church. As he did so, he heard the minister talking about "a burning fiery furnace." This had a very strange effect upon him. He thought of his great wickedness, and trembled like a leaf. He slipped quietly into the church, and took a seat near the door. The minister was preaching about Daniel's three friends, who were cast into Nebuchadnezzar's fiery furnace. The baker was fearfully frightened. At the close of the sermon, according to the custom in that church, the minister asked any person who desired to be prayed for to come up to the chancel. The baker was the first to go. We can imagine the surprise of his wife when she saw him there. When the church was out, he walked back with his wife. On reaching home, he begged her pardon for his cruel treatment of her, and asked her to pray with him. She did so, and he soon became a Christian.'

And there was this strange thing to mention in connection with this story : the minister who preached that night was not the pastor of the church, but a stranger who was supplying for him. It was the well-known Rev. John Fletcher of Madeley. He had prepared himself to preach on another subject that night. But, on reaching the church, he had entirely forgotten the text and the subject on which he had intended to preach. He was troubled to know what to do. He lifted up his heart in prayer to God, and asked for direction. And while they were singing the opening hymn, the thought came into his mind to preach about Nebuchadnezzar's furnace and the three men who were cast into it. And this led to that baker's conversion.

How interesting it is to think how strong God made that brave woman, under those trying circumstances, and what a blessing followed from it, both to herself and her husband.

The first wonderful thing about the eagle is—its strength.

The second wonderful thing about the eagle is—ITS SIGHT.

If you and I were walking out at noonday, and should attempt to look up towards the sun, we should find its light too strong for us, and we should be obliged to shut our eyes, or to put our hands over them, to protect them from its glare. But it is very different with the eagle. It can rise from its nest at noon, and go soaring up towards the sun. It can go on, rising higher and higher, and yet all the time be gazing steadily at the full-orbed splendour which is shining round it. We watch the noble bird till it has soared quite out of our sight. We cannot see that eagle any more. And yet, if in the field far below where we are there is a little hen walking about, the eagle will see it from its towering height, and, swooping down on the poor creature, will make a meal of it. The eagle is wonderful in its sight. And it is God who gives to the eagle this power of seeing.

And if we ask Him, God will do the same for us. I do not mean by this that God will give to our bodily eyes such wonderful sight as the eagle has. We do not need this, and it would do us no good if we had it. God has not promised to give us this kind of sight. What we most need is sight for the eyes of our minds or souls. I mean by this the power to understand the truths of the Bible ; so that we may see and know what our sins are, the danger into which they have brought us, and how through Jesus we may be pardoned, and have grace to serve Him faithfully in this life, and be happy with Him for ever in the life to come. This is eyesight more wonderful than that which the eagle has ; and God can give us just this kind of eyesight. David was seeking for this when he offered such prayers as these : 'That which I see not, teach Thou me.' 'Open mine eyes that I may behold wondrous things out of Thy law.' And to have our eyes opened in this way, or to have spiritual eyesight given to us, is the greatest blessing we can ask of God, or that He can give to us.

I have only one story for this part of our sermon. It shows us the kind of sight which God gives to His people, and the good effect which it has upon them. We may call it—

THE YOUNG GIRL'S SIGHT, OR ABOUT THE HEN AND THE EGG.

A young man from a town in England went over to Paris to learn the French language and to finish his education. He spent several years there, and became acquainted with a number of gentlemen who were infidels. At home he had been taught by his mother to read the Bible and to believe its teachings. But, after hearing what those Frenchmen had to say about it, he gave away his Bible, and became an infidel.

Shortly after his return home, he was invited to spend an evening with an intelligent family in their neighbourhood. There was a large company present, and different sets of them were amusing themselves in various ways.

As this young man was walking through the parlour, he saw two young girls, one about twelve and the other about fifteen or sixteen years old, sitting in a bay window, earnestly engaged in reading. Going up to them, he said, 'Well, young ladies, what novel is that you are reading ?'

'It is not a novel, sir,' said the elder girl. 'We are reading God's book, the Bible.'

' Oh, then, do you believe there is a God?' asked the young man.

The girls looked at each other in astonishment. Then the elder girl said to him, 'And is it possible, sir, that you don't believe it too?'

' I used to believe it once,' he said ; 'but, after living in Paris, and studying science and philosophy and mathematics, I learned that this is all a mistake. There is no God!'

' I never was in Paris,' said the young girl, 'and never studied those important things that you speak of. I only know my catechism and my Bible. But, since you are so learned, may I ask you a question?'

' Certainly. Just as many questions as you please.'

' You say there is no God. Now, suppose there was an egg here, could you tell me where it came from?'

' What a funny question! Why, of course the egg comes from a hen.'

' And which of them existed first, the egg or the hen?'

' I really don't know what you mean by this question. I suppose, of course, the hen existed first.'

' Well, that must have been a hen that did not come from an egg. Can you tell me where that hen came from?'

' Beg your pardon, miss. I was mistaken. Of course the egg existed first.'

' Then that must have been an egg that did not come from a hen. Well, where did that first egg come from?'

The young man got excited, and said, 'What's the use of asking such questions as these?'

' The use is just this,' said the young girl. 'If the first hen did not come from an egg as other hens do, then somebody must have made it ; that somebody must be God. If you cannot explain how the first hen, or the first egg, existed without God, can you explain how the world existed without God?'

That is a question which all the infidels in the world cannot answer. The young man had nothing more to say. He turned away from the girls, took his hat, and went home.

Now that young girl, like the eagle in the air, had a wonderful sight, only of a different kind from that which the eagle has. God had opened the eyes of her soul to see what that young man, with all his education and learning, could not see at all. And that is the sight which we all need, and should earnestly desire to have. And if with all our hearts we ask God for it, He will certainly give it to us. The second wonderful thing about the eagle is—its sight.

The third wonderful thing about the eagle is—ITS TRAINING.

Our infant schools and Kindergartens are places in which young children are taught, or trained to know and serve God.

And the young eagles in their nests have a remarkable sort of training which they go through. This training we see in the efforts which the parent eagles make to teach them how to fly, so that, when they grow up, and have to leave their nest, they may know how to take care of themselves.

If you and I could stand somewhere in sight of an eagle's nest, and watch the parent birds training their young ones to fly, this is what we should see. The time has come when the young must be taught to fly. Their parents wish to show them how, and they do it in this way. They shake their wings over the nest to wake up their young ones. Then they fly about, very near the nest, to show their children how to fly. And then, by sounds and motions which the young birds understand, they call on them to come out of their nest and learn to fly. When the young eagles come out and begin to use their wings, the parent birds keep close to them and watch them carefully. If one of the young eagles does not use his wings right, and is beginning to fall, the mother bird flies under it, gets it on her back, and takes it to the nest. Then the mother tries again with that bird, and keeps on trying, till the young one succeeds in learning how to fly. This is the training which the young eagles have to go through.

And God compared the training which He gave to the children of Israel to this which the young eagles receive, when He said : 'As the eagle stirreth up her nest, fluttereth over her young, spreadeth abroad her wings, taketh them, beareth them on her wings ; so have I done for my people Israel.'

And so He does for all His people. While we are in this world we are in God's school. He is training us and teaching us, that we may know how to love and serve Him here, and be happy with Him for ever in heaven.

When God was leading the children of Israel through the wilderness, all that He did to them was to train them to be ready to go in and possess the good land of Canaan, which He had prepared for them. And so, all that God is doing for us in this world is to train us for heaven. And this is what the Apostle Paul means when he says that 'God is making all things work together for good to them that love Him.'

Here are some illustrations of the way in which God does this. Our first incident may be called—

A LESSON FROM THE VINE.

A faithful minister of the gospel called one day to visit a member of his church, who had lately met with a great trial, and was very impatient under it, and complained of being hardly dealt with. On reaching the house of his friend, the servant said that her master was working in the garden. On going there, the minister found his friend engaged in trimming a vine, the leaves and branches of which had grown too thick and close. After a few kind words spoken to him, the minister asked him what he was doing.

'I find,' said he, 'that, owing to the late rains, the branches and leaves of this vine have grown so much as to prevent the rays of the sun from reaching and ripening the grapes. So I am pruning the vine, and taking away these leaves, that the rays of the sun may be able to reach and ripen the grapes that are growing upon it.'

'Very good,' said the minister. 'And now, my friend,' he went on to say, 'don't you know that we Christians are all vines in God's garden? And that when He sends trials or afflictions upon us, as He has lately done to you, He is only doing for us just what you are doing for that vine. He is pruning us, and taking away unnecessary leaves, in order that the fruits of the Spirit may ripen better in our hearts and lives.'

'Thank you, sir, for this lesson,' said the minister's friend. 'I never thought of that before. And now I won't complain of God's dealings with me any more.'

This is a good lesson from the gardener and his work. And we may get another from the sculptor and his works.

A sculptor is one who works in stone. He takes blocks of marble or other stone, and makes busts or figures of men or women out of them. When the sculptor has a block of marble before him, with his mallet or hammer in one hand, and his chisel in the other, he will go to work upon it. Day after day, for weeks and months, he will keep on pounding and chiselling, till at last he brings forth out of that unshapely mass of stone the beautiful figure of a man or woman. And this illustrates what God is doing in training us for heaven. The afflictions and trials which we meet with in this life are like the mallet and chisel of the sculptor in God's hand, and by them He is making us what He wishes us to be.

Our next story may be called—

A LESSON FROM THE SCULPTOR.

This story refers to a good Christian mother. She had been visited with a long and painful illness, which she bore with great patience and cheerfulness. Her sufferings were so great at times as to make it very trying to her family to witness them, and they could not keep from weeping.

One day, when her daughter was waiting on her, she was so distressed at the sight of her mother's suffering, that she could not keep back the tears from flowing down her cheeks.

When her mother saw those tears, she looked tenderly at her, and said, 'Don't cry, my darling child. Remember I am in the loving Saviour's hands ; and this is only the chiselling that He is giving me, to make me ready for heaven.'

That good mother had learned well the lesson from the sculptor, and was making a proper use of it.

When the sculptor is going on with his work, he never gives one blow with his mallet or chisel to the block of stone before him, but what he sees is necessary in order to accomplish the object he has in view. And it is just so with God—our great heavenly Sculptor.

I have only one other short story to use here. We may call it—

THE SUCCESSFUL TRAINING OF A BOY.

A little boy, about twelve years old, was tempted one day to pluck some cherries from a tree which his father had told him not to touch.

'You needn't be afraid,' said his companion, who was standing near him. 'Your father is not here, and won't know anything about it. And if he should find it out, he is too good to hurt you.'

'Yes,' said the brave little fellow, 'I know it ; and that's the very reason why I won't take any. He wouldn't *hurt me*, but it would *hurt him* to know that I didn't mind him.'

That boy had been properly trained, and he was making a right use of his training.

And so we see that the third wonderful thing about the eagle is—its training.

And then the fourth wonderful thing about the eagle is—ITS SAFETY.

I refer especially here to the safety which the eagle finds in its nest. This is generally built on the top of a steep mountain peak, so far up as to be out of the reach of harm or danger. Other birds do not visit the eagle's nest ; while animals and men find it almost impossible to climb up the tall peak to the spot where its nest is built. And so this noble bird can sit calmly on its nest, in the high place where it is built, and feel perfectly safe there. Here is a short story to illustrate this point. We may call it—

THE EAGLE'S LESSON TO A KING.

There was a king once, who ruled over a large and powerful nation, and who was very rich. But the burden of cares connected with his kingdom made him so unhappy that his riches gave him very little comfort. He had heard of an old man, famous for his wisdom and piety, who lived as a hermit, all alone by himself, in a cave on the borders of a forest, some miles distant from the king's palace. The king went to see him one day, and found him in his cave.

'Holy man,' said the king, 'I have come to see you, and to ask if you can tell me how I may be happy.'

Without making any reply, the wise old man led the king along a rough path, till he brought him in front of a very high, perpendicular rock, on the top of which an eagle had built her nest.

Pointing to it, he asked, 'Do you know why the eagle builds her nest so high?'

'Certainly,' said the king; 'she does it in order to be safe from harm and danger.'

'Then imitate that bird,' said the wise old man : 'build your home in heaven ; let your treasure and your heart be there, and then you will be safe and happy.'

That was good advice to the king, and it is good advice for us all. When we think of the safety of the eagle in its nest far up the mountain's side, we see in it a good illustration of the safety which attends us if we are true servants of God. This safety is found in the presence and power of God, and His faithfulness in fulfilling His promises. Here are some of the promises which God has given to show how safe His people are under His care. In one place we read : 'The beloved of the Lord shall dwell in safety by Him' (Deut. xxxiii. 12). The 91st Psalm seems to have been written on purpose to show how safe God's people are. Here God says to each of them : 'Because thou hast made the Lord, even the Most High, thy habitation ; there shall no evil befall thee, neither shall any plague come nigh thy dwelling. For He shall give His angels charge over thee, to keep thee in all thy ways.' With angels watching over us as our keepers, we must be safe indeed.

There are many more promises of the same kind in the Bible, but these are enough.

And then we find in the Bible interesting illustrations of the safety which God's people find in Him. Look at Abraham. Four great kings were offended at him once for something that he had done, and he was very much afraid of them. But God said to him, 'Fear not, Abraham, I am thy shield.' With God for our shield, how safe we are ! God would not let those kings do anything to hurt Abraham.

How safe Daniel was even in the den of lions, because God was his shield ! And how safe his three friends were, though they were cast into Nebuchadnezzar's fiery furnace. God was their shield there, and so the flames could not hurt them.

And here are some short illustrations outside of the Bible. The first may be called—

PROTECTED FROM A ROBBER.

An interesting Christian young girl was confined for several years to a sick-bed. She was generally left by herself all night. On one occasion, about midnight, she was lying awake on her bed. The rest of the family were asleep in their own rooms. She saw the door of her room open, and a robber came in. He stopped a moment on entering. Her little lamp was shining on them both, from the stand by her bedside. He looked at the young girl, and was surprised to find her awake, and yet perfectly calm. She uttered no cry or scream, but, as the robber stood there, looking at her, she simply raised her hand, with her finger pointing towards heaven, and said, 'Man, do you know that God is looking at you?'

The man stood still for a moment, and then, without speaking a word, quietly turned round and went out of the house.

The God of Abraham was the shield of that sick girl, and we see how safe she was under His protection!

Our next story may be called—

SAFE WITH FATHER.

On one occasion there had been heavy rains in a certain neighbourhood. These rains had caused dangerous floods, which were sweeping through that part of the country. A labouring man, who lived in a lonely cottage with his little boy about seven years old, woke at midnight and found the water coming into the cottage. Then he got up and dressed himself and his little boy, and started to go to the house of a friend, about a mile off. They had to walk through the water nearly all the way, and at times it was up to the little boy's waist. On reaching the house of their friend, the father told about the difficulty they had met with in getting there. On hearing this, the mother of that family laid her hand on little Johnny's head, and said, 'Well, my boy, weren't you afraid in going through the water?'

'Not at all,' said the brave little fellow, 'for I was walking by the side of father. He had hold of my hand, and I knew he wouldn't let the water drown me.' And this is just the way we should feel towards our heavenly Father. He is always at our side. He has our hand in His, and *this* is what makes us safe.

I have only one other short illustration. We may call it—

THE MESSENGER OF GOD.

A good man, who had served God for many years, was sitting one day, with several other persons, eating a lunch on a bank very near a deep mining pit. He was the nearest of them all to the mouth of the pit. As he sat there eating, a little bird came and fluttered in his breast, and gently pecked at his shoulder, and then flew away. Presently it came again, and did the same thing. Then the old man said, 'I'll follow you, little birdie, and see where you came from.' He rose to follow the bird, and, while he was away, the bank of the pit fell down into the mine, and those who had been sitting by him were carried with it and killed. God knew the danger to which that faithful servant of His was exposed, and He made that little bird His messenger to save him.

The fourth thing for which the eagle is wonderful is—its safety.

Where is our text to-day? Proverbs xxx. 19. What the words of the text? 'The way of the eagle in the air is wonderful.' What is the sermon about? The eagle and its wonders. How many wonderful things about the eagle did we speak of? Four. In the first place, it is wonderful for what? *For its strength.* In the second place, for what? *For its sight.* In the third place, for what? *For its training.* And in the fourth place, for what? *For its safety.*

David's prayer to God was, 'Open Thou mine eyes that I may behold wondrous things out of Thy law' (Psalm cxix. 18). This a good prayer for us all to offer. And then let us pray that God may help us 'both to perceive and know what things we ought to do, and also to have grace and power faithfully to perform the same.' Then we shall be God's loving servants, and, like the eagle, we shall have wonderful strength, and sight, and training, and safety.

The following are some of the references to the eagle in the Bible :—

The Lord shall bring a nation against thee from far, as swift as an eagle flieth (Deut. xxviii. 49).

As an eagle stirreth up her nest, fluttereth over her young, spreadeth abroad her wings, taketh them, beareth them on her wings : so the Lord alone did lead him, and there was no strange god with him (Deut. xxxii. 11, 12).

They are passed away as the swift ships, as the eagle that hasteth to the prey (Job ix. 26).

Doth the eagle mount up at thy command, and make her nest on high? She dwelleth and abideth on the rock, upon the crag of the rock, and the strong place. From thence she seeketh the prey, and her eyes behold afar off (Job xxxix. 27-30).

Riches certainly make themselves wings; they fly away as an eagle toward heaven (Prov. xxiii. 5).

The way of an eagle in the air is wonderful (Prov. xxx. 19).

O thou that dwellest in the clefts of the rock ; though thou shouldest make thy nest as high as the eagle, I will bring thee down from thence, saith the Lord (Jer. xlix. 16).

Thus saith the Lord, A great eagle with great wings, full of feathers, which had divers colours, came unto Lebanon, and took the highest branch of the cedar (Ezek. xvii. 3).

Though thou exalt thyself as the eagle, and though thou set thy nest among the stars, thence will I bring thee down, saith the Lord (Obad. 4).

Ye have seen what I did to the Egyptians, and how I bare you on eagles' wings, and brought you to myself (Ex. xix. 4).

Bless the Lord, O my soul, who satisfieth thy mouth with good things, so that thy youth is renewed like the eagle's (Psalm ciii. 5).

But they that wait upon the Lord shall renew their strength; they shall mount with wings as eagles; they shall run, and not be weary; and walk, and not faint (Isaiah xl. 31).

VIII.

THE ANT.

'Go to the ant, thou sluggard; consider her ways, and be wise.'—
PROVERBS vi. 6.

OUR subject to-day is the ant. The ant is one of the most wonderful of insects, and insects are in many ways the most wonderful of all God's creatures; there are more wonders about the insect world than about any other; God seems to have provided for these little creatures the most marvellous means of getting on in life. Their instincts, their principles, their powers of reasoning, make them even more wonderful than the larger animals.

The celebrated naturalist, Sir John Lubbock, has recently written a wonderful book, entitled *Wasps, Ants, and Bees*, in which very many interesting and curious incidents are given of the wonderful habits of these little creatures. One of these stories is as follows:—

'An old friend of mine told me that, being at a friend's house one dry summer, when all the field flowers were nearly scorched up, he saw thousands of bees busy in a field of clover then in bloom.

'"I wish my bees were here," said my friend.

'"Probably they are," replied the gentleman.

'"What, at forty miles' distance?"

'"Yes," said his friend. "On your return home, dredge the backs of your bees with flour as they issue from the hives in the morning, and we shall see."

'This was done, and his friend wrote to him directly: "There are plenty of your white-jacket bees here in the clover."'

But, whatever is the fact with bees, ants follow their noses much more than their eyes. In my garden I saw a train of ants, ascending an apple tree, go up by one track, and descend by another. As in ascending they passed between two small shoots that sprang from the bole, I stopped their passage with a piece of bark. The ants did not see this obstruction with their eyes, but ran bump against it, and stood still, astonished. Soon a crowd of them had thus been suddenly stopped, and were anxiously searching about for a passage. By various successive starts forward, they eventually got around the obstruction, and reached the track on the other side. The line of scent was renewed, and thenceforward, on arriving at the barricade, they went, without a moment's hesitation, by the circular track. I then took my penknife, and pared away a piece of the outer bark on the open bole where the ants were descending. The effect was the same. The scent being taken away, the ants came to a dead stand, and there was the same spasmodic attempt to regain the road, which being effected in the same way, the scent was carried over the shaven part of the bark, and the train ran on as freely as before.

The ant is a Bible insect. There are two short passages in the Old Testament, both found in the book of Proverbs, around which an animated controversy has long raged. The first is found in chap. vi. 6–8 :—

'Go to the ant, thou sluggard ; consider her ways, and be wise :

' Which, having no guide, overseer, or ruler,

' Provideth her meat in the summer, and gathereth her food in the harvest.'

The second passage is as follows :—

'There be four things which are little upon the earth, but they are exceeding wise.

'The ants are a people not strong, yet they prepare their meat in the summer.'

The Rev. J. G. Wood, in his 'Chapter on the Ant' in his book on Bible Animals, says :

'It has been objected to this passage, that the ant is a carnivorous insect, and therefore could not gather her food in the harvest, and that the very nature of that food would prevent it from being laid up in store.'

But the writer of the book of Proverbs was right when he alluded to the vegetable stores in the nest, and only spoke the truth when he wrote about the ant that was 'exceeding wise.' Any one who wishes to test the truth of his words, can easily do so by watching the first ants' nest which he finds ; the species of ant not being of much consequence. The nests of the white ant are perhaps the best suited for investigation ; first, because the insect and its habitation are comparatively large ; and second, because so much of the work is done above ground.

The most wonderful ant in the world is one which hitherto is only known in some parts of America. Its scientific name is *atta malefaciens*, and it has been called by various popular names, such as mound-making ant, and agricultural ant, on account of its habits; the stinging ant, on account of the pungency of its venom. This characteristic has gained for it the scientific name of *malefaciens*, or villainous.

The economical habits of this wonderful insect far surpass anything that Solomon has written of the ant, and it is not too much to say that if any of the scriptural writers had ventured to speak of an ant that not only laid up stores of grain, but actually prepared the soil for the crop, planted the seed, kept the ground free from weeds, and finally reaped a harvest, the statement would have been utterly disbelieved, and the credibility—not only of that particular writer, but of the rest of the Scripture—severely endangered.

We all know that Solomon's statement concerning the ant has afforded one of the stock arguments against the truth of the Scriptures; and here we have his statement not only corroborated to the very letter by those who have visited Palestine for the express purpose of investigating its zoology, but far surpassed by the observations of a scientific man, who has watched the insects for a series of years.

These ants of Palestine belong to the same genus as the agricultural ant, as may be inferred from the above description.

The habits of ants vary greatly, according to their species, and the climate in which they live. All, however, are wonderful creatures. And, whether we look at their varied architecture, their mode of procuring food, or the system of slave-catching adopted by some; or whether we look at the milking of aphides practised by others, or at their astonishing mode of communicating thought to each other, and their perfect system of discipline; we feel how true were the words of the royal naturalist: 'That the ants are little upon the earth, but they are exceeding wise.'

There is one point in their economy in which all known species agree. Only those which are destined to become perfectly developed males and females attain the winged state before they assume the transitional or pupal condition. Each spins around itself a slight but tough silken cocoon, in which it lies secure during the time which is consumed in developing its full perfection of form. When it is ready to emerge, the labourer ants aid in freeing it from the cocoon, and in a short time it is ready to fly.

The males of these winged ants rise into the air, seeking their mates, and as they are not strong on the wing, and are liable to be tossed about by every gust of wind, vast numbers of them perish. Whole armies of these ants fall into the water and are drowned, or devoured by fish, while the insectivorous birds hold great festivals on so abundant a supply of food. As soon as they are mated, they bend their wings forwards, snap them off, and pass the rest of their lives on the ground.

In consequence of the destruction that takes place among the winged ants, the Arabs have a proverb which is applied to those who are ambitious: 'Though God purposes the destruction of an ant, He permits wings to grow upon her.' Beyond the knowledge of the astonishing fact of the ant in the East laying up food for winter, modern research has proved the wisdom and instinct of these little creatures to be far in advance of that of any other known insect, not even excepting the bee. Their skill in architecture is wonderful and varied. Some species build their labyrinths of bits of kneaded clay, arched and fitted like the most skilful masonry. Others employ rafters and beams for their roofs, and others excavate the trunks of trees. They fortify their passages against rain and enemies; closing them every night, and opening them in the morning. Like the bees and wasps, their communities are composed of males, females, and neuters, the latter being both workers and rulers. Those receiving the eggs watch over them with unceasing care, and bring the larvæ to enjoy the heat of the sun, then carry them back to their chambers as the day declines. They gather food for them, and supply them incessantly. They tear the cases away from the cocoons when the perfect insect is ready to emerge. They spread and dry the wings, which the males and females alone possess, and they only in the perfect state. They afterwards tend the females, feed and wash them, and keep continual guard over them.

They rear myriads of aphides, or small plant parasites, from the egg, to supply food for the young, and they keep them like cows.

Some species, like the Amazon ants, organize regular marauding expeditions, attacking the colonies of other ants, and carrying off the larvæ to be their slaves.

In fact, had not the habits of the ants been verified by the observations of the most careful and truthful naturalists, they would have been incredible. Truly, indeed, did Agur pronounce them to be 'exceeding wise.'

So much, then, for the history of the ant, this wonderful Bible insect.

Let us now find out the lessons which we learn from this little monitor.

The first lesson we learn from the ant is—THE LESSON OF WHAT LITTLE PEOPLE CAN DO. They are a very little race of people, something like the pigmies found in Lilliputia, according to the story of *Gulliver's Travels*. The ants are the littlest kind of insects, the very weakest specimen of the animal creation which can be found. They are so small that we can hardly call them animals, and yet we are told that they are very wise. It is not big people that are necessarily great or wise. Wisdom is a matter of quality, not of quantity.

When we are young we are a people not strong; but we can surely do something ourselves while we are little; we don't have to wait until we are grown. Our first lesson, then, is from what the ants *are:* they are little people—a people not strong—and yet they are wise.

If the ants were to wait until they grew up to be big, before they began to be wise, they would always remain little and foolish.

I suppose the little baby ants grow up into what they call big ants; but then they are all little, whether we call them little or big.

When an ant sees one of us walking along, we must look like moving mountains; and the garden where his ant-hill is, must seem to him as our world. The ants are a people not strong, but they do what they can.

If you were to study out an ant-hill, you would find that it is built just like a city. There are streets in it, and gates; and it is full of little holes,—where the different ants live,—and these are like our houses.

They build their cities according to some plan of their own, and they have their storehouses and places of supplies, in which they keep their food for the winter, just as we find food kept in the storeroom of some fort.

I was reading the other day a story about what a boy could do, which showed that it was his own confidence in himself which secured for him his future.

'Sir,' said a boy, coming to one of the wharfs in Boston, and addressing a well-known merchant,—'sir, have you any berth for me on your ship? I want to earn something.'

'What can you do?' asked the gentleman.

'I can try my best to do whatever I am put to,' answered the boy.

'What have you done?'

'I have sawed and split all mother's wood for nigh two years.'

'What have you not done?' asked the gentleman, who was a queer sort of a questioner.

'Well, sir, I have not whispered once in school for a whole year,' answered the boy, after a moment's pause.

'That's enough,' said the gentleman. 'You may ship aboard this vessel, and I hope to see you master of her some day. A boy who can master a wood-pile, and bridle his tongue, must be made of good stuff.'

Another illustration of this same principle that little people can accomplish great things, is found in the life of the celebrated missionary, Dr. William Carey, the keynote of whose life was the motto—

'I CAN PLOD.'

The Rev. Dr. William Carey, who was the originator of the Baptist Missionary Society of England, and the great pioneer of mission work in India, was born in obscurity. His father was a poor man, and could afford him but little assistance. At an early age he was apprenticed to a shoemaker, and even after he was licensed to preach, in consequence of his poverty, he continued to work at his trade. Notwithstanding the difficulties which surrounded him, he was diligent in the improvement of his mind, and embraced every opportunity which presented itself for the acquirement of useful knowledge.

When he first proposed his plans to his father in reference to his great missionary work, he replied,—

'William, are you mad?' And ministers and Christian people replied to his proposition, 'If the Lord should make windows in heaven, then might this be.'

His discouragements in first entering upon his work in India were appalling. When he found himself without a roof to cover his head, without bread for his sickly wife and four children, he made up his mind to build a hut in the wilderness, and live as the natives did around him. 'There are many serpents and tigers, but Christ has said that His followers shall take up serpents,' said the undaunted man.

God did not call him to this sacrifice, but to others which required wonderful courage and persistence, before he achieved his final success, which has made him famous the world over.

What was the secret that enabled the shoemaker's apprentice to become one of the most distinguished men of the age? What brilliant gift raised him from an obscure position to one of honour and fame, as the author of grammars and dictionaries, translations of the Bible and other books? He either translated or assisted in the completion of twenty-seven versions of the Scriptures, requiring a knowledge of as many languages or dialects.

He betrays the secret. In giving an estimate of his own character, he speaks of himself with Christian humility, but with full consciousness of the honour put upon him in the wonderful results he has been permitted to achieve. While not laying claim to brilliant gift or genius, he says, 'I can plod; I can persevere.'

He does not say, as we see too often now-a-days, 'I could always manage to get along, and keep up with my class in

some way, without much study. I could jump at the meaning
of my lesson ; or I can catch up a trade without years of hard
labour ;' but 'I can persevere.'

Plodding boys, hold up your heads ! You may seem to be
left behind in the race by your so-called 'smart' companions.
Plod on. Your progress may be slow, but do not be. discouraged. Remember 'the race is not always to the swift.'

Now, my dear children, such stories as these about little
people, who are not very great or strong, and yet who accomplish good, show us that, like the ants, we can become little
and wise in doing well that which lies in our power.

The first lesson, then, from the ants is found in what they
are—they are a people not strong, yet they are wise.

The second lesson we learn from the ant is—A LESSON OF
INDUSTRY.

The ants prepare their meat.

When a vessel goes to sea on a long voyage, the steward, who
has charge of all the provisions, puts plenty of prepared food
on board, such as canned vegetables and fruits, and salted meat
and fish. Those are called 'prepared vegetables,' or 'prepared
meats.'

They are put up long before they are used, and are preserved
from the air and from all possibility of decay. And so, too,
when an army marches, there is one very important branch
called the commissariat department. It is in charge of an
officer called the quartermaster, and it is his duty to provide
suitable food and provisions for the men and horses, and all the
different parts of the army. This takes a great deal of planning
and forethought. A quartermaster-general must see a long way
ahead : he must provide not only for the day, or the week, or
even the month to come ; he must provide for months ahead.
For if the men and horses do not have food enough, they cannot
march or fight, and there will surely be trouble. Just think,
then, how very wise these little insignificant ants must be to
think of the future in the way they do, and prepare for it when
it is afar off.

We know in an ant-hill, which is an ant-city, that they have
soldiers, and policemen, and hard-working day-labourers, whose
business it is to go out and bring home food, and store it
away in their barns for winter. In Africa, and in the eastern
countries, travellers who have watched all sorts of ants tell
us that sometimes different tribes of ants have regular pitched
battles. They meet and fight by the thousands, and then the
conquering army takes possession of the captured city, and
carries off the food that has been stored there, and makes slaves
of the poor defeated ants, just in the way that Alexander the

Great, or King Cyrus, or Julius Cæsar did with cities and men in their days. How very wonderful all this is! How strange a thing it is to see all this system and forethought among such little bits of creatures as the ants. This is one of the great works of the ants, then, to provide or prepare their food. They cannot work in the winter time. There is no food for them when the snow is on the ground, and so they plan for their underground cities in the summer, and send out their thousands of day-labourers to hunt for little particles of food to store away in their granaries for the winter, just in the way in which Joseph sent out the Egyptians to gather food in the years of plenty before the days of famine came. And here it is that the lesson comes home to us all. We must prepare for our future; we must not live only for the present. And there are three kinds of meat we must get, for meat means strength, you know, and these are: meat for the body, meat for the mind, and meat for the soul.

Here is a story which shows us how it is that all growth in character comes slowly, but surely, by little habits.

A boy watched a large building as the workmen from day to day carried up the brick and mortar.

'My son,' said his father, 'you seem taken with the bricklayers. Do you think of learning the trade?'

'No, sir; I was thinking what a little thing a brick is, and what great houses are built by laying one brick upon another.'

'Very true, my son; never forget it. So it is in all great works. All your learning is one lesson added to another. If a man could walk all around the world, it would be by putting one foot before another. Your whole life will be made up of one moment upon another. Drops added to drops make the ocean.

'Learn from this not to despise little things. Be not discouraged by great labours; they become easy if divided into parts. You could not jump over a mountain, but step by step takes you to the other side. Do not fear, therefore, to attempt great things. Always remember that the large, large building went up only one brick upon another.'

The ants teach us, then, the great lesson in life of preparing for the future—the lesson of industry. Now, then, my dear children, try for this good habit; try to have it in your life; pray for it; seek to get good habits for life. Be as busy as the hard-working bee is for the food it gathers from flower to flower; or as busy as the industrious little ant is, who tries so hard to prepare its own meat. The ants are a people 'not strong, yet they prepare their meat in the summer.'

*The third lesson we learn from the little ants is—*THE LESSON OF PERSEVERANCE.

Once upon a time, according to an old fable, there was a merry grasshopper, who chirruped away and hopped about through the grass all summer as happy as he could be.

A big bumble-bee saw him, and said, 'Look out for the winter, my friend, or you'll starve.'

Then a hard-working ant asked him to help him roll along a great big piece of bread which he had found.

'Not I,' said the grasshopper; 'I'm no fool. You don't catch me working like a slave with such lovely sunshine as this all about us.'

'But there's a winter coming on,' said the ant; 'and what will you do then, with the cold weather and the snow on the ground?'

'Oh, I'll wait till it comes,' replied the grasshopper; 'and, besides, I never saw a winter, and I don't believe it is as bad as people say.' And away he jumped over the tall grass.

But at last the leaves fell, and it grew very cold, and the snow came, and the poor grasshopper had the rheumatism in his fine legs, and he did not know how he was to live.

He went to the beehive, and begged them to take him in; but they said they were all full in there, and had no room for loafers.

Then he went to the ant-hill, and tried to get in; but he was told at the door that they had no food to spare for those who would not work. And so the poor grasshopper died.

The grasshopper died because he had no end or aim in life; he was not persevering: but the bees lived on, because of their incessant perseverance.

A lady once said of her boy,—

'When our Tom was six years old, he went into the forest one afternoon to meet the hired man, who was coming home with a load of wood. The man placed Master Tommy on the top of the load, and drove homeward. Just before reaching the farm, the team went pretty briskly down a steep hill.

'When Tommy entered the house, his mother said, "Tommy, my dear, were you not frightened when the horses went trotting so swiftly down Crow Hill?"

'"Yes, mother, a little," replied Tom honestly. "I asked the Lord to help me, and hung on like a beaver."'

Now that was sensible in Tom, because he joined working to praying. Let his words teach us a life-lesson in all our troubles. Let us pray and hang on like a beaver. By which I mean that while you ask God to help you, you must help yourself with all your might.

A gentleman travelling in the northern part of Ireland heard the voices of children, and stopped to listen.

Finding the sound came from a small building used as a

schoolhouse, he drew near. As the door was open, he went in, and listened to the words the boys were spelling.

One little fellow stood apart, looking very sad.

'Why does that boy stand there?' asked the gentleman.

'Oh, he is good for nothing,' replied the teacher. 'There's nothing in him. I can make nothing out of him. He is the most stupid boy in the school.'

The gentleman was surprised at his answer. He saw the teacher was so stern and rough that the younger and more timid were nearly crushed. After a few words to them, placing his hand on the noble brow of the little fellow who stood apart, he said,—

'One of these days you may be a fine scholar. Don't give up; try, my boy, try.'

The boy's soul was aroused. His sleeping mind awoke. A new purpose was formed. From that hour he became anxious to excel. And he did become a fine scholar, and the author of a well-known Commentary on the Bible; a great and good man, beloved and honoured. It was Dr. Adam Clarke.

The secret of his success is worth knowing: 'Don't give up; but try, my boy, try.'

The third lesson which we learn from the ants is—the lesson of perseverance.

The fourth lesson which we learn from the ants is—THE LESSON OF LAW AND ORDER.

When the children of Israel were in Egypt, we read that they were compelled by their hard taskmasters to make bricks without straw; they were sent over the country to gather stubble instead of straw.

Now it is very poor kind of brick which is made out of stubble. We read in the book of Exodus that the children of Israel were in 'evil case,' when they were compelled to gather stubble instead of straw.

And it is very much the same way with us through life: if we want to have rich results in our lives, we must be careful about the details, just as the children of Israel were, when they were compelled to get whatever material they could, out of which to make their bricks. There is nothing like being careful in the matter of the details of life.

If we want to make our lives rich, and true, and strong, we must be careful what material we put into our lives.

It will never do to make our bricks out of any stubble that we happen to find; we must look out for that straw which will produce the strongest and best kind of brick. Mr. J. T. Field, the well-known author, writes in one place what he would do if he were a boy again. He says:

'If I were a boy again, I would practise perseverance oftener, and never give a thing up because it was hard or inconvenient to do it. If we want light we must conquer darkness. When I think of mathematics, I blush at the recollection of how often I "caved in" years ago. There is no trait more valuable than a determination to persevere when the right thing is to be accomplished. We are all inclined to give up too easily in trying or unpleasant situations, and the point I would establish with myself, if the choice were again within my grasp, would be never to relinquish my hold on a possible success, if mortal strength or brains in my case were adequate to the occasion. That was a capital lesson which Professor Faraday taught one of his students in the lecture-room after some chemical experiments. The lights had been put out in the hall, and by accident some small article dropped on the floor from the professor's hand. The professor lingered behind, endeavouring to pick it up. "Never mind," said the student. "It is of no consequence to-night, sir, whether we find it or no." "That is true," replied the professor; "but it is of grave consequence to me as a principle that I am not foiled in my determination to find it." Perseverance can sometimes equal genius in its results. "There are only two creatures," says the Eastern proverb, "who can surmount the Pyramids—the eagle and the snail."

'If I were a boy again, I would school myself into a habit of attention oftener. I would let nothing come between me and the subject in hand. I would remember that an expert on the ice never tries to skate in two directions at once. One of our great mistakes while we are young is that we do not attend strictly to what we are about just then, at that particular moment. We do not bend our energies close enough to what we are doing or learning. We wander into a half-interest only, and so never acquire fully what is needful for us to become master of. The practice of being habitually attentive is one easily obtained if we begin early enough. I often hear grown-up people say, "I couldn't fix my attention on the sermon or book, although I wished to do so." And the reason is, a habit of attention was never formed in youth.

'If I were to live my life over again, I would pay more attention to the cultivation of memory. I would strengthen that faculty by every possible means and on every possible occasion. It takes a little hard work at first to remember things accurately; but memory soon helps itself, and gives very little trouble. It only needs early cultivation to become a power. Everybody can acquire it.'

These, then, are the four lessons which we learn from the ants, who are a people not strong, yet who prepare their meat in the summer.

The first lesson we learn from the ants is *the lesson of what little people can do.*

The second lesson we learn is *the lesson of industry.*

The third lesson we learn is *the lesson of perseverance.*

The fourth lesson we learn is *the lesson of law and order.* And in this way the little insignificant ant, which we can scarcely see except through a microscope, teaches us the four great lessons for our everyday work in life.

IX.

THE BEAR.

WE come to-day to the subject of the Bear. We always like to go to see animals in the Zoological Gardens. There is something about animals which is very attractive to us. Perhaps it is because we feel that in a certain way we are one with them; perhaps it is because we see in the animals certain traits which we see and feel to be in ourselves. In this way we cannot help feeling that in some way they are our first cousins.

This course of sermons is a sort of 'Moral Zoological Garden,' and to-day we come to the lessons which we learn from the bear.

Bears are very curious animals; we can learn a great many lessons from the ways and habits of bears. Bears are what they call 'Plantigrade' animals, that is, they place the whole of their feet upon the ground as they walk.

Most parts of the globe are inhabited by some species of bear. They are nearly always found where the deep woods are. We have always called the bear a rude animal, and say of man that 'he is as cross as a bear.' But the bear, while he is not fond of miscellaneous society, is a devoted parent, and a model of parental responsibility.

Sometimes the education of the bear is taken up by accomplished hands, and he turns out a capital pupil.

There was a bear once which was kept by some students at Oxford, who was the most gentlemanly specimen of his race on record. The students called him 'Tiglath-Pileser,' after the name of the Syrian monarch, but they always called him 'Tig.' He was a Syrian bear, the kind mentioned in the book of Kings as the destroyer of the children that mocked Elisha. Tig was taught to stand on his hind legs, and walk through the quadrangle of the University, decked in a cap and gown like the other students. He used to be invited to parties, where he would sit in a chair and make himself very much at home; and he was particularly fond of ice-cream and beer.

Tiglath-Pileser was a great character at Oxford, and lived in a yard where there was an eagle, a tortoise, and a monkey for his companions.

Tig did not enjoy their society, for the monkey used to pull his ears and hair, while the eagle, being unconversational in his habits, stood on the tortoise almost all the time, and beguiled the hours by trying to eat it. Finally, Tig could not stand his companions' low habits, and he climbed over the fence and escaped through the streets of Oxford, where he did so much harm to the shopkeepers' windows that he was ordered out of town, and sent to a Zoological Garden. This was too much for poor Tig after having been an Oxford student, and in a month or two he died of a broken heart.

Of all the bear tribe, the grizzly bear is the most dangerous. The common black bear is a very knowing animal, but the bears which we read about in the Bible are perhaps the fiercest of all the Bruin family.

We read a great deal about the bear in the Bible. Sometimes the bear, not content with the fierce wild animals which he can secure, descends to lower planes, and seizes upon goats and sheep in the pastures. This habit is referred to by David in his well-known speech to Saul, when the king was trying to dissuade him from going to fight Goliath (1 Samuel xvii. 33–36). 'And Saul said to David, Thou art not able to go against this Philistine to fight with him : for thou art but a youth, and he a man of war from his youth. And David said unto Saul, Thy servant kept his father's sheep, and there came a lion, and a bear, and took a lamb out of the flock : and I went out after him, and smote him, and delivered it out of his mouth : and when he arose against me, I caught him by his beard, and smote him, and slew him. Thy servant slew both the lion and the bear : and this uncircumcised Philistine shall be as one of them, seeing he hath defied the armies of the living God.'

Though not generally apt to attack the human family, it will do so if first attacked, and then it becomes a most dangerous enemy.

The Prophet Amos, who was a husbandman, and knew the habits of bears, says in one place (Amos v. 18, 19): 'Woe unto you that desire the day of the Lord ! to what end is it for you ? the day of the Lord is darkness, and not light. As if a man did flee from a lion, and a bear met him ; or went into the house, and leaned his hand on the wall, and a serpent bit him.'

Another reference to the dangerous character of the bear is made in 2 Kings ii. 23, 24, where we read the following words : 'And he went up from thence unto Bethel : and as he was going by the way, there came forth little children out of the city, and mocked him, and said unto him, Go up, thou bald head ; go up, thou bald head. And he turned back, and looked on them, and cursed them in the name of the Lord. And there came forth two she-bears out of the wood, and tare forty and two children of them.'

As the bear is not swift of foot, but rather clumsy in its movements, it cannot take nimbler animals in open chase. It prefers to lie in wait for them in the bushes, to strike them down with a sudden blow of its paw ; a terrible weapon, which it can wield as effectually as the lion uses its claws. A reference to this habit of the bear is made in Lamentations of Jeremiah iii. 10 : 'He was unto me as a bear lying in wait, and as a lion in secret places.'

Harmless to man as it generally is, there are occasions in which it becomes terrible, and not seeking to avoid his presence, but even searching for him, and attacking him as soon as seen.

In the proper seasons of the year, hunters, or those who are travelling through those parts of the country infested by the bear, will sometimes find the cubs, generally two in number, their mother having left them in the den while she has gone to search for food.

'To all animals that rear their young,' says a writer on natural history, 'is given a sublime and almost supernatural courage in defending their offspring. And from the lioness, that charges at a host of armed men when her cubs are in danger, to the hen, which defies the soaring kite or the prowling fox ; or to the spider, that will give up her life rather than abandon her yet unhatched brood, the same self-sacrificing spirit actuates them all.'

That the sight of a bear bereaved of her young was well known to both writers and contemporary readers of the Old Testament, is evident from the fact that it is mentioned by several writers, and always as a familiar illustration of furious anger. See for example 2 Samuel xvii. 8, when Hushai is dissuading Absalom from following the cautious counsel of Ahithophel : 'For thou knowest thy father and his men, that they be mighty men of war, and they be chafed in their minds, as a bear robbed of her whelps in the field.'

Solomon also, in Proverbs xvii. 12, uses the same image : 'Let a bear robbed of her whelps meet a man, rather than a fool in his folly.'

When a bear fights it delivers rapid strokes with its paws, tearing and rending away everything that it strikes.

A blow from a bear's paw has several times been known to strip the entire skin, together with the hair, from a man's head ; and when fighting with dogs it is known to tear its enemies open, as if each claw were a chisel.

This mode of fighting is clearly alluded to by the Prophet

Hosea, who seems, from the graphic force of his sentences, to have been an actual spectator of such a combat: 'I will meet them as a bear that is bereaved of her whelps, and will rend the caul of their heart,' etc. (Hosea xiii. 8).

That the bear was a well-known animal, both in the earlier and later times of the Scripture, is also evident from the fact that it was twice used as a symbol, exhibited to a seer in a vision. The first of these passages occurs in the book of Daniel, vii. 5, when the prophet is describing the wonderful vision of the four beasts: 'And behold another beast, the second, like to a bear, and it raised itself up on one side, and it had three ribs in the mouth of it between the teeth of it : and they said thus unto it, Arise, devour much flesh.'

The second illustration occurs in the book of the Revelation of St. John : 'The seven-headed and ten-crowned beast: having a form like that of a leopard, but feet like those of a bear.'

Having now had something of the history and nature of the bear, let us learn the lessons which this Bible animal teaches us.

We learn four lessons from the bear.

First of all, we learn THE LESSON OF DOCILITY.

Bears can very easily be taught. In the city of Berne, in Switzerland, there are a great many bears which are cared for at public expense. The name of the city, Berne, is taken from the Burgundian word for bear. Many hundred years ago, a Burgundian duke killed a bear on that spot; and when he founded the city, he named it Berne. As I looked at the statue one time, in the market-place, I found that there was a motto on it, which I put in my note-book. The motto is as follows : '*E Bellua cæsa sit nomen urbis,*' 'From a bear slain, let the city take its name.'

Some time ago, when I was in Vermont, I was very much struck with a performing bear that I saw in a certain town. Two men had charge of this bear. One of the men blew a bugle, and the other man led the bear and his dancing-pole, the bear performing all sorts of antics. He stood up on his hind legs, and danced, and drank beer, and ate pretzels, and did all sorts of strange things.

The bears in Berne in the bear-pit are a great object of curiosity to visitors. They are taught all manner of tricks, and are very much sought after by the people who come to that place.

By docility we mean the spirit of teachableness. We can never get on in life without a habit of docility : for we must be always learning from others if we want to succeed in life. The splendid horse who does such wonders in harness, the patient oxen with their yoke, the trained birds and horses and dogs which we see in many of the shows, all teach us that the first step towards success in life is the possession of the faculty of docility.

Somebody has said that every person who would be happy in this world must keep *two pet bears.* They are called Bear and Forbear ; that is, each one of us, if we expect to have friends and happy homes, must learn to *bear* patiently unpleasant things, and *forbear* doing or saying things unpleasant to others.

A gentleman was once making inquiries in Russia about the method of catching bears in that country.

He was told that to entrap them a pit was dug several feet deep, and after covering it over with turf, leaves, etc., some food was placed on top. The bear, if tempted by the bait, easily fell into the snare ; but he added,—

'If four or five happen to get in together, they all get out again.'

'How is that ?' asked the gentleman.

'They form a sort of ladder by stepping on each other's shoulders, and thus make their escape.'

'But how does the bottom one get out ?'

Ah ! these bears, though not possessing a mind and soul such as God has given us, can yet feel gratitude, and they won't forget the one who has been the chief means of procuring their liberty.

'Scampering off, they bring the branch of a tree, which they let down to their poor brother, enabling him speedily to join them in the freedom in which they rejoice.'

Sensible bears, we should say, are a great deal better than some people we hear about, who never help anybody but themselves.

If dogs and oxen and horses could talk and tell all they know, would not some people be astonished !

If the horse could tell at night how many miles he had travelled, and how many blows his cruel driver had struck him, the whip would not be used quite as freely as it is. If the patient ox could come home and tell his owner just how he had been overloaded, and yelled at, and beaten, and whipped about the eyes and ears by the cruel little wretch who was set to drive him, there would be likely to be a new driver the next day, or probably the little rascal might get a taste of his own cart-whip.

Well, beasts cannot talk, but they can feel and hear and understand a deal more than some suppose. They are given to us by God to serve us, and not to be abused, and He notices all that they suffer ; for God cares for oxen and sparrows and ravens, as well as for men : and if we serve God, and treat His creatures wisely, as old Eliphaz says, even the 'beasts of the field shall be at peace' with us (Job v. 23), and we shall find that they can serve us in very many ways, as the following story will show.

'When the English steamer *Eira* was nipped in the polar ice in 1881, the crew of twenty-two men made their way over the ice to a point of land where they could find driftwood for fuel. There they built a hut, but were short of meat. There were only bears for game, and in the three-months' night of the Arctic winter, the bear and the ice were so much the same shade of white that the hunters could see him only a short distance away, and the bear stood the better chance to catch the hunters. Famine stared them in the face, and the men sat down and talked of what was to be done.

'One that listened, and seemed as deeply concerned as any, was a dog. His name was Oscar. They did not know that he understood their talk, but presently he started up, and made them open the door of the hut and let him out. He went over the ice till he met a bear, then he barked at the beast, and made it run after him, stopping now and then to bark, and so keep the bear following till they came close to the hut. The men heard Oscar barking, took their guns, came out, and shot the bear. Oscar kept on leading up the bears, who thought they were going to make a meal of him ; and he and the ice-bound crew had plenty of meat all winter.

'In the spring, Captain Gray, of the *Eclipse*, was appointed to go in search of the missing *Eira*. The two vessels met, and came home together, and Oscar's owner made a present of the dog to the other captain, hoping that if he ever got into any difficulty, Oscar would render him as good service.'

The spirit of teachableness is the first step in the pathway of success. Without docility, we can never learn anything in life, and without learning in life we never can acquire power. The beautiful thing about military life is that it teaches those who enter it to be docile. Grant and Sherman and Sheridan, the great American generals, acquired their power through the possession of docility. They were ready and willing to be taught at any time in their life, and it was this spirit of teachableness which finally gave them their power.

The bear is possessed of several valuable accomplishments, which he has learnt from man : he is a wonderful climber of trees and rocks, he is an excellent swimmer, and a first-class digger. When we see a trained bear standing on his hind legs, with a staff in his hand, and walking about like a man at a country fair with such airs and graces as Tiglath-Pileser the Oxford student had, we learn a great lesson from this Bible animal—the lesson of docility.

The second lesson we learn from the bear is—A LESSON OF

PARENTAL RESPONSIBILITY. This is a long word, but it means taking care of one's children.

The mother bear does the best she can to educate her young. She licks her little cubs into shape when they are very small, and in this way makes them presentable to the rest of the family.

Bears are very fond of one another, and show great affection for members of their own family. Two brown bears which were born in captivity in the London Zoological Garden were exceedingly fond of each other. One of these two was sold, and removed from its companion, which immediately became uneasy at the protracted absence of its playfellow. So deeply was its affectionate heart wounded by the separation, that it became nearly mad, and at last contrived to make its escape from its place of confinement, evidently with the intention of searching after its lost friend. It was captured, and replaced in its cage, but its health became so seriously affected, that its owners were obliged to re-purchase its companion, and restore it to its disconsolate relation.

After a mother bear has spent all her skill and energy in licking her bears, they are supposed to be educated, and to be fitted for the duties and responsibilities of bear society. I was reading the other day a fable about this habit among the bears. It appears a mother bear was very much afraid that a great lion, who lived in the forest near them, might some day devour her young ones when they were off at play, or had gone on errands. So she told her fears to the lion one day, when he was paying the bear family a social call. The lion in a very polite way declared that nothing would be further from his intentions than to hurt her children, if he could only tell how he was to know her cubs.

'Oh,' replied the mother bear, ' nothing can be easier. You will know my little dears at once ; they are the most beautiful cubs in the world. Their education is all over ; I have just finished licking them into shape.'

The lion bade the family adieu, and set off on his journey home through the forest. Feeling very faint and hungry, he was at a loss to know how he was to find any refreshment, when all of a sudden he came upon two fat little cubs waddling home. He fell upon the cubs, and, after a few short struggles, made a good meal out of them, and then pursued his way home.

The next day he was called upon by the stricken mother, who expressed her surprise at his unfeeling action, whereupon he replied, 'My dear madam, nothing can give me greater pain than to think of the unfortunate mistake which has been made ; but I really found it quite impossible to see in the ugly little cubs which I devoured, the beautiful creatures which you so eloquently described to me.'

Now, my dear children, there is no mistaking the fact that many boys are little else than young bears who need to be trained into shape. This is what school does for us; this is what our true friends do for us; this is what society does for us. All education—and all Christian education—is intended to mould us into fitting shape. The only use of a parent, or of a grandparent, is to see that their children and grandchildren are trained into shape for the great duties of life.

The bears do not have a varied curriculum of education, but they do the best they can for their cubs. They paw over them, and maul them, and lick them into shape, and so we learn from the bears—the lesson of parental responsibility.

The third lesson we learn from the bear is—THE LESSON OF ADAPTABILITY. Bears can run on their four legs, or stand up on their hind legs and walk like a man; they can dig with a shovel, sit up at a table, and eat and drink with a tumbler, knife and fork, though they prefer to drink what they have out of a bottle. During the time when it is engaged in feeding, the bear is constantly in the habit of climbing up all kinds of lofty spots, for the purpose of obtaining food.

Trusting to its powers of swimming, the bear does not hesitate to cross rivers in search of food, or in order to escape from its enemies. It is in the habit of taking frequent baths during the hot months of the year for the sake of cooling its heated frame.

They have the thickest kind of fur clothing, which they cannot put away in camphor when the summer comes on, as we do; yet they don't seem to mind their fur.

When they are in the woods they walk on all-fours, like the other animals. When they are exhibited in the menageries they try to make the best of it, and adapt themselves to their surroundings.

If *we* cannot adapt ourselves to our surroundings, the bear does. We generally become first-class fretters in life, if things do not come out as we desire, and there is nothing so disagreeable as the fretter.

A certain lady writes:

'A young friend who has been visiting me was a fretter. She fretted when it rained, and fretted when it shone. She fretted when others came to see her, and fretted when they did not. It is dreadful to be a fretter. A fretter is troublesome to herself, and troublesome to her friends. We, to be sure, have our trials; but fretting does not help us to bear, or get rid of them.

'I have lately come across a short rule for fretters, which

they shall have.   Here it is : Never fret about what you can't help, because it won't do any good.   Never fret about what you can help, because if you can help it, do so.

'Say this when you get up in the morning, say it at noon, and say it at night ; and not only say, but do ; and that will be, do not fret at all—a fine doing.'

'But we have our trials,' my young readers say.

Yes, you have ; and your little trials are as hard to bear as your big ones.   But fretting does not help them ; nor wishing we were somewhere else, or somebody else, or dwelling upon them until they look a great deal bigger than they really are.

Did you ever read the fable about the toad and the plantain leaf ?

A toad used to live under a stone beside the brook.   He was a pretty fat toad, and got along in the world as well as toads generally do.   One day he went out to find something to eat, and, hopping out among the leaves by the creek's side, he heard a rustle among the leaves.   He said to himself, 'There's a beetle !   I like beetles.   I'll be quiet and catch him.'

So he crept along till he came to it, and stuck out his tongue to get it ; but it happened to be a bumble-bee !   He dropped it like a hot coal, and had to cry out in the way toads cry, and hop back to his hole under the stone.   He suffered with the pain, and his tongue swelled up, and he was obliged to lie by for two or three days.   Hopping back to his home, he plucked a leaf of plantain, and took it home for his medicine, and put it in his mouth to cure the sting of the bee.   He stayed at home for two or three days, and began to get hungry, and poor, and lean.   As he hopped along, he came under the leaf of a plantain, and, being very hungry and tired, he stopped under the leaf, and, looking up, said, 'Oh, what a nice time you plantains have !   I should like to change places.   Toads have a hard life.'

The plantain said, 'Friend toad, I should like to change too.   I don't see what toads have to complain of.   I think they must have a fine time of it.'

'Let me tell you,' said the toad : 'in the first place, we have to work for our living, and find all we get to eat ; and sometimes, when we think we are going to get a beetle, we get a bumble-bee.   Then, again, in winter time we are frozen up, and when we come out the boys come along and stone us, and the crows pick us up.   Isn't that trouble ?   While you plantains have just to sit by the river, and don't have to work.   I should like to change places with you.'

'Stop ! let me tell you my side,' cried the plantain.   'We cannot hop about as you can, but have to stay where we are put.   If we want a drink of water, we can't go to the creek and get it. We can't move an inch to go and see the world, and visit our next neighbour. Then the sun shines hot all day, and we have to bear it, and can't hop under a cool leaf, as you do. Then, by and by, comes along a cow, and nips off our head ; or a little worm, and eats into our heart, and we have no power to shake him off. I should like to change places with you : you take mine, and I will take yours ; for I am so anxious to hop down to the creek, and get a drink.'

'Stay ! stay !' cried the toad. 'I hear a cricket. Let me get it ;' and off he went after the cricket, and never came back.

So it appears everybody does have trials ; and the only right way of getting along is not to wish ourselves somebody else, and fret ourselves because we are not, but contentedly bear our lot, and be satisfied with what God has given us. The third lesson we learn from the bear is—the lesson of adaptability.

The fourth and last lesson which we learn from the bear is— THE LESSON OF THE ADVANTAGES OF HUMOUR IN GETTING US OUT OF THE HARD PLACES OF LIFE.

It is very curious to think of the occupations of animals. Bears are philosophers ; the stork and the heron are fishermen. Bees are geometricians ; their cells are so constructed as, with the least quantity of material, to have the largest-sized spaces and least possible loss of interstices. So, also, is the ant-lion ; his funnel-shaped trap is exactly correct in its conformation, as if it had been made by the most skilful artist of our species, with the aid of the best instruments. The mole is a meteorologist. The torpedo, the ray, and the electric eel, are electricians. The nautilus is a navigator ; he raises and lowers his sail, casts and weighs his anchor, and performs other nautical evolutions. Whole tribes of birds are musicians. The beaver is an architect, builder, and wood-cutter. He cuts down trees, and erects houses and dams. The marmot is a civil engineer : he not only builds houses, but constructs aqueducts and drains to keep them dry. The white ants maintain a regular army of soldiers. The East India ants are horticulturists ; they make mushrooms, upon which they feed their young. Wasps are paper manufacturers. Caterpillars are silk-spinners. Some birds are tailors ; they sew the leaves together to make their nests. The bird *ploceus textor* is a weaver ; he weaves a web to make his nest.

The squirrel is a ferryman : with a chip, or a piece of bark for a boat, and his tail for a sail, he crosses a stream. Dogs, wolves, jackals, and many others are hunters. The ants are regular day-labourers. The monkey is a rope-dancer. The association of beavers present us with a model of republicanism. The bees live under a monarchy. The Indian antelopes furnish

an example of patriarchal government. Elephants exhibit an
aristocracy of elders. Wild horses are said to select their
leaders. Sheep, in a wild state, are under the control of a
military chief ram.

But let us come back to the bears, and we will find that they
teach us a lesson of the advantages of humour. The bear is a
regular philosopher, and his philosophy helps him along over
the hard places of life.

Somebody asked Edward Hyde, Earl of Clarendon, how it
was that he was able to keep his head through all the changes
and vicissitudes of fortune through which he passed. He was
in power during the reign of Charles the First, and Charles the
Second, and James the Second, and William and Mary. Part
of the time he was in power, and part of the time he was
banished from the country. When asked how it was that he
maintained himself through all these changes, he replied, that
he had observed that the mood of humour was the mood of
right reason, and that he had never been placed in any position
in life in which he did not see the humorous side. In this
way his humour was to him what the oil-can and the wad of
cotton are to the hot-box of a car.

An Irish girl, giving evidence in a court of justice against a
lad who had committed a theft, and was a constant source of
uneasiness to his parents, said, ' Arrah, sir, I'm sure he never
made his mother smile.'

What a sad testimony to be given against any boy is this !

Let us preserve the sense of humour, which has been given
to us by God, to oil the heated and creaking places in life. It
helps the bear over some very hard places in life, and it will
help us in the same way if we do not part from this faculty
which God has given us.

These, then, are the four lessons which we learn from the
bear :

First, we learn *the lesson of docility*. Second, we learn *the
lesson of parental responsibility*. Third, we learn *the lesson of
adaptability*. And fourth, we learn *a lesson of the advantages of
humour*.

In this way even the awkward and ungainly bear, strolling
down the mountain pass, and looking out from behind rock
and stump at the far-off habitation of civilised man, can go
into pulpit and preach a sermon for us.

X.

THE STORK.

'The trees of the Lord are full of sap; the cedars of Lebanon, which
He hath planted ; where the birds make their nests : as for the stork,
the fir trees are her house.'—PSALM civ. 16, 17.

WE come to-day to the lessons which we learn from the stork,—
the large, wide-winged, migratory bird so frequently alluded to
in the Bible.

The stork has very many interesting and singular qualities :
to-day we will study some of these, and find out what we can
about the stork.

There are a number of references to the stork in the Bible ;
one of these is in Jeremiah viii. 7 : 'Yea, the stork in the
heaven knoweth her appointed times ; and the turtle and the
crane and the swallow observe the time of their coming : but
my people know not the judgment of the Lord.' Another
mention of this bird occurs in Zechariah v. 9 : 'Then lifted
up I mine eyes, and looked, and behold, there came out two
women, and the wind was in their wings ; for they had wings
like the wings of a stork : and they lifted up the ephah between
the earth and the heaven.' Still another place where the stork
is mentioned is in the 11th chapter of Leviticus, 19th verse :
'And the stork, the heron after her kind, and the lapwing, and
the bat.' Still another reference to the stork is in Job xxxix.
12 (Revised Edition) : 'The wing of the ostrich rejoiceth, but
are her pinions and feathers kindly,' or, as it is in the margin,
'are her feathers like the stork ?' which shows us that the stork
was considered as the symbol of the bird that was kind or
benevolent.

From all these passages we learn, in the first place, that the
stork was a bird, as it is mentioned in connection with other
birds, and is said to have wings and feathers. We find out
from these passages that the stork is a migratory bird ; that it
builds its nest upon fir trees, or high places, and that it is a
very large-winged bird. The word used for stork in the
Hebrew is Chasaidah ; and it comes from the word Chesed,
which means benevolence ; this contains the idea of mercy,
and benefit, and pity.

According to some writers, the name was given to the stork
because it was supposed to be a bird remarkable for its filial
piety. For the storks in their turn support their parents in
their old age ; they allow them to rest their necks on their
bodies during their flight ; and if the elders are tired, the

H

young ones take them on their backs. According to others, this name is given to the stork because it exercises kindness towards its companions, in bringing them food. But in all cases the derivation of the word comes from the idea of bene-volence, or kind-heartedness.

Birds have a way of communicating their ideas to one another, and of showing kindness to their companions and friends. A gentleman who has been studying bird habits, writes in one place :—

'I have closely observed the woodcock's system of telegraphy. The bird's mandibles are furnished with extremely sensitive nerves, so arranged that when the point of the bill rests upon the ground, the slightest sounds are conveyed to its brain. Standing upon the water-saturated earth of a spouty bog, our bird utters a faint, keen cry, scarcely audible at two rods' distance, then immediately lets fall his head till the tip of his bill touches the ground, and listens attentively. If his mate hears him, she replies, puts her bill on the ground and listens in turn. So the love-messages go back and forth as long as the birds have anything to say. This sort of thing usually happens in the soft twilights from May to the middle of August, though occasionally I have seen and heard it in the broad light of a summer day.'

Partly on account of this idea, of the storks being kind to their young,—which is a very old idea,—and partly on account of their services as scavengers of the streets, the stork has always been protected through the East, as it is at the present time in some parts of Europe. The slaughter of a stork, or even the destruction of its eggs, would be punished with a heavy fine.

In consequence of the kind treatment it enjoys, the stork loves to haunt the habitations of mankind.

A celebrated naturalist says of the storks :—

'In many of the continental towns, where sanitary regula-tions are not enforced, the stork serves the purpose of a scavenger, and may be seen walking about the market-places, waiting for the offal of fish, fowls, and the like, which are simply thrown on the ground for the storks to eat. In the Eastern lands the stork enjoys similar privileges, and we may infer that the bird was perfectly familiar both to the writers of the various scriptural books in which it is so mentioned, and to the people for whom these books were intended. When they settle upon a tract of ground, the storks divide it among themselves in a manner that seems to have a sort of system in it, each bird appearing to take possession of a definite amount of ground. By this mode of proceeding, the ground is rapidly cleared of all vermin. The storks examine their allotted spaces with the keenest scrutiny, devouring every reptile, mouse, worm, grub, or insect that they can find upon it. Sometimes the storks will spread themselves in this way over a vast extent of country, arriving suddenly, remaining for several months, and departing without giving any sign of their intention to move.'

The wings of the stork, which are mentioned in the Bible, are very conspicuous and striking, an adult bird measuring about seven feet across when flying. As the body, large though it be, is comparatively light when compared with the extent of wing, the flight is both lofty and sustained, the bird flying at a very great height, and when migrating, it is literally 'the stork in the heavens.'

The naturalist Tristram says: 'The stork has a very great attachment to locality, and nothing but unremitting persecution can drive them from the spot which has once been selected for a nest. Year after year—indeed, generation after generation— a pair of birds return every spring to the same place, and either rebuild, or thoroughly repair, the old nest. If any accident happens to one of the pair, its place is speedily supplied, and the succession of tenants maintained.

'The one instance of a breeding-place being deserted, which ever fell under my own observation, was under curious circumstances. On the highest point of a large mass of ruin at Rabbath Ammon, were the remains of a deserted pile of sticks —an old stork's nest. One of the birds had got its leg entangled and broken in a chink of the ruin, where it had perished miserably; and its gaunt skeleton, with the pinion feathers still remaining on the wing-bones, swayed to and fro, suspended in mid-air; and it effectually scared all its fellows from the spot.'

In almost every country in the old world the stork is a welcome and cherished visitor, not only from its character, but from the services it renders to man. The periodical return of the stork is noticed in Jeremiah viii. 7.

In the countries where the stork lives, it is protected by the citizens. Boxes are provided on the tops of the houses for it, and he considers himself a fortunate man whose roof the stork selects. In the city of Strasburg, in the district of Alsace and Lorraine, there are many visitors who go there on purpose to see the storks on the chimney-tops. There is a well-authenticated account of the devotion of a stork, which, at the burning of the town of Delft, in Holland, after repeated and unsuccessful attempts to carry off her young, chose rather to remain and perish with them than to leave them to their fate. Well may the Romans call the stork *Pia avis*, the pious bird.

Storks have some very curious habits.

A pair of storks built a nest on one of the chimneys of a mansion near Berlin. Having a curiosity to inspect it, the owner climbed up, and found in it one egg, which, being about the size of a goose's egg, was replaced by one belonging to that bird. The storks seemed not to notice the exchange; but no sooner was the egg hatched, than the male bird, perceiving the difference, rose from the nest, and, flying round it several times with loud screams, disappeared, and was not seen for three days, during which time the female continued to tend her off-spring as usual. Early on the fourth morning, however, the inmates of the house were disturbed by loud and discordant cries in the field fronting the house; when they perceived about five hundred storks assembled in a dense body, and one standing about twenty yards before the rest, apparently haranguing its companions, who stood listening, to all appearance, with great emotion. When this bird had concluded, it retired, and another took its place, and seemed to address them in a similar manner. This proceeding and noise was repeated by several successive birds, until about eleven o'clock in the forenoon, when the whole flock simultaneously arose in the air, uttering dismal cries. The female all this time was observed to remain on her nest, watching their motions with apparent trepidation. In a short time the body of storks made towards her, headed by one bird, supposed to be the male, who struck her vehemently three or four times, and knocked her out of the nest. The whole mass then followed the attack, until they had not only destroyed the female stork, who made no attempt either to escape or defend herself, but the young gosling, and utterly removed every vestige of the nest itself. Since that time no stork has been known to build there.

This anecdote appears to demonstrate a power of combination and a kind of moral government among storks, which will startle readers who have hitherto believed that the lower animals are destitute of mental capacity.

The nearest approach to the stork that we have in this country is the long-legged heron, which we sometimes find near our mountain lakes; they wander through the forests, and wade in water, but they are smaller in size, and not as interesting in character, as is this Bible bird, the stork, which is the subject of our thoughts to-day.

We learn three important lessons from the stork.

First, we learn THE LESSON OF BEING FOND OF OUR HOMES. The storks are not gadders; they are not travelling and paying calls all the time. They stay at home and attend to their families.

They make their nests with great care, and, when they have made them, there is no place so dear to them as their homes. This nest idea is one which we ought to cultivate in life. Before very long we will leave our homes, and have to go out in the

world to make our own living, and our home will be taken away from us.

A child was once speaking of his home to a friend, who asked him, 'Where is your home?'

Looking up with loving eyes to his mother, he replied, 'My home is where my mother is.'

On a tombstone in an old church in England is the following epitaph: 'During sixty years of wedded life, she always made my home happy.' This was a husband's tribute to a devoted wife.

The storks go away from their homes for the winter, but early in the spring they always come again, glad to find their old nests. The way in which they care for their homes, and show their love for them, teaches us a lesson, which we ought not to be slow to learn.

Six of the seven wise men of Greece give their opinion of what constitutes a happy home as follows:—Solon thought the house most happy where the estate was got without injustice, kept without distrust, and spent without repentance. Bias said, 'That house is happy where the master does freely and voluntarily at home what the law compels him to do abroad.' Thales held that house most happy where the master had most leisure and respite from business. Cleobulus said, 'That in which the master is more beloved than feared.' Pittacus said, 'That is most happy where superfluities are not required and necessaries are not wanting.' Chilo added, 'That house is most happy where the master rules as a monarch in his kingdom.' And he proceeded, 'When a certain Lacedæmonian desired Lycurgus to establish a democracy in the city, "Go you, friend," replied he, "and make the experiment first in your own house."'

The first lesson which we learn from the stork is—the lesson of being fond of our homes.

The second lesson we learn from the stork is—THE LESSON OF FILIAL DEVOTION.

Filial love, or the love which we have, as children, to our parents, is the first indication which comes to us in life of our moral nature. The boy who is a good son will probably be a good brother, a good husband, and a good father; but when he is ungrateful to his parents, he will probably be false in every other relationship in life.

The ancients always honoured those who were devoted and true to their parents. And the hero of Virgil's great poem, Æneas, was called 'pious Æneas,' because, when Troy was burning, he went out from Troy with his wife following in his footsteps, his boy Ascanius at his side, and his father Anchises on his shoulders.

The Chinese to-day rate all goodness as beginning with devotion to parents. Now the storks teach us this lesson of filial devotion. When they go on their flight to the south for the winter, they do not leave the old folks behind; they care for their parents quite as much as they do for their children, and they insist upon taking the old people with them.

I knew a family once, where the children used to say, when they had anything given to them, and were asked to divide it among the different members of the family, 'Anything will do for the old man.' By which they referred to the fact that anything would suit their father. There is no worse vice in the world than filial ingratitude. It is the hot-bed out of which all other vices grow; and Satan is pretty sure to eventually possess the boy and girl who do not honour their parents, and who show ingratitude to them.

There was once a man who had an only son, to whom he bequeathed everything. When his son grew up, he was unkind to his father, refused to support him, and turned him out of his house. The old man said to his grandson, 'Go and fetch the covering from my bed, that I may go and sit by the wayside and beg.' The child burst into tears, ran for the covering, took it to his father, and said to him, 'Pray, father, cut it in two: the half of it will be large enough for grandfather; and perhaps you will want the other half when I grow a man and turn you out of doors.' The words of the child struck him so forcibly, that he ran to his father, asked his forgiveness, and took care of him until his death.

The second lesson that we learn from the stork is—the lesson of filial devotion.

The third and last lesson which we learn from the stork is—THE LESSON OF FOLLOWING OUR BEST INSTINCTS.

The Rev. Dr. H. Pritchard, who is fond of dogs as well as of preaching, once taught his congregation a good lesson by a simple remark on the faithfulness of this animal. He went to his pulpit, and had begun his sermon, when his dog, which had got out from home, slipped into the church, walked up the aisle and into the pulpit, looked up at his master, and began to whine. The congregation tittered. Instantly stopping, the Doctor walked out of the pulpit and down the aisle to the door, and, letting the dog out, returned. Leaning over the pulpit, he said, '*O that this congregation were as faithful to their Master as that dog is to his!*' Quiet reigned, and he proceeded with his sermon without further interruption.

We can learn a great many lessons from the habits of animals.

Animals get rid of their parasites by using dust, mud, and

clay. Those suffering from fever restrict their diet, keep quiet, seek dark, airy places, drink water, and sometimes plunge into it. When a dog has lost its appetite, it eats that species of grass known as dog's-tail grass, which acts as an emetic and a purgative. Cats also eat grass. Sheep and cows, when ill, seek out certain herbs. An animal suffering from chronic rheumatism always keeps as far as possible in the sun. The warrior ants have regularly organized ambulances. The naturalist Latreille cut the antennæ of an ant, and other ants came and covered the wounded part with a transparent fluid secreted from their mouths. If a chimpanzee is wounded, it stops the bleeding by placing its hand on the wound or dressing it with leaves and grass. When an animal has a wounded leg or arm hanging on, it completes the amputation by means of its teeth.

The stork teaches us this lesson of following our best instincts in two ways. The first way the stork teaches us this lesson of following our best instincts is in the way it has of going south to escape the storms of winter.

It is a great thing in life to get out of stormy weather. There is no use in fighting a storm. There is no use in defying the winter. We ought to go out of the path of temptation, as Solomon says in the book of Proverbs, when speaking of the way of temptation : 'Avoid it, pass by it, turn from it and go away.'

The storks do not try to fight the winter, but they go out of the way of the winter. It is their instinct which teaches them to do this ; and in the same way, in life, we will find that we can get out of a great many troubles by simply turning away from them, as the storks escaped the cold weather, which they knew was surely coming on, by simply spreading their broad wings, and flying to the south, away from it.

Another way in which the storks teach us the lesson of following our best instincts, is the way they have of building their nests very high.

The bird that builds its nest low on the ground is never safe, never secure. The foot of the adventurous traveller may at any moment crush its eggs, and break up its home life.

The scent of the dog may soon detect the hidden nest on the lowland, or in the bushes ; but the hawk and the eagle, the falcon and the stork, are birds which build their nests so very far from man, that man cannot disturb them. And in the same way in life, my dear children, unless we put our affections on things that are above, we will never be safe and secure from harm.

Remember that hymn which we sometimes sing, which shows

us, after all, how our safety is in building our hopes high in heaven :

When I can read my title clear
To mansions in the skies,
I'll bid farewell to every fear,
And wipe my weeping eyes.

Should earth against my soul engage,
And fiery darts be hurled,
Then I can smile at Satan's rage,
And face a frowning world.

Let cares like a wild deluge come,
And storms of sorrow fall,
May I but safely reach my home,
My God, my heaven, my all.

There shall I bathe my weary soul
In seas of heavenly rest,
And not a wave of trouble roll
Across my peaceful breast.

These, then, are the lessons which we learn from this wonderful Bible bird, the stork :

It is a bird which is large of wing, large of heart, which builds high, and blesses all about it. It destroys the germs of evil and poisonous insects.

It cares for its own, it lives at home.

It is devoted to its parents.

It follows its best instincts in building its home high above the ground.

Remember the words of the Prophet Jeremiah, when he said, contrasting the knowledge of this bird with that of God's people Israel,—

'The stork in the heaven knoweth her appointed times ; and the turtle, the crane, and the swallow observe the time of their coming : but my people know not the judgment of the Lord.'

XI.

THE ASS.

'And the ass saw the angel of the Lord.'—NUMBERS xxii. 27.

IN going on with our study of Bible Natural History, the next animal that we take up is the ass. The ass is an animal well worthy of our study.

We find the ass spoken of in the Bible between sixty and

seventy times. These animals were held in great estimation in the Eastern countries where the Bible was written. They were the favourite beasts on which kings and members of the royal family were accustomed to ride. Among these animals there was one portion, or tribe, whose hair was always white. And these white asses were the favourite ones, especially used by the distinguished persons of whom I have just spoken.

When our blessed Saviour made His last public entrance into Jerusalem, before His crucifixion, He chose to ride upon an ass. The Prophet Zechariah had foretold, hundreds of years before the time of Christ, that He, the king of Zion, 'should come, riding upon an ass, on a colt the foal of an ass.' And He came in just that way. So this prophecy was literally fulfilled.

Our sermon to-day is about what sort of an animal the ass is.

And there are three things about the character of the ass of which I wish to speak.

In the first place, I desire to show that the ass is A SENSIBLE ANIMAL.

People generally have a very different opinion about the ass from this. If you see a boy doing some silly, foolish thing, you will be very apt to hear some one near him say, 'You stupid ass, what did you do that for?' The saying, 'stupid as an ass,' is one that we often hear. And yet, properly considered, it is not true. In this country, where the ass is so often overworked, ill-used, and almost starved, no doubt it often becomes ill-natured and stupid. But in Eastern countries, where it is not overworked, but is well fed and kindly treated, the ass is a bright, intelligent, and sensible creature. And when the kings of those countries, with their princes and great men, ride upon the ass, the richest kind of harness is put upon it, and the appearance which it presents is very pleasing and attractive. The people there never think or speak of the ass as a stupid animal. On the contrary, they prize it very much, because they know it is an animal of good sense.

We have an excellent illustration of the good sense of the ass in connection with the incident spoken of in our text.

The children of Israel were finishing their long journey through the wilderness, and getting ready to enter the land of Canaan. They were still on the other side of the river Jordan. Balak, the king of Moab, through whose country they were about to pass, was very much afraid of them. Now it happened that there was a famous prophet, named Balaam, who lived near the river Euphrates, in the country of Mesopotamia. Balak had great confidence in that prophet. He believed that if he blessed any people, they would be blessed, and that if he cursed any persons, they would surely be cursed. So he made up his mind to try and get Balaam to come and curse the Israelites. Then he sent a committee of his princes to Balaam. In the name of the king they asked him to come and curse the Israelites, and told him that if he did so the king would make him a rich man. Now Balaam had a great love of money. He wanted very much to go and get what the king promised him. But God told him that he must not go. So he had to send the messengers back to tell the king that God would not let him come. Then the king sent other messengers, who urged him still more strongly to come, and promised him yet greater riches if he would only come and do what the king wanted him to do.

Then Balaam made up his mind to go to King Balak. He mounted his ass to ride there, but, as he was riding along, God sent an angel, who stood before him in the way, with a flaming sword in his hand. Now Balaam's mind was so occupied in thinking about the money he expected to get from Balak, that he did not see the angel. But, as our text says, 'the ass saw the angel of the Lord,' and turned aside several times to get out of his way. Balaam smote the ass with his staff each time that it turned aside. At last the ass spoke to him, and asked him what he had smitten him for. Some people think that this is not a real, true story. But I am quite sure that it is. For the Apostle Peter refers to this story in one of his epistles, and tells us that 'the dumb ass, speaking with man's voice, forbade the madness of the prophet.' The apostle would not have thus referred to this story unless he had known that it was true. It was God who taught Balaam's ass to bray; and when He wanted that ass to speak with a man's voice, it was just as easy for Him to teach it to speak as to bray. And when the ass saw the angel of the Lord, and saved his master's life by turning out of the angel's way, he proved very satisfactorily that he had more sense than his master. This is a good Bible illustration of the point now before us—that the ass is a sensible creature. And outside of the Bible we find plenty of such illustrations. Here are two.

The first may be called—

A DONKEY'S GOOD SENSE.

Several years ago, in Kansas City, an old horse and an old donkey, who had served their master faithfully, were kept together in a stable, and were well taken care of. They became well acquainted, and got to be quite fond of each other.

One day they were both turned into a field near the stable that they might feed on the grass. In the middle of this field was a large pond, which was sometimes filled with water, and

at other times with deep mud. In trying to get across this
pond, the old horse sunk down into the mud, and stuck fast,
so that it could not get out.

As soon as the donkey saw the trouble his companion was
in, he started off, and ran to the stable. He put his head in
the office door, and brayed as loudly as he could. After doing
this for some time, he started to run back for the pond, waving
his tail over his back. On looking round, he saw that no one
was following him. Then he returned to the office, put his
head in the door, and brayed again, longer and louder than
before. After this he started again for the pond. In a little
while he stopped and looked back to see if anybody was coming.
The stable-keeper had been watching him. Feeling sure that
there was something wrong, he told one of the stable-boys to
follow him, and see what was the matter. The boy went to the
pond, and saw the trouble the poor horse was in. Then he
returned and reported about it, and three men were sent to get
him out, which was soon done.

Now certainly that donkey showed his good sense in the way
in which he went to work to save the life of his companion.
You or I could not have acted more sensibly under the
circumstances than he did.

Our next story may be called—

THE MILKMAN'S DONKEY.

This story was told by an American gentleman who spent
several years in Spain, engaged in business. He found that
with the peasantry of Spain the donkey is a special favourite,
and is treated almost as a member of the family. The women
and children of the household feed him from their own hands,
and pat him, and speak kindly to him. He knows them all,
and loves them all. He will follow his master, and come and
go at his bidding, just as an intelligent child or servant would
do. He loves to have the baby placed on his back, and then he
will walk gently round with him on the grass-plot in front of
their cottage. The gentleman of whom we are speaking was
told of a peasant, in the neighbourhood where he lived while in
Spain, who had for many years carried milk into the city of
Madrid, to supply a set of customers. Every morning he and
his donkey, with panniers well loaded, went their accustomed
round. One morning the peasant was attacked by sudden illness, so that he was unable to go round with his milk, and had
no one to send in his place. His wife advised him to trust
their faithful donkey to go by himself, as he always knew just
where to stop. The panniers were accordingly filled with cans
of milk, and the priest of the village wrote, in a large hand, on

a card which was fastened to the donkey's neck, a request to the customers to measure out their own milk, and send back the empty cans. Then the donkey was told what to do, and set off with his load. The door-bells in Spain have a rope hanging outside the house, to which a wooden handle is fastened. The donkey would stop before the house of each customer, and, after waiting what he thought was a sufficient time, would pull the bell-rope with his mouth. And, when he had gone through the entire round, he trotted home with the empty milk-cans on his back. He continued to do this for several days, till his master got well again, and he never missed a single customer. And these incidents make it perfectly clear that the ass, when properly treated, is a sensible animal.

In the second place, the ass is A USEFUL ANIMAL.

No one doubts this, and it needs no argument to prove it. The ass is useful in the heavy burdens which it carries for its owners. It is useful for the long journeys it can accomplish for those who ride upon it. It can travel as far as the horse or the camel, only not quite as rapidly. And in Switzerland and other countries, where mountain ranges like the Alps or the Andes are found, the ass is. useful for the safe way in which it carries passengers over the most steep and dangerous mountain paths. The ass is so careful and sure-footed, that it goes over the narrowest and most dangerous paths, along the sides of the steepest mountains, without stumbling or falling. This makes it very useful in those countries.

We read of one man in the Bible, whose history was connected with this animal in a very strange way. I refer to Saul, the first king of Israel. His father, Kish, was a farmer, and kept cattle of different kinds. On one occasion some of his asses strayed away and were lost. He sent his son Saul, with one of his servants, to try and find the lost asses. After hunting for them a long time, and not finding them, they came near the place where Samuel the prophet lived. Saul's servant suggested to his master that it might be well for them to call on the prophet and make inquiries about the lost asses. They did so, and the prophet told them not to trouble themselves about the lost asses, because they had been found and taken back to their home. Then Samuel took Saul apart by himself, and told him that the people of Israel had asked God to let them have a king, as other nations had, and that God had chosen him to be the first king of Israel. After this, Samuel poured oil on Saul's head, and anointed him to be king in the name of the Lord. How strange this was! Saul had set out to find the lost asses of his father. He did not find them, but while seeking for them he found a crown and a kingdom. He must always have thought of those lost asses with great interest. Certainly the ass had proved itself a useful animal to him.

Here is an incident to show how useful the ass can show itself to be. This story may be called—

SAVED BY A DONKEY.

Dr. Hammond, a surgeon in the United States army, tells this story as occurring in connection with himself. At the time here referred to, Dr. Hammond was stationed at Fort Webster, in that part of the country which is now called Arizona.

On one occasion the doctor wished to make a journey to a small settlement, some miles distant from the fort. He started on a fine large donkey that belonged to him. His path lay down a steep valley between two high mountains. After going two or three miles from the fort, the donkey suddenly stopped, and would not go on another step. The doctor jerked the reins, and said, 'Go 'long!' but the donkey wouldn't go. Then he dashed the spurs against his side, but yet he stood still. Then he whipped him severely, but he would not move a step. Then the doctor had to turn the donkey round, and go back to the fort. The next day it was found out that just beyond where the donkey stopped there was a company of Apache Indians hidden behind the bushes, waiting to shoot any one who might come along. The donkey, either by his quick scent or sharp hearing, had found out that the Indians were there, and this made him unwilling to go any nearer to them. And here we see how the good sense of that donkey made him useful to his master, in saving his life.

And now we may look at some illustrations of the different ways in which we may imitate this feature of the ass's character, and make ourselves useful.

Our first story may be called—

WHAT A LITTLE GIRL DID.

A good many years ago, a little girl twelve years old was passing the old brick prison in the city of Chicago, on her way to school, when she saw a hand beckoning to her from a cell window, and heard the weary voice of a prisoner asking her to please bring him something to read.

The next Sunday she went to the prison, and carried that poor prisoner a book to read from her father's library. And then she kept on doing this every week. Several months after this, she was sent for to go and see that poor prisoner on his death-bed.

When she entered his room, he said to her, 'Little girl, you have saved my soul. And now, before I die, I want you to promise me that you will keep on visiting the prison, and try to do for the other poor people in prison the good you have done for me.'

She promised to do so ; and she has kept her promise. Her name is Linda Gilbert. She has been for many years the stedfast friend of the prisoners. And how very useful she has been in carrying on this work, it is impossible to tell. She has been the means of establishing good libraries in many prisons. She has visited and helped great numbers of prisoners. From among these she has a certain knowledge of not less than six hundred who are now living honest and useful lives. Men who were once prisoners in all parts of the country know her, and love her for the good she has done them. And this life of great usefulness all grew out of that little girl hearing the prisoner's call, and trying to help him in his need.

Our next story may be called—

HOW A CHINESE BOY MADE HIMSELF USEFUL.

A wealthy Virginia planter was lying very ill in the city of Richmond. He had a dangerous and infectious fever, and his physician thought that he was dying.

He had no knowledge of religion, and had lived without any thought of God, or his soul. When the doctor told him he had not long to live, he swore about it, and said, 'It's too bad, so young as I am, with so much to live for, to think of dying now! But it's always been so. Everything is against me.' At length the nurse was afraid of catching the fever, and she left him. Then the doctor asked him if he might get a Chinese lad to wait on him. 'Oh, it makes no difference,' said the sick man ; 'you may as well let me die like a dog. It will soon be over, anyhow.'

In another part of the city of Richmond there was a large Chinese laundry. One of the boys connected with this laundry was named Ching. He was a native of China, but had learned to read and love the Bible, and had become a Christian. The love of Jesus in his heart, and the hope of going to heaven when he died, made him very happy ; and the great desire of his heart was to get an education, and go back to China, and tell his countrymen about Jesus and His great salvation. But he saw no way yet of getting an education.

The doctor was acquainted with Ching. He called at the laundry, and asked him if he would be willing to wait on a patient of his who was sick with a dangerous fever. 'He is a rich man, and will pay you well.' Ching expressed his willingness to go, for he felt sure that God would take care of him.

Then the doctor took him, and introduced him to his patient. A few days after this, the sick man lay dozing on his bed, while Ching was sitting in the corner opposite to him reading his Bible. Presently the sick man opened his eyes, and, seeing what Ching was doing, he said, 'What confounded book is that you are always reading?'

This hurt Ching very much; but he meekly said, 'This no confound book; this my Jesus' book; this my passport.'

'Ha! your passport!—what do you mean by this?'

And then Ching merely read these two short verses:

'"There is no other name under heaven, given among men, whereby we can be saved, but the name of Jesus."

'"The blood of Jesus Christ cleanseth us from all sin."'

'Did you say "all sin," Ching? Read that again. Would it cleanse my sin?'

He read it again, and then said, 'Yes, sir, it will cleanse your sin, and satisfy all your hopes and longings.'

And then, at the sick man's request, Ching knelt down by his bedside, and prayed that God would pardon his sins, and give him a new heart, and make him a happy Christian.

This was repeated day by day, for some time. And then a great change came over that sick man. He found pardon, and peace, and salvation in Jesus. And a change came over his body as well as over his soul. His fever was broken, and he soon got quite well again. And when he learned that Ching was anxious to get an education, and go and preach the gospel to his countrymen, he gave him money enough to pay for his education. And then he himself joined the Church, and became an active and devoted member of it. And to-day that once wicked man is one of the noblest Christians in the country, and is using his money to promote the interests of religion and education in the South; while Ching is one of the most honoured and successful missionaries among the Chinese, and is labouring faithfully to make Christ known among his countrymen.

Thus we have seen that the second lesson which we learn is —the lesson of usefulness.

And thinking of this should lead us all to try and make ourselves useful.

In the third place, the ass is A GRATEFUL ANIMAL.

I mean by this that when kindness is shown to the ass, he is sensible of it, and remembers it, and makes some acknowledgment of it. We have no examples of this given us in the Bible, but we meet with many cases outside of the Bible.

Here is one that we may call—

A DONKEY'S GRATITUDE TO HIS HORSE FRIENDS.

An English farmer had three fine horses and a donkey on his farm. These animals were often put to graze together in the same field. Now it generally happens that horses do not like to have a donkey near them, and they will show their dislike by kicking him, and trying to drive him away.

But it was not so with those English horses. They treated the donkey kindly, and let him share with them the best grass to be found in the field. The donkey seemed to feel their kindness to him, and he showed his gratitude to them for it in the following way.

One day the donkey was put by himself into a field which had a remarkable growth of the very finest grass, and he was enjoying it greatly. His three friends the horses were in an adjoining field, where the grass was very poor and scanty. There was a high, thick hedge of hawthorn bushes separating those two fields. The horses came and looked over the hedge to see their friend the donkey having such a good time enjoying that green grass. He knew, from the way they looked at him, that they wanted to come into his field and share the pleasure which he felt in eating that excellent grass. Then the donkey went to a gate near by, which led into the field where he was grazing. That gate was fastened by a round piece of wood, which was put through an iron staple in the post of the gate. He had often seen his master fasten or unfasten that gate by putting in or pulling out that piece of wood. So he took hold of it with his teeth, and tried to pull it out. It was very tight, and he had to keep on trying for a good while; but finally he got it out. Then the gate swung wide open, and the horses came in, leaping about joyfully, as if to thank their donkey friend for his kindness in letting them in.

And here we see the gratitude of that donkey to his friends the horses, for the kindness they had showed to him.

And when we think of all that our blessed Saviour has done for us, what a debt of gratitude we owe to Him, and how gladly we should improve every opportunity of showing it.

Here is a story which may be called—

A SAVED SINNER'S GRATITUDE TO THE MAN WHO BROUGHT HIM TO JESUS.

That good man, the late John B. Gough, used to tell this story:—'One day,' said Mr. Gough, 'I was going to meet an engagement to lecture at a town in England. I had six miles

to ride so as to reach the nearest station, in order to catch the train which I was to take. A man sat by my side, who was driving me in a little one-horse hack. I noticed that he sat leaning forward in an awkward manner, with his face close to the glass of the window. I asked him if he was cold.

'"No, sir," he said. Then he placed a handkerchief round his head, and I asked him if he had the toothache.

'"No, sir," was his reply. Still he sat leaning forward. At last I said, "Will you please tell me why you sit leaning forward in that way, with a handkerchief round your head and neck, if you are not cold, and have no toothache?"

'He said, very quietly, "The window of the carriage is broken, the cold wind is coming in, and I am trying to keep it from you."

'I said, in surprise, "You are not putting your face to that broken pane to keep the wind from me, are you?"

'"Yes, sir, I am."

'"Why do you do that?"

'"God bless you, sir! I owe everything I have in the world to you."

'"Why, I never saw you before!"

'"No, sir; but I have seen you. I was a ballad singer once,—a poor, wretched creature. I went to hear you preach in Edinburgh. You told me that I was a man, and that if I came to Jesus, He would pardon my sins, give me a new heart, and help me to live like a man. I came to Jesus. He did for me as you said He would. And now I am living like a man. I have a happy wife, and a comfortable home. But I owe it all to you. God bless you, sir! There's nothing in the world I would not gladly do, to show my love for you, if it would do you any good."'

Now certainly that man showed his gratitude to Mr. Gough for bringing him to the Saviour.

I have only one other illustration. We may call it—

'I LOVE TO PINT HIM OUT.'

A gentleman, while travelling through one of the Southern States of America, came to a river, which he had to cross in order to pursue his journey. Joe Brown, a coloured boatman, who had charge of a ferry-boat, offered to take him over. The gentleman took a seat in the bow of the boat, while Joe, stepping into his place, began to pull on the oars, and the boat was soon gliding swiftly out into the stream. Several sloops were in sight, going up and down the river. All at once Joe stopped rowing. He pulled in the oars, and, springing to his feet, took off his ragged old straw hat, and, shading his eyes with his hand, looked earnestly at some object on one of the sloops in the distance.

Then he cried out, 'As I'm a libbing man, dat am de Captin!'

The gentleman started from his musing, and looked towards the distant vessel, but could not see anything very distinctly.

'Don't you see him, mister?' said Joe. 'He dat strong, good-looking man leaning against de mast.'

'Perhaps I'll see him when the vessel gets a little nearer,' said the gentleman.

'I want yer to see de Captin,' said Joe.

'Who is the Captain?' asked the gentleman.

'De Captin?' said Joe, with a look of surprise. 'He am de man what sabed me. I can't miss seeing him while he am in sight.'

'How did he save you, Joe?'

'He strip off his coat and jumped into de ribber, and cotch hole of dis chile wid his strong arm, just as he was sinking into the great depths, with the ropes around his feet. Dat am de way he sabed me,' said Joe, with very great feeling.

'You have not forgotten to be grateful, I see.'

'Grateful! Why, I'd breave every breff I draw for him, if I could. I tole him I would work all de rest of my days for him without pay. But he wouldn't let me. So I stay as close to him as I ken. He runs by here 'bout ebery two weeks. So I allus watches for him, and I love to pint him out. It's all dis poor nigger can do.'

And if that poor man felt so much gratitude to him who saved his body from drowning, by simply plunging into the water, how much gratitude do we owe to the blessed Saviour, who died in agony upon the cross in order to save our souls from everlasting death?

Now, where is our text to-day? Numbers xxii. 28. What are the words of the text? 'And the ass saw the angel of the Lord.' What is the sermon about? What sort of an animal the ass is. How many things about it did we speak of? Three. What was the first? It is *a sensible animal.* What is the second? It is *a useful animal.* What is the third? It is *a grateful animal.* Let us all ask God by His grace and blessing to make us sensible, useful, and grateful: then we shall be happy in serving God while we are here on earth, and when we die we shall find a glorious reward awaiting us in heaven.

XII.

THE ELEPHANT.

'Once in three years came the navy of Tharshish, bringing gold, and silver, ivory, and apes, and peacocks.'—1 KINGS x. 22.

THE elephant is an animal which is not mentioned directly in the Bible. There are frequent references made to ivory, the product of that animal, but the word elephant is nowhere found in Holy Writ. Some writers have thought that the 'behemoth,' described in the book of Job, was the elephant, but it is now generally considered that the animal described in this book is the hippopotamus, or great water-horse of the river Nile. It was because this animal had tusks that it was supposed to be the elephant; but, now that people have been able to see the hippopotamus for themselves, and have compared it with the wonderful description in Job, they have come to the conclusion that it is not the elephant which is meant.

The words from the book of Job are as follows :—

'Behold now behemoth, which I made with thee ; he eateth grass as an ox.

'Lo now, his strength is in his loins, and his force is in the navel of his belly.

'He moveth his tail like a cedar.

'His bones are as strong pieces of brass ; his bones are like bars of iron.

'He is the chief of the ways of God : He that made him can make His sword to approach unto him.

'Surely the mountains bring him forth food, where all the beasts of the field play.

'He lieth under the shady trees, in the covert of the reed, and fens.

'The shady trees cover him with their shadow ; the willows of the brook compass him about.

'Behold, he drinketh up a river, and hasteth not : he trusteth that he can draw up Jordan into his mouth.

'He taketh it with his eyes: his nose pierceth through snares.'

The earliest mention of ivory in the Scriptures is to be found in 1 Kings x. 18 : 'Moreover the king made a great throne of ivory, and overlaid it with the best gold.' We see, then, that ivory was considered of great value in the days of King Solomon. The words of our text to-day show us this.

King Solomon, and Hiram king of Tyre, had each of them a navy, and the vessels in this navy went every three years as far as India, or Tarshish, 'bringing gold, and silver, ivory, and apes, and peacocks.' These animals, no doubt, were brought to Jerusalem for King Solomon's Zoological Gardens there. The Hebrew names given to the apes, the peacocks, and the ivory are almost identical with the words used in the Cingalese language of the present day. We nowhere read in the Bible that any elephant was ever brought to Jerusalem, but we read a great deal about ivory, the product of the elephant, being brought there.

The Hebrew word for ivory is *shen, i.e.* a tooth. The Israelites knew perfectly well that ivory was the product of a tooth of some great animal, and not of a mere horn, like a goat's horn or cow's horn.

In the marginal reading of our text to-day, about the ivory coming into Jerusalem, along with the apes and the peacocks for King Solomon's garden, the word translated 'ivory' reads 'elephants' teeth;' so that, while we do not read of elephants in the Bible, we do read of the ivory which was manufactured out of their tusks. There are a number of places in the Bible in which ivory is distinctly mentioned as forming part of the adornment of houses.

One of these is in Psalm xlv. 8: 'All thy garments smell of myrrh, aloes, and cassia, out of the ivory palaces whereby they have made thee glad.'

Another instance is that found in 1 Kings xxii. 39: 'Now the rest of the acts of Ahab, and all that he did, and the ivory house which he made, are they not written in the book of the Chronicles of the Kings of Israel?'

The use of ivory as an article of luxury is also mentioned in Amos vi. 4: 'Woe to them that lie upon beds of ivory, and stretch themselves upon their couches.'

And in Ezekiel xxvii. 6, in the description of the costly materials out of which the Assyrians built their ships, we read that the very benches on which the rowers sat were inlaid with ivory.

There is only one place in the New Testament in which ivory is mentioned. It is found in Revelation xviii. 11, 12: 'And the merchants of the earth shall weep and mourn over her'; for no man buyeth their merchandise any more: the merchandise of gold, and silver, and precious stones, and all manner vessels of ivory.'

The elephant is put to many uses. If he cannot thread a needle, he can pick one up from the ground with his trunk. His sense of touch is very delicate.

An elephant was once left to take care of a little boy baby. This he did with wonderful care and gentleness. If the baby strayed off too far, the elephant would stretch out his long trunk and bring the little wanderer back.

In the year 1863 an elephant was employed at a station in India to pile up heavy logs, a work which these animals will do with great neatness and speed. The superintendent suspected the keeper of stealing the rice given for the animal's food. The keeper, of course, denied the charge, but the elephant, who was standing by, laid hold of a large wrapper which the man wore around his waist, and, tearing it open, let out some quarts of rice, which the fellow had stored away under the folds.

So closely do elephants remember the meaning of the signs which have been taught them, that they will instantly obey the gentlest signal, such as the lifting of a finger, or the slightest touch on their ears.

Mr. Jesse, the keeper of an elephant in London, was once giving him some potatoes, when one fell on the floor, just beyond the sweep of the creature's trunk. There was a wall a few inches behind the potato, and, blowing strongly, the sagacious animal sent it so hard against the wall that the potato rebounded, and on the recoil came back near enough for the elephant to seize it.

The elephant likes music, easily learns to mark the time, and to move in step to the sound of drums. His smell is exquisite, and he likes perfumes of all kinds, and, above all, fragrant flowers; he chooses them, picks them one by one, and makes bouquets of them, and, after having relished the smell, carries them to his mouth, and seems to taste them.

The elephant is a very interesting animal, and teaches us four important lessons.

First of all, the elephant is AN EXAMPLE OF BRAVERY.

All boys like to be considered brave. To be called a coward is the most horrible disgrace.

The elephant is a very brave animal, and in olden times was used as an engine of war.

In the book of Maccabees, which is found among the books known as the Apocrypha, we find that the elephant is mentioned as the very embodiment of all that is brave.

In the first book of Maccabees, first chapter, verses sixteen and seventeen, we read as follows :—

'Now when the kingdom was established, before Antiochus, he thought to reign over Egypt, that he might have the dominion of the two realms.

'Wherefore he entered into Egypt with a great multitude, with chariots, and elephants, and horsemen, and a great navy.'

We see by this that the elephant was considered a very beneficial engine of war; and the king of Egypt was so frightened by these invaders that he took to flight, and allowed Antiochus to take possession of the country.

After this, we read that Antiochus marched against Jerusalem with a vast army, which is described as follows :—

'The number of his army was an hundred thousand footmen, and twenty thousand horsemen, and two and thirty elephants exercised in battle.

'And to the end that they might provoke the elephants to fight, they showed them the blood of grapes and mulberries.

'Moreover, they divided the beasts among the armies, and for every elephant they appointed a thousand men, armed with coats of mail, and with helmets of brass on their heads; and besides this, for every beast were ordained five hundred horsemen of the best.

'These were ready at every occasion : and wheresoever the beast was, and whithersoever the beast went, they went also, neither departed they from him.

'And upon the beasts were there strong towers of wood, which covered every one of them, and were girt fast unto them with devices : there were also upon every one two and thirty strong men, that fought upon them, besides the Indian that ruled him.

'As for the remnant of the horsemen, they set them on this side and that side at the two parts of the host, giving them signs what to do, and being harnessed all over amidst the ranks' (1 Maccabees vi. 30–38).

We can see by this quotation from the Maccabees that the thirty-two elephants were looked upon in very much the same way that the Romans regarded their chariots of war, or as in the present day we think of the artillery of the army. In olden days, the mention of the Indian that ruled the elephant shows us that the present custom of having men sit on the elephant's head to guide him runs back through centuries.

When Julius Cæsar crossed the Alps and conquered Gaul, and when Hannibal crossed the same mountains to attack Rome, we read of the elephants which they had in their armies, and they were always looked upon in the light of artillery.

One of the old writers, in describing the elephant as a fighting force in the army, writes :—

'The military elephant did carry four persons on his bare back; one fighting on the right hand, and another on the left hand; the third, which stood fighting on the back of the elephant, and the fourth in the middle of these, guiding and holding the reins, and guiding the beast in the transaction of the objects; as vital in this, especially wherein was needed equal knowledge and dexterity. For when the Indian which ruled them said, Strike here on the right hand, or else on the left hand, or refrain, and stand still, no reasonable men could yield obedience.'

This old writer, whose name was Topsel, seems to have been greatly interested in the description of the elephant as a fighter in the army, and further describes the courage of the elephant as follows :—

'They did fasten iron chains fast all upon the elephant that was to bear ten to fifteen, twenty, or thirty men ; on either side they put panniers of iron, bound underneath their belly ; upon them all like panniers of wood, hollow, wherein they placed their men at arms, and covered them over with small boards ; for the trunk of the elephant was covered with a mail for defence, and upon that a broad sword two cubits long. This, as also the wooden castle, or pannier aforesaid, first to the neck, and then to the back of the elephant. Being thus armed, they entered the battle. And they showed unto the beasts, to make them ferocious, wine and liquor made of rice, and a white cloth ; for at the sight of any of these, his courage and rage increaseth above measure. And his horrible voice is wonderful ; his body is a terrible force ; his admirable skill, his ready and inestimable obedience, is a strange sight, seldom seen, especially as produced in battle.'

We read a great deal about the elephant as a military arm, or weapon, in the book of Apocrypha, in the wars which the Maccabees were waging with their Syrian enemies. No other method of checking the elephant, except by self-sacrifice, could be found ; and in 1 Maccabees vi. 43–46, we read how Eleazar, the son of Matthias, nobly devoted himself for his country. Eleazar, also named Savaran, perceived 'that one of the beasts, armed with royal harness, was higher than all the rest, and supposing that the king was upon him, put himself in jeopardy, to the end that he might deliver his people, and get himself a perpetual name : wherefore he ran upon him courageously in the midst of the battle, slaying on the right hand and upon the left, so that they were divided from him on both sides. Which done, he crept under the elephant, and thrust him under, and slew him : whereupon the elephant fell down upon him, and he died.'

Now, my dear children, we all ought to be as brave in fighting evil, as the elephant is in fighting the side to which he is opposed. An old hymn says that

> Satan trembles when he sees
> The weakest saint upon his knees.

The only way to overcome Satan is by fighting him, and never giving in, in the conflict.

A young lady, who had been a very earnest Christian, began to grow cold and indifferent, and a great change came over her. This was observed with a great deal of sadness by her friends ;

and her minister, who happened to see her, said to her, 'My dear young friend, how comes it that you have changed so much of late? You were one of the most zealous of Christians, and now you seem to have lost all interest in religion.'

'I will tell you,' she replied. 'When I first became a Christian, I made it a practice to read my Bible regularly, and to pray every night before going to sleep. During the past winter it has been very cold, and I thought that it would be just as well if I prayed in bed. And now I want to tell you that it is these feather-bed prayers that have done the mischief.'

We can never drive off Satan by feather-bed prayers. We have got to use stronger weapons than that.

Many a time has Satan succeeded in his efforts to overcome frail humanity, but in no case could he have done so if always and ever his victims had known how to use the 'sword of the Spirit, which is the word of God.' '*It is written,*' said our Saviour in the wilderness, and 'Satan departed from Him.'

'What's wrang wi' ye noo? I thought ye were a' richt,' said one Scotch boy to another who had recently been converted, but who was still disquieted and desponding. 'What's wrang wi' ye noo?'

'Man, I'm no' richt yet,' replied the other, 'for Satan's aye tempting me.'

'And what dae ye then?' asked his friend.

'I try,' said he, 'to sing a hymn.'

'And does that no' send him awa'?'

'No, I'm as bad as ever.'

'Weel,' said the other, 'when he tempts ye again, *try him wi' a text;* he canna staun that.'

This is the great remedy for temptation; and we can only conquer our adversary the devil by the word of truth, by the power of God, by the armour of righteousness on the right hand and on the left.

Here is the way in which a little girl fought Satan :—

A little girl sat upon the large stone doorstep of her father's house, and beside her was a boy of about the same age. He had been eating a fresh, rosy apple, and had thrown the core into the gutter beyond the walk, and watched it as the muddy water carried it from his sight; then, turning back to his playmate, who seemed absorbed in the pictures of a new book, he said,—

'Give me your apple, Katie; mine's all gone.'

'Not now; wait a little while,' was the reply.

But the greedy little fellow, not willing to wait, took the apple up, turned it round and round, smelled it, and then tossed it up lightly in his hands, each time catching it again.

I expected his teeth would go into it, but he was too honest for that.

At last it dropped from his hands, rolled into the gutter, and was borne away.

His cry brought the eyes of the little girl upon him. The blood mounted to her brow; she was at once upon her feet, with one hand raised, apparently to strike the shrinking form beside her. But the hand did not fall; and she stood, her face and form showing the struggle within. I prayed that she might not be too strongly tempted.

A moment more, and her voice fell on my ear:

'Go away, Satan! go away!'

The mother within heard the words too, and, coming out, asked what they meant. A blush was upon the brow of the child, but it was humility and shame that caused it, while, with drooping head, she answered, 'Satan wanted me to strike Freddy; but I didn't.'

The mother drew her within her arms, and kissed her, saying, 'That is right, my child; resist him, and he will flee from you.'

Now, my dear children, the wonderful thing about bravery is, that wherever it appears in life it holds on to your nature to the very end. Here is a story which will illustrate this.

'At the close of 1793, the Indian fleet was detained in the Downs and at Spithead from Christmas to April following. During the detention a mutiny broke out on board the *Dutton*, which threatened to be attended with serious consequences. The captain and lieutenant had left the vessel, and the inferior officers, having lost their command, were firing pistols overhead. Serious apprehension was felt lest the men should gain access to the powder magazine, and madly end the strife by their own death and that of all on board.

'It was at this critical moment that Captain Haldane, of the *Melville Castle*, appeared at the side of the vessel. His approach was the signal for renewed and angry tumult. The shouts of the officers, "Come on board; come on board!" were drowned by the cries of the mutineers, "Keep off, or we'll sink you!"

'The scene was appalling; and to venture into the midst of the angry crew seemed to be an act of daring almost amounting to rashness. Ordering his men to veer round by the stern, in a few moments Captain Haldane was on the quarter-deck. His first object was to restore to the officers composure and presence of mind. He refused to head an immediate attack on the mutineers, but very calmly reasoned with the men, sword in hand, telling them that they had no business there, and asking what they hoped to effect in the presence of twenty sail of the line.

'The quarter-deck was soon cleared, but, observing that there was still much confusion, and inquiring where the chief danger lay, he went down immediately at the very point of alarm. Two of the crew, intoxicated with spirits, and more hardy than the rest, were at the door of the powder magazine, threatening with horrid oaths that, whether it should prove heaven or hell, they would blow up the ship. One of them was in the act of wrenching off the iron bars from the doors, whilst the other had a shovel full of live coals ready to throw in. Captain Haldane, instantly putting a pistol to the breast of the man with the iron bar, told him that if he stirred he was a dead man. Calling for the irons of the ship, he saw them placed, first on this man, and then on the other. The rest of the ringleaders were also secured, and the mutiny was quelled through the courage and energy of Captain Haldane.'

Quitting the navy, Captain Haldane devoted his fortune and his life to the cause of Bible truth. The same energy and zeal marked his career, as he fought the Lord's battles with weapons which were not carnal.

The first lesson which we learn from the elephant is—the lesson of bravery.

The second lesson which we learn from the elephant is—THE LESSON OF GENTLENESS.

I was reading the other day about the elephant as a gentle nurse, and the story is found as follows :—

A large elephant showed, by the constant flagellation of his person, that he was much annoyed by his persecutors the mosquitoes ; and just at that time the keeper brought a little naked black thing, as round as a ball, which in India I believe they call a child, and laid it down before the animal with two words in Hindustanee, 'Watch it,' and then walked away in the town. The elephant immediately broke off the larger part of a bough, so as to make a smaller and more convenient whisk, and directed his whole attention to the child, gently fanning the little lump of India ink, and driving away every mosquito which came near it. This he continued for upwards of two hours, regardless of himself, until the keeper returned. It was really a beautiful sight, causing much reflection. Here was a monster, whose weight exceeded that of the infant by at least a thousand times, acknowledging that the image of his Maker, even in the lowest degree of perfection, was divine ; silently proving the truth of the sacred announcement, that God hath 'given to man dominion over the beast of the field.' And here, too, was a brute animal setting an example of devotion and self-denial that but few Christians, none indeed but a mother, could have practised.

For an elephant to be gentle is the greatest lesson to us all to follow the example of this mammoth beast. We would expect that the elephant could be strong, or of service in moving logs ; but for an elephant to be gentle seems to us something very surprising.

Wise men are members of the Wisconsin Dairymen's Association. Upon the wall of the room in which its annual meeting was recently held was hung this motto:

' Talk to your cow as you would to a lady.'

The dairyman who wrote that motto has, consciously or unconsciously, applied the Hebrew proverbs about 'a soft answer,' and 'a soft tongue,' to the management of cows. We doubt not that his cows are not only good milkers, but gentle.

A gentleman's horses and cattle will be gentle, for he treats them with a consideration similar in spirit to that which he metes out to his neighbours. They know that their master is also their friend, and therefore they heed his words and return his friendship. Boys sometimes ornament the barn with pictures and posters. We wish they would hang over the stable and cow-shed these proverbs :

' A soft answer turneth away wrath, but grievous words stir up anger.'

' By long forbearing is a prince persuaded, and a soft tongue breaketh the bone.'

As every schoolboy knows, a gentle answer calms an irritated companion. Even the most obstinate, who would resist opposition as a bone withstands the strongest jaws, is overcome by winning words. Let our farmers' boys try the influence of Solomon's proverbs upon the stock they care for.

The other day I was reading a wonderful account of the power of gentleness as shown by a little girl. The story is as follows :—

' There is a little girl of six years of age, a daughter of Mr. David Thomas, who lives on the borders of a pond which supplies water for the furnace works at Weare River, who has a most wonderful control over a class of animals hitherto thought to be untameable. For a year or two past, the little girl has been in the habit of playing about the pond and throwing crumbs into the water for the fishes. By degrees these timid creatures have become so tame as to come at her call, follow her about the pond, and eat from her hand.

' A gentleman went down there a few days since with his young daughter, to see the little creatures and their mistress. At first the fishes were deceived, and came up to the surface of the water as the gentleman's daughter approached, but in a moment they discovered their mistake, and whisked away from the stranger in high dudgeon.

'Their own mistress then came up and called, and they crowded up, clustering about her hands to receive the crumbs. She had, besides, a turtle, or tortoise, which has been maimed in the leg. This creature lives in the pond, and seems to be entirely under the control of the little girl, obeying her voice, and feeding from her hand. We have just returned from a visit to the pond, and have seen the little bright-eyed girl sporting with her obedient swarms of pickerel, pout, and shiners, patting them on the head, stroking their sides, and letting them slip through her hands. She has her favourites among them. A pout, which has been marked on the head in some way, and the turtle we spoke of, are remarkably intelligent. A more beautiful instance of the influence of kindness and gentleness can hardly be found.'

And we all ought to strive to imitate the gentleness of the elephant; and, above all other places, we ought to try to be gentle at home. It is shameful to think that at times a person will act more impolitely to his wife or his sister than he would to a stranger. A gentleman, or a gentlewoman, is not one who is polite in company alone, but is one who shows that he possesses a gentle spirit, by being kind and gentle to the weak, the poor, and the suffering.

The second lesson which we learn from the elephant is—the lesson of gentleness.

The third lesson which we learn from the elephant is—THE LESSON OF COMMON-SENSE.

The elephant has a good business head. Strange as it may seem, lazy, clumsy-looking as elephants are in our menageries, where he is merely an object of curiosity, in Asia he is as useful an animal as the horse, and he is employed in a greater variety of ways. There are few or no tasks which the horse can be trusted to perform without constant guidance, whereas the elephant may be given as much freedom as many men would have, to perform the same task. This is notably the case in the lumber yards of Rangoon, where the entire operation of moving heavy timber is by male elephants, without any supervision of the men. It is strange to think of elephants as being in the lumber business, but this is really the case. In Rangoon, the logs to be moved are teakwood, which is very heavy. They are cut into lengths of twenty feet, with a diameter, or perhaps a square, of about a foot. An elephant will go to a log, kneel down, thrust his tusks under the middle of it, curl his trunk over it, test it to see that it is evenly balanced, and then rise with it, and easily carry it to the pile which is being made. Placing the log carefully on the pile in its proper place, the sagacious animal will step back a few paces, and measure with his eye to determine whether or not the log needs pushing the one way or another. It will then make any necessary alteration of position. In this way, without a word of command from its mahout, or driver, it will go on with its work.

To do any special task, it must, of course, be directed by the mahout; but it is marvellous to see how readily this great creature comprehends its instructions, and how ingeniously it makes use of its strength. If a log too heavy to be carried is to be moved a short distance, the elephant will bend low, place his great head against the end of the log, and then, with a sudden exertion of strength and weight, throw his body forward, and fairly push the log along; or, to move the log any great distance, he will encircle it with a chain and drag his load behind him.

As a rule, however, the work of dragging is done by the female elephants, since, having no tusks, they cannot carry logs as the male elephants do. A man could hardly display more judgment in the adjustment of the rope or chain around a log, nor could a man with two hands tie and untie knots more skilfully than do the elephants with their trunks.

The elephant is a great example for those of us who want to be common-sense Christians. The world of common-sense and the world of Christian living lie very close together. It was when our Lord saw that the scribe answered discreetly that He said, 'Thou art not far from the kingdom of God.' Common-sense and the Spirit of God keep very close company.

I was reading a short time ago about a servant girl who showed her common-sense in religion.

The story is called—

'I HANGED ON AND PRAYED.'

A few days since, a gentleman, aged, but ambitious, was engaged in painting his house. A portion of the cornice seemed to be quite inaccessible, but, by placing a ladder on the roof of a piazza, it could be reached. This could be accomplished, however, only by extreme carefulness, and the ascent would be attended with great risk, as the ladder was almost perpendicular, and liable to fall back.

The old gentleman entered, and requested the servant girl of the family to come out and hold the ladder steadily at its base, while he ascended it. She was frightened at the idea of his attempt, and entreated him to relinquish it. He stubbornly refused to follow her advice, and commanded her to take a position on the roof by means of a chamber window. Trembling

K

and terrified, she obeyed. Step by step he climbed, until he reached the topmost round. She held her breath as he reached up with his brush to paint the ornament which extended out beyond the cornice, fearing every moment that he would fall to the ground and be instantly killed. She grew dizzy with excitement, her lips were colourless, and her face became as pale as the snow. But still she clung to the ladder, and held it firmly. If she had loosened her grasp for a moment, too well she knew what the result would be. Finally her suspense was over, for he descended safely, having executed his design.

Soon afterward the servant might have been heard repeating this adventure to her mistress.

'What did you do?' exclaimed the old lady in frightened tones, fully realizing a sense of the danger past.

'Why, I *just hanged on and prayed*,' said the girl feelingly.

'The hanging on was probably the most efficient,' said the old gentleman, somewhat sceptically.

'Oh, I prayed, so that I *could* hang on,' said the girl.

The third lesson which we learn from the elephant is—the lesson of common-sense.

The fourth lesson which the elephant teaches us is—THE LESSON OF OBEDIENCE.

An elephant in Calcutta had a disease in his eyes. For three days he had been completely blind. His owner, an engineer officer, asked the doctor if he could do anything to relieve the poor animal. The doctor said he would try the nitrate of silver, which was a remedy commonly applied to similar diseases in the human eye. The large animal was ordered to lie down, and at first, on the application of the remedy, raised a most extraordinary roar at the acute pain which it occasioned. The effect, however, was wonderful. The eye was in a manner restored, and the animal could partially see. The next day, when he was brought, and heard the doctor's voice, he lay down of himself, placed his enormous head on one side, curled up his trunk, drew in his breath just like a man about to endure an operation, gave a sigh of relief when it was over, and then, by trunk and gesture, evidently wished to express his gratitude.

A great blessing always comes to the obedient boy. The disobedient boy is a hard case, and it is not easy to do anything with him. And we don't like such a boy, and we don't like to think about him; but a truly obedient boy is the delight of our eyes. He will come out right, and make a man.

Once upon a time a circus came to town, and everybody knows how the music and the grand tent and horses set all the little boys agoing. Sixpences and shillings are in great demand, and many a choice bit of money have the circus riders carried away, which was meant for better purposes.

A little boy was seen looking around the premises with a great deal of curiosity. 'Halloa, Johnny,' said a man who knew him, 'going to the circus?'

'No, sir,' answered Johnny; 'father don't like 'em.'

'Oh, well! I'll give you money to go, Johnny,' said the man.

'Father don't approve of them,' answered Johnny.

'Well, go for once, and I'll pay for you.'

'No, sir,' said Johnny; 'my father would give me money if he thought it was best; besides, I've got a shilling in my strong box—twice enough to go.'

'I'd go, Johnny, for once; it is wonderful the way the horses do,' said the man. 'Your father needn't know it.'

'I sha'n't,' said the boy.

'Now why?' asked the man.

''Cause,' said Johnny, twirling his bare toes in the sand, 'after I've been I could not look my father right in the eye, and I can now.'

The man gave up, and didn't try any more. Johnny was a brave and plucky little fellow. But he was brave because he was obedient.

When the late Horace Maynard, U.S. Minister to Turkey during the days of the great Rebellion, entered Amherst College, he placed a big letter 'V' over his door; and for a time considerable curiosity was aroused on the part of his college mates, to know the meaning of it. But all inquiry failed, and the subject was finally forgotten. At commencement, when the young man graduated, he was appointed to deliver the valedictory address, and during the address he said: 'My young friends, I will now explain to you what that mysterious letter "V" signified. It meant "Valedictory;" and from the time I entered this college, I determined that I would bend all my efforts to secure this honour; and I kept myself obedient to this object which I had placed before me as the end of my college life.'

I was reading the other day a funny fable about two men and a bear. It seems that two men had to go through a great wood. One of them was short and stout, and one was tall and slim.

'I could not run fast or climb well,' said the short one; 'if a foe, man or beast, came on me, I should have to stand my ground.'

'Have no fear,' said the slim man. 'I can run fast and climb well; but still it is my rule to stand my ground—I would fight for you to the last. I fear no man or beast, not I. Hark! what is that noise?'

'I am sure,' said the short man, 'that is the growl of a bear; I know there are bears in this wood.'

The bear was soon in sight. The tall man ran a short way and hid in a tree. The short one fell flat on his face on the ground, and held his breath. The bear came to him, smelt him, and thought he was dead. So he left him, and with a gruff growl or two went his way.

When the bear was out of sight, the short man rose from the ground, and the tall one came down from the tree.

'What did the bear say to you, my friend?' said the tall man to the short one. 'I saw him put his mouth close to your ear.'

'He told me,' said the short man, 'to put no trust in one who brags in the way you do, for those who boast so much are not brave.'

My dear children, let us learn not to talk about our faith, or to sing about our faith, or to preach about our faith, but let us learn to *act our faith*, and to practise our Lord's words: 'If ye know these things, happy are ye if ye do them.'

These, then, are the four lessons which we learn from the elephant:—

The first lesson we learn from the elephant is *the lesson of courage.*

The second lesson we learn is *the lesson of gentleness.*

The third lesson we learn is *the lesson of common-sense.*

The fourth lesson we learn is *the lesson of obedience.*

Not long ago, one of Barnum's elephants was in danger of losing his sight, and the surgeon who had been called to examine the huge animal induced him to submit to an operation, that the eye might be saved. Accordingly the poor animal was tied down, and some caustic fluid was dropped into his eye. The elephant roared with pain; but on the following day the eye that was treated was much better. The surgeon thought he would have a terrible time operating on the other eye; but his surprise can be imagined, when the great beast stretched himself out and submitted readily to the operation. The elephant had recognised the skill of the operation performed by his benefactor.

Now, my dear children, whenever you see an elephant, be it as big as Jumbo or as small as the Baby Elephant, let that big waddling animal stand to you as an object lesson of God's wisdom in creation; and bear in mind that this object lesson, the elephant, who rolls along the sawdust ring like an old sailor who has just landed, teaches us these four lessons: *To be brave; to be gentle; to use common-sense; and to be obedient.*

XIII.

THE SCORPION.

'That great and terrible wilderness wherein were fiery serpents and scorpions.'—DEUTERONOMY viii. 15.

OUR subject to-day is the scorpion—a dreadful insect, which is as full of lessons as it is of venom.

The scorpion is a reptile of which we frequently read in ancient history. They are exceedingly common in Palestine, and they are a constant source of terror to the travellers there until they become accustomed to them.

The scorpion is in reality a terrible kind of spider, and has the venom claw at the end of its body, and not in its jaw. Scorpions do not look unlike lobsters, as we see them collected in a basket, on their way to the market. These uncomfortable creatures, the scorpions, manage in some way to secrete themselves in hidden nooks and corners, and one experienced in travelling in the East—where scorpions abound—will be careful where he takes his seat, until he has discovered whether there are any scorpions or venomous spiders hidden under the rocks near where he may happen to be.

Nooks and corners in walls are the places where scorpions delight to take refuge; so that one who travels in the East learns very soon the places in which to expect these insects. The scorpion has a peculiar venom, some of the larger scorpions being able to make a man very ill, and even to kill him, if he should be one subject to inflammation.

The scorpions were so much feared by the early Christians and the apostles of our Lord, that we find He promised them safety from their stings, and the bite of poisonous reptiles.

A writer of natural history says,—

'After a person has been stung once by a scorpion, he suffers comparatively little the second time, and that if he be stung three or four times, the only pain that he suffers arises from the bite, which is like a mosquito bite. Sailors say that after a week at sea, the poison of a scorpion loses its power, and they care nothing about the scorpions which are sure to come aboard, inside of the bundles of firewood.'

We will now take a few passages from the Word of God, wherein reference is made to the scorpion. As might be expected, most of these references are to the poisonous quality of the scorpion's sting, but one or two allude to its habit of dwelling in desert places.

Deut. viii. 15 : 'Who led thee through that great and terrible wilderness, wherein were fiery serpents, and scorpions, and drought, where there was no water.' Another place where they are described in the Bible, is in Ezekiel ii. 6 : 'And thou, son of man, be not afraid of them, neither be afraid of their words ; though briars and thorns be with thee, and thou dost dwell among scorpions ; be not afraid of their words, nor be dismayed at their looks, though they be a rebellious house.'

The passages which mention the poison of the scorpion occur in the New Testament. One of these is found in Rev. ix. 5 : 'And to them it was given that they should not kill them, but that they should be tormented five months ; and their torment was as the torment of a scorpion, when he striketh a man.' Also in verse 10 of the same chapter we read : 'And they had tails like unto scorpions, and there were stings in their tails ; and their power was to hurt men five months. Another passage is that used by our Lord, Luke xi. 12, where He says : 'Or if he shall ask an egg, will he offer him a scorpion ?' And in St. Luke x. 19, our Lord says : 'Behold, I give unto you the power to tread on serpents and scorpions, and over all the power of the enemy, and nothing shall by any means hurt you.'

There is a famous story in the Old Testament in which a scorpion is concerned ; it forms a part of the angry counsel given to Rehoboam by his friends, when there was a threatening of revolt in the united kingdom of Israel. The old men counselled him to be kind and tender, in the words that he uttered to those who were contemplating revolt, but Rehoboam yielded to the advice of his young friends and companions, and said to those who asked him for favour, 'And now, whereas my father did lade you with a heavy yoke, I will add to your yoke. My father hath chastised you with whips, but I will chastise you with scorpions. So Jeroboam and all the people came to Rehoboam the third day, as the king had appointed, saying, Come to me again the third day. And the king answered the people roughly, and forsook the old men's counsel that they gave him ; and spake to them after the counsel of the young men, saying, My father made your yoke heavy, and I will add to your yoke ; my father also chastised you with whips, but I will chastise you with scorpions' (1 Kings xii. 12–14).

What Rehoboam meant by these words is plain enough, namely, that he was going to be more severe than his father had been ; but what he really meant by 'whipping the rebels with scorpions,' was probably a reference to a terrible kind of whip called a scorpion, which is something like the knout used in Russia at the present day.

This fearful instrument—the scorpion—was made on purpose to punish slaves, so that merely to refer to the scorpion was itself an insult. It was made up of a number of thongs of leather, each of which ended with a knob of metal, tipped with metal hacked, so that it looked like the jointed and hacked tail of the scorpion. This fearful weapon of punishment could kill a man in a moment, by two or three blows, and it was sometimes used in the amphitheatres : a gladiator armed with a scorpion being matched against one armed with a spear.[1]

That many scorpions were found in Palestine and its neighbourhood, may be seen from the fact that a 'pass' between the south end of the Dead Sea and Mount Zion was named for it. The southern boundary of Judah is said to be 'Maaleh-acrabbim.'

The words in the Bible where it is described are as follows : 'And it went out to the south side to Maaleh-acrabbim, or the mountain of scorpions, and passed along to Zin, and ascended up on the south side unto Kadesh-barnea, and passed along to Herzon, and went up to Adar, and fetched a compass to Karkaa' (Joshua xv. 3). The literal translation of these words, Maaleh-acrabbim, is, 'they are sent of scorpions,' or 'the scorpion pass.'

We have allusions in the Scriptures to other poisonous insects, such as the spider, the worm, and the horse-leech ; but the scorpion is the most dreadful of all Bible insects. So that to say of any animals, that they had tails like unto scorpions, and that their stings were in their tails, is to say the most dreadful thing that is possible of any living creature.

Lobsters look fierce enough as we see them in the baskets, but if we add to lobsters the power of a venomous sting, we will have some idea of what a scorpion is like. The nearest approach to a scorpion which it was my fortune to have, was a South American tarantula. This insect was as large as my doubled-up fist, and was given to me by a sea-captain who got it from Brazil. He brought it in a little cage, such as the canary birds are brought in when they are taken to market to be sold.

This tarantula had been forty days at sea without eating or drinking anything, and I supposed that he was dead. I took him out of the cage, and put him on the mantelpiece, keeping him there as a sort of dead curiosity.

One warm day in June, when I came home, I found my tarantula walking around the mantelpiece quite lively. He had six or eight legs, covered with hair and bristles, and had two big eyes in the centre of his body, and he looked like the pictures of the devil-fish, as described by Victor Hugo. I tied a piece of string around one of his legs, and took him out for a

[1] *Bible Animals*, by J. G. Wood, p. 643.

walk across the room. He hadn't anything to eat for about
fifty days, but he seemed very lively, and after he had straight-
ened out his legs and got them limbered into use, he fairly ran
across the floor. My tarantula soon became an object of terror
to the household, and my friends and family would not come
into the room where he was, as he had an awkward way of
jumping about, and pouncing down on my desk, as a monkey
would swing from bough to bough in the forest. When the
very hot weather came on, in July, he became so venturesome
that he thought nothing of walking down-stairs to the dining-
room, to put in an appearance at the dinner-table ; this was
too much for the peace and well-being of the family, so the
tarantula was drowned in a quart of alcohol, and was presented
to the Academy of Natural Sciences, where he now adorns
one of the shelves in their new building in Philadelphia.

This was the nearest approach I ever had in my life to any
experience with a scorpion. The naturalist Tristram, in his
Review of the Physical Geography of the Holy Land, says :
'Scorpions are carnivorous, feeding chiefly on beetles and
locusts ; they swarm in every part of Palestine, and are found
in houses, chinks of walls, among rocks and under stones,
whether in dry or moist situations. It is always necessary,
before pitching tents, to turn up every stone, however small,
lest scorpions should be secreted ; as when disturbed or aroused
by the warmth of the camp, they will strike at and sting any
person or object within reach. So numerous are they, that in
the warmer parts of the country, every third stone is sure to
conceal one. Eight species have already been described from
Palestine, and we find several additional kinds varying in
colour and in size. The largest and most dangerous species is
black, and about six inches long. Others are yellow, brown,
white, and reddish. Others are striped and banded. They lie
dormant during the cold weather, but are very easily roused
and excited. The young are carried for some days on the back
of the female, until they are old enough to provide for themselves.'

So much then for the scorpion ; let us now learn the lessons
which this venomous creature teaches us.

First of all, we learn from the scorpion—THE LESSON OF THE
HIDDEN POWER OF VENOM.

By venom we mean poison, or virus, or any noxious matter
which is secreted in any part of our being. Venom comes from
the Latin word *venenum*, which means drug or poison.

Venomous thoughts are thoughts of malice, and spite, and
malignity ; that is why we always want to kill a viper, or a
snake, or a black spider, because we know that it is filled with

venom, or poison, or some noxious material which will give us pain, or perhaps cause us death. A venomous writer is one who is malignant and mischievous. A venomous neighbour is one who is spiteful, and has evil designs upon us.

We don't know how it is that we have this evil within us, but it is very evident that in some way venom is within us, just as truly as it is within the poisonous scorpion.

There was a rich nobleman in England who had a little daughter named Anne. They were very fond of her, for she was a fine little creature, very lively and merry and affectionate, and exceedingly beautiful. But she had a very bad temper. When anything vexed her, she would fly into a rage, and turn and strike any one that provoked her. After every fit of anger she would be ashamed and sorry, and resolve never to do so again. But the next time she was provoked, it was all forgotten, and she was as angry as ever.

When she was between four and five years of age, her mother had a little son, a sweet little tender baby. Anne's nurse, who was thoughtless and wicked, loved to tease her, because she was so easily irritated, and so she told her that her father and mother would not care for her now, because all their love and pleasure would be in this little brother, and they would not mind her. Poor Anne burst into a flood of tears, and cried bitterly, saying, 'You are a naughty woman to say so! Mamma will always love me; I know she will, and I'll go this very moment and ask her.'

And she ran out of the nursery, and hastened to her mother's room. The servant called after her, 'Come, miss, you needn't go to your mother's room; she won't see you now.'

Anne burst open the door, but was instantly caught hold of by a strange woman she had never seen before.

'My dear,' said this woman, 'you cannot see your mother just now;' and she was going on to tell that it was because she was very sick, and could not be disturbed. But she was too angry to listen, and she screamed and kicked at the woman, who was obliged to take her by force and carry her back to the nursery. When she put her down, she gave the servant a charge not to let her go to her mother's room. This added to her rage. But the thoughtless, wicked servant, instead of trying to soothe and quiet her, burst out into a laugh, and said, 'I told you that, miss; you see your mamma does not love you now.'

Then the poor child became mad with fury. She seized a smoothing-iron, and, darting forward, threw it upon the baby's head, as it lay in the cradle. The child gave one struggle, and breathed no more.

Anne's mother died that night of grief. Anne grew up in

the possession of great riches. She had every outward comfort about her that money could procure, but she was a very unhappy and miserable woman. She was never known to smile. The thought of the terrible consequences of that one outburst of passion pressed upon her like a heavy burden, all her days. Ah ! what a saddened woman this girl became ! She was a child of sorrow to all about her. Her venomous hate had made her so.

If you give way to such tempers, my dear young friends, you will certainly come to be like the scorpion; but if you strive and pray against such feelings, and try to be gentle, kind, and pleasant to those around you, then you will be children of blessing to your parents.

Let us beware of this hidden power of venom within us, for the poison as ' of asps ' is indeed under our lips.

The first lesson of warning which the scorpion teaches us is —the lesson of the hidden power of venom.

The second lesson we learn from the scorpion is—THE LESSON OF THE POISONING POWER OF SIN.

The following illustrates what we mean. It is a story entitled—

ONE DROP OF EVIL.

' I don't see why you won't let me play with Will Hunt,' pouted Walter Kirk. ' I know he doesn't always mind his mother, and smokes cigars, and once in a while swears just a little ; but I have been brought up better than that, he won't hurt me. I should think you would trust me ; I might do him some good.'

' Walter,' said his mother, ' take this glass of pure water, and put just one drop of ink in it.'

' Oh ! mother, who would have thought one drop would blacken the whole glass so ! '

' Yes, it has changed the colour of the whole, has it not ? It is a shame to do that ; just put a drop of clear water in it, to restore its purity,' said Mrs. Kirk.

' Why, mother, you are laughing at me ! One drop, nor a dozen, nor fifty, won't do that.'

' No, my son, and therefore I cannot allow one drop of Will Hunt's evil nature to mingle with your careful training ; many drops of which will make no impression on him.'

And this was perfectly true. In the chemical laboratories of our colleges, there are many experiments made which show us the wonderful power of a single drop of poison. A great bottle of colourless water will become a thick and clouded white in an instant by the addition of a single drop of the prepared chemical ; and one drop of poison such as strychnia will paralyze in an instant, a living being—such as the gold-fish, turtles and tadpoles, which we see in a vase of water.

But none of these poisons are so powerful as the poison of sin. St. James says in his Epistle : 'Then when lust hath conceived, it bringeth forth sin : and sin, when it is finished, bringeth forth death' (James i. 15).

I was reading, some time ago, a story which shows us the poisoning power of sin.

A man who wished to buy a handsome ring, went into a jeweller's in Paris. The jeweller showed him a very ancient gold ring, remarkably fine, and curious on this account, that on the inside of it were two little lion's claws. The buyer, while looking at the others, was playing with this. At last he purchased another, and went away. But he had scarcely reached home, when first his hand, then his side, then his whole body became numb and without feeling, as if he had a stroke of palsy ; and it grew worse and worse, till the physician, who came in haste, thought him dying.

'You must have somehow taken poison,' he said.

The sick man protested that he had not.

At length some one remembered this ring ; and it was then discovered to be what used to be called a death-ring, and which was often employed in those wicked Italian States three or four hundred years ago. If a man hated another, and desired to murder him, he would present him with one of them. In the inside was a drop of deadly poison, and a very small hole out of which it would not make its way except when squeezed. When the poor man was wearing it, the murderer would come and shake his hand violently, the lion's claw would give his finger a little scratch, and in a few hours he was a dead man.

Now you see why I tell you this story. For four hundred years this ring had kept its poison, and at the end of that time it was strong enough almost to kill the man who had unintentionally scratched his finger with the claw ; for he was only saved by great skill on the part of the physician, and by the strongest medicines. I thought, when I read that story, how like this poison was to sin. You may commit a sin now, and for the present forget it ; and perhaps, ten or twelve years hence, the wound you then gave yourself may break out again, and that more dangerously than ever. And the greatest danger of all is lest the thoughts of sin we have committed, and the pleasure we had in committing them, should come back upon us in the hour of death.

The second lesson which we learn from the scorpion—is the lesson of the poisoning power of sin.

The third and last lesson that we learn from the scorpion is—
THE LESSON OF THE MISERY OF SPITEFULNESS.

There is nothing in life so miserable and contemptible as the spirit of spitefulness; that is, the spirit of envy at another's success.

There is something spiteful and venomous about the bite of an insect or reptile; a bite from a mosquito, a spider, or a snake will always make us think of the *spitefulness* of the creature that has bitten us.

The wasp and the hornet seem spiteful in their hate; while the busy bee gives us his buzz as a note of warning.

I was reading some time ago a story of how a boy secured a prize through spite. He had passed every other boy in the class, with the exception of one student, whom he never could excel. Do what he would, he had to come in second with his hated rival always first. At last he discovered that his antagonist had a way of fingering a certain button on his coat, the top button on his jacket, and that when he was reciting or speaking a piece for a prize, or coming in to an examination, he would be always fingering this top button.

One day, as they were going into the examination room, this envious boy clipped off the button with a pair of scissors unknown to his companion, and when the boy came to make his recitation, and found that his metal button was gone, he was thrown off his guard, stumbled—faltered—took his seat—and failed! His rival gained the prize, but he gained it because of the scorpion-like sting of spitefulness, whereby he overcame his adversary.

I was reading the other day a story of the effect of spitefulness, or how it was that a girl suffered from retributive providence.

'Three girls were schoolfellows, two of whom by superior goodness and diligence advanced rapidly in their classes. The third, too indolent and careless to endeavour to excel, notwithstanding indulged in the most evil feelings against her more fortunate companions. She hated the one who bore off the premiums, and envied the other whose amiability had won for her the love of the whole school. Day by day these wicked passions grew stronger in her breast, until they ended in a burning desire to revenge herself on her innocent schoolfellows, who had no suspicion of her feelings with regard to them, but ascribed her dark looks and bitter words to ill-temper. The wretched girl, in her desire for vengeance, determined upon a plan as cruel as it was awfully wicked, and with desperate coolness she pursued her design. At various times she procured small quantities of poison, until she thought she had obtained sufficient to destroy life, and then watched for a favourable opportunity to bring her design to bear. It came sooner than she had hoped for, for the girl who had incurred her hatred had taken cold, her amiable friend attending upon her with a sister's care. One evening, as she was preparing a cooling drink for the invalid, the miserable victim of envy took advantage of a moment when her attention was withdrawn, and mixed the deadly poison with the drink.

Quite unsuspicious of what had taken place, the kind-hearted girl bore the drink to her friend, who, fortunately for herself, had fallen into a profound sleep. A servant, coming into the room soon after, carried away the cup with others.

Fancying the draught was already doing its deadly work, the would-be murderess was proceeding to her room, when, passing an open door, she saw a cup of lemonade, as she thought, on a table, and, feeling thirsty, she drank it and hastened up-stairs. But judgment had overtaken her; it was the very drink she had poisoned for the invalid, and of which, with such consummate art, she had made her friend the bearer, intending her to fall under suspicion of the deed.

Sharp screams of anguish soon rang through the house as the poison began to take effect; and when both the objects of her rancorous feelings stood with the other inmates of the house beside the dying girl, they were horrified to learn from her lips the fate she had designed for them, and to see the awful malignity of the looks she cast upon them.

Death itself did not obliterate the traces of her violent sufferings, which left their mark on her distorted face, made still more frightful by the stamp of hate and envy.

These, then, are the lessons which we learn from the venomous scorpion, whose sting is in its tail, and who is itself the very embodiment of venom.

First, we learn *a lesson of the hidden power of venom.*

Second, we learn *a lesson of the poisoning power of sin.*

Third, we learn *a lesson of the misery of spitefulness.*

It is said of St. Patrick, the apostle to Ireland, that he drove out the snakes from that country.

Let us learn to drive the serpents and scorpions out of our own nature, and to realize our Lord's words when He said,—

'Behold, I give unto you power to tread on serpents and scorpions, and over all the power of the enemy, and nothing shall by any means hurt you.'

XIV.

THE DOVE.

'Be ye harmless as doves.'—MATTHEW x. 16.

THE dove is oftener mentioned in the Bible than any other bird, or than all the other birds put together.

We find it spoken of for the first time in the eighth chapter of Genesis. The deluge had then taken place, by which all the inhabitants of the earth had been drowned except Noah and his family, who were saved in the ark. After the waters of the flood had been decreasing for some time, Noah wanted to find out whether the earth was dry enough for himself and family to leave the ark, and venture on the land again. He first sent forth a raven to find out how things were on the land. But the raven kept on flying about, and did not return to the ark. Then he sent out a dove, and finding that the earth was still covered with water, and that there was no place where it could rest, the dove returned at once to the ark. It had nothing to say to Noah, but he understood what was meant by its coming back to him. After this he waited for seven days more, and then sent out the dove again. In a little while it came back to the ark once more, holding the leaf of an olive tree in its bill. On seeing this, Noah knew that the water was gradually going off, and that the trees were beginning to appear. After this he waited seven days more, and then sent out the dove again. But, finding that the earth was dry, the dove lodged on the branches of the trees, and did not return again to the ark. Then Noah knew that the waters of the flood had disappeared from the earth, but still he waited till God told him to take his family and go out of the ark.

The dove was the only one among all the birds that was allowed to be offered as a sacrifice to God. When infants were presented for the first time to God in the temple, if their parents could afford it, they were required by the Jewish law to offer a young lamb as a sacrifice. But if they were too poor to buy a lamb, they were allowed to bring two doves as a sacrifice instead of the lamb, as they were much cheaper. When our blessed Saviour, as an infant, was first presented to God in the temple at Jerusalem, His parents could not afford to buy a lamb for a sacrifice, and so, instead of that, they offered a pair of turtle doves. And thus the dove was connected in this interesting way with the early history of our Saviour.

And when He became of age, and was about to enter on His

public ministry after He had been baptized in the river Jordan by John the Baptist, we are told that the heavens were opened above Him, and the Holy Spirit came down in the shape of a dove, and abode upon Him. And it is pleasant to find the dove connected in these two ways with the person and work of Jesus.

The dove is not a large bird. It is about the size of an ordinary pigeon. But it has a pleasing shape, and its colour is very beautiful.

David speaks of the dove's wings as looking like silver and its feathers like gold (Psalm lx. 13).

Our sermon to-day is about the lessons taught us by the dove. And in studying the habits and character of the dove, we find illustrations of three good lessons.

The first of these is—THE LESSON OF GENTLENESS OR KINDNESS. When we look at the dove, it seems to stand before us as the very image of kindness and gentleness.

Compare the dove with the eagle or the hawk, and how very different it appears! When we look at the strong beak or the great sharp claws of the eagle or the hawk, we see in a moment that they were made for fighting. But it is very different with the dove. It has no strong beak, and no great sharp claws. This shows that fighting is not the dove's mission in life. It is gentle, and loving, and kind. Here is an illustration of this. We may call it—

THE CRIPPLED DOVE.

One day a dove was flying about, trying to get food for her young ones in the nest. While it was thus engaged, a boy who was passing along threw a stone, and hit it on the wing. This crippled the poor bird, and it fell to the ground. That boy ought to have been ashamed of himself. He did not belong to 'The Band of Mercy,' or else the pledge of that band—'I will try to be kind to all living creatures, and protect them from cruelty'—would have kept him from throwing that stone.

The poor bird lay fluttering on the ground, and trying in vain to get back to its nest. Presently some of its mates gathered around it, and seemed anxious to help it; but they could not tell how to do this. Their cooing and chattering drew together a number of their companions from a large dove-cot near by. One seemed to think that this ought to be done, and another that something else would be better. Some tried to lift the helpless bird by taking hold of its wings with their beaks. But they could not do this; so they kept on cooing and chattering.

Presently two of the birds flew away, but came back in a little while, bringing with them a twig about six inches long and an ·eighth of an inch thick. They laid this down before their poor crippled companion, and got her to take hold of it at one place with her beak, and at another with her two claws. Then two of the larger birds each took hold of one end of the twig, and, rising on their wings, bore their wounded mate home to her nest ; and as they laid her down there, she cooed and chirped out her thanks to them in the liveliest possible way.

And when we learn this lesson of gentleness, or kindness, which the dove teaches us, we shall find it very useful. Here is an illustration of this. We may call it—

USING THE OIL.

'I was trying, one day,' says a mechanic, 'to drive an iron bar through a heavy piece of timber. I bored a hole of the right size, but the bar was rusty, and the hole was rough. I kept on pounding away, but made slow progress, and I saw that the wood was beginning to split. Then I thought of the oil can. I got it, and oiled the iron bar, and poured some oil into the hole, and then a few blows of the hammer sent the iron through to its place, without any trouble.'

The oil had not lessened the size of the bar, nor increased that of the hole. It had only relieved the friction. It had smoothed both the surfaces. A few drops of oil were more effective than many blows of the hammer would have been. And so, if we learn to make a right use of the oil of kindness, or gentleness, we shall find it a great help to us in boring our way through the troubles and trials of our daily life.

I have just one other story to tell here. This shows us how much good may be done by a little use of the oil of kindness. We may call it—

COALS OF FIRE.

Farmer Dawson kept missing some corn, that was taken every few nights from the crib in his barn, although the door was well secured with lock and key.

'Who can have stolen it ?' asked his wife.

'It's that lazy Tom Slocum,' he said. 'I've suspected him all the time, and I won't bear it any longer !'

'What makes you think it's Tom ?' she asked.

'Because he's the only man around who hasn't any corn, or anything else, indeed. He spent last summer in the saloons, while his neighbours were at work. Now they have plenty, and he has nothing.'

'But his family are suffering,' said the wife. 'They are sick, and in need of food and medicine. Don't you think we ought to help them?'

'No!' said the farmer; 'for if he finds that we take care of his family, it will encourage him to spend the next summer as he spent the last. The best thing will be to send him to jail, and his family to the poorhouse, and this is what I'm going to do. I've laid a plan to trap him this very night.'

His wife pleaded earnestly with him for Tom's poor family, and begged him to try the Scripture rule of heaping coals of fire on his head, by showing him kindness. As her husband went out of the house, she said,—

'Do try the coals of fire first.'

The farmer went to examine his barn, and find out how the corn was stolen. Very soon he found a hole near the crib, large enough for a man to put his hand through. So he set a trap inside of the hole, which would catch the thief's hand as soon as it was put through the hole, and keep him there till the trap was unfastened.

Early the next morning he started for the barn, to see what had taken place. On his way there, he said to himself, 'Shall I try my plan or my wife's? Will the jail or the coals of fire be the best? I think I'll try the coals.'

On reaching the barn, he found Tom Slocum with his arm through the hole, and his hand caught in the trap.

'Hullo, neighbour, what are you doing here?' he asked.

Poor Tom felt too much ashamed to say anything.

Farmer Dawson loosed his hand from the trap, and, taking Tom's sack, told him to hold it, while he filled it with the grain which he desired.

'There, Tom, take that,' said the farmer; 'and, after this, when you want corn, come to me, and I will let you have it on trust, or for work. I need another hand on the farm, and will give you steady work with good wages.'

'Oh, sir!' said Tom, quite overcome, 'I've been wanting work, but no one would hire me. My family are suffering, and I am ashamed to beg.'

'Very well, Tom,' said the farmer; 'now take this corn to the mill, and make things comfortable about home to-day, and to-morrow we'll begin. But there's one thing we must agree about first.'

Tom looked at him earnestly, as if he meant to say, 'And what's that?'

'You must let whisky alone,' said the farmer; 'and promise me never to take another drop.'

The tears sprang into Tom's eyes, and his voice trembled as he said, 'You've been so kind to me, that I am willing to do

L

anything you ask me. I make the promise now, and, by the help of God, I'll try to keep it.'

Farmer Dawson took Tom to the house, and gave him his breakfast, while his wife put up a basket of food for the suffering family in the poor man's home.

Tom went to work the next day, and kept steadily on with it. He stopped drinking and stealing, attended church and Sunday-school with his family, and became a respectable and useful member of society.

'How changed Tom Slocum is from what he once was!' said the farmer's wife one day.

'Yes,' replied her husband. 'It was the coals of fire that did it.'

The first lesson we learn from the dove is—the lesson of gentleness, or kindness.

The second lesson we may learn from the dove is—THE LESSON OF FAITHFULNESS.

Some of the Jewish writers have had a good deal to say about the reason why the dove was chosen by God to be used in sacrifice to Him, rather than other birds; and the reason they give for it is,—that the habits and character of the dove are so different from those of the others. There is the raven, for instance, and other birds of its tribe, as the crow and the magpie. These are all cunning, and deceptive, and thievish. But the dove, on the other hand, is always kind, and loving, and true. When a male and female dove agree to live together as heads of a family, they never change, but remain true and faithful to each other as long as they live.

And then they show the same faithfulness in the care of their little ones. Here is a good illustration of this part of our subject.

We may call it—

THE DOVES' FAITHFULNESS TO THEIR YOUNG.

A gentleman in New Hampshire had a large dovecote near his house, in which he kept a number of doves; and he gives this account of an incident which took place one winter in connection with those doves.

Two of them had built their nest in the top storey of the dovecote, and had hatched their young ones, which came out of the eggs about the middle of February 1876.

On the seventeenth day of that month, a very severe snowstorm set in at the close of the day. Now the door of the dovecote looked towards the north-west. That was the quarter from which this storm was coming, so that the snow was blowing directly into the door of the dovecote in which these little ones, only a few days old, were lying.

The storm was very severe. It was the worst that had been known in that part of the country for many years. Exposed to that heavy storm, the young doves would have been frozen to death, if it had not been for the faithfulness of the father-bird in trying to protect them. He stood in the doorway of his little home with his back toward the wind. He spread out his tail, so as to cover up the door, and kept fluttering his wings to shelter his poor little ones from the snow, and keep the cold wind from blowing on them.

If it had not been for the faithful efforts of that father-bird, the little doves would all have been frozen to death. He stood there for hours with his tail and back all covered with the cold snow, and yet perfectly willing to bear all the suffering which it brought upon him, for the love which he had for his young ones, and his desire to protect them from harm.

Certainly this was a very good illustration of the faithfulness of that dove. And the lesson thus nicely illustrated is one of the most important lessons for us to learn in the discharge of all our duties. Our success in life depends on this more than anything else.

Here are two other illustrations of the good that resulted from learning and practising the lesson of faithfulness.

The first of these may be called—

THE REWARD OF FAITHFULNESS IN A GREAT THING.

The great thing here referred to was the proper observance of the Fourth Commandment, about keeping the Sabbath-day holy.

'It was late one Saturday evening,' says an English gentleman, 'when the stage in which I was travelling, over an American road, stopped, as I thought, only to change horses.

'"How long do you stay here?" I asked the driver.

'"Until morning," was his answer.

'This was a great disappointment to me. The little town to which I was going was only about twenty miles farther, and I wanted very much to get there that night. I made up my mind to try and hire a private carriage, and finish my journey before the Sabbath began. But I found it was impossible to do this. Then I concluded to spend the Sabbath there, before journeying any farther.

'At the hotel where I was staying, I met a merchant whom I knew. Like myself, he was a professing Christian, but his views about the Sabbath were very different from mine. I found that he was going to start on his journey the next

morning, which was Sunday, and he tried to persuade me to
do the same. We had a long argument on the subject, bu
could not agree about it. He told me that if I didn't start on
Sunday morning, I should not be able to go till Wednesday
I told him I would rather wait that long, than dishonour Go
by breaking the Sabbath.

'We each pursued our own course ; but see what the resul
was. He started on his journey the next morning. At the
close of the day, just as they came in sight of the town to
which he was going, the stage was attacked by robbers, and
the Sabbath-breaking merchant lost a large sum of money
which he had taken with him for making purchases. That wa
the result of his unfaithfulness to God's command about the
Sabbath.

'I stayed in that village till the following Wednesday,' say
this gentleman, 'and while there, I made the acquaintance o
several persons, who have been warm friends of mine eve
since ; and I was able to make arrangements for starting a
Sunday-school on the next Sabbath. It was greatly needed
there, and proved a blessing to the village. That was my
reward for honouring God's holy day.'

God's command about the Sabbath is a great thing. And
thus we see how faithfulness in this great thing was rewarded.

And here is an incident that shows us how faithfulness in a
little thing was rewarded.

This story is told by a New York merchant.

'One morning, some years ago,' says this gentleman, 'I wa
preparing to go down town to my business, when the servan
told me that a man was waiting at the front door to see me.

'"Tell him I'll be down in a moment,' I said.

'On going to the door, a man of tall stature and healthy
look called me by name, and asked me for help, saying that h
had a large family and a sick wife, and no means to get foo
for them.

'"You seem to be strong and healthy ; why don't you work ?'
I asked.

'"Simply, sir, because I cannot get work."

'"If I give you work, what pay do you want?"

'"Anything, sir, you please to give me, so that I can only
get help for my suffering family."

'I thought I would try and find out if he really meant wha
he said. "Very well," I said ; "I will give you twenty-five
cents an hour if you will carry a brick on your arm around
this block for five hours without stopping."

'"Thank you, sir ; I will do it."

'I got a brick, and placed it on the man's arm, started him
on his walk, and then went down town to my business.

'I never supposed for a moment that the man would keep on all day doing what he had promised to do. I did not expect to find him there when I came back in the afternoon. But, as I came in sight of my house, I saw him walking steadily along, with the brick on his arm. The neighbours were looking at him from their windows and doors as he paced along; some thought he was crazy, and a lot of boys were following him and making fun of him. But if any one spoke to him, his only answer was,—

'"Don't stop me; it's all right."

'I went up to him, and, taking him quietly by the arm, walked with him to my house. The poor fellow was very tired. I gave him a seat in the hall, and asked my servant to bring him something to eat. Then I gave him a dollar and a half for what he had done. He told me that in one of his walks a lady came out of a house and asked him what he was carrying that brick for. He told her the reason, and she gave him a dollar. And when it was known why he was doing this, small sums of money were given him by different persons, so that it had been quite a profitable day to him. "But what am I to do to-morrow?" he asked.

'"Why," I said, "go to some of the persons from whom you received help to-day, and ask for work, and come to-morrow afternoon and tell me how you get on."

'The next afternoon he came, and told me that he had found steady employment at a store in the neighbourhood, for a dollar a day. Before leaving, he asked for the brick which had made him so successful. I gave it to him, and he took it home. Not long after, he called again, and told me that he then had a better situation in a larger firm, where his salary was a thousand dollars a year.

'Three or four years after this,' said the gentleman, 'I was riding in a street car, when a well-dressed man spoke to me, with a smile, and asked if I knew him. Seeing me hesitate, he said, 'Don't you remember the man who carried the brick?' He then told me that he was now doing a prosperous business on his own account, that he had laid up considerable money, and was going to build a nice house for himself up town.

'"And what became of the brick?" I asked.

'"That brick, sir, has always occupied a place on our mantel-piece. We value it as the most precious of all our possessions. It has made our fortune."'

But it was not the brick which made that man's fortune. It was God's blessing on his faithfulness in doing his duty, that made him so successful. And if we learn to be faithful, we may be sure that God will bless us.

The second lesson we learn from the dove is—the lesson of faithfulness.

The third lesson we may learn from the dove is—THE LESSON OF PEACEFULNESS.

The dove, with an olive leaf in its bill, is always considered as the emblem of peace. There is something peaceful in the very appearance of the dove. Its nicely rounded form, the smoothness of its feathers, and the calm, quiet expression of its eye, all seem to tell of peace. And then the soft, low, gentle voice, with which we hear it cooing, always suggests the idea of peace. Audubon, the well-known traveller and ornithologist, tells a story that comes in very well to illustrate this part of our subject. We may call it—

THE PIRATE AND THE DOVES.

'I knew a man,' says Mr. Audubon, 'who had been connected with a band of pirates for some years. At the time to which I refer, he was an honest, useful man, at the head of a happy family. In a conversation which I had with him on one occasion, he gave me this account of the way in which he was led to give up being a pirate, and lead a different sort of life.

'"Our vessel was anchored once, for some time, in a snug little harbour, on a good-sized island in the Gulf of Mexico, off the coast of Florida. We had several tents pitched on shore, and spent most of our time there. We used to get our supply of drinking water from a fountain that flowed out from a beautiful grove of trees, not far from our camp. In the grove surrounding that fountain, a number of doves had their nests. The gentle cooing of those doves used to have a strange effect on me. One day, having nothing to do, I went and took a seat by that fountain, and spent some time there in watching the motions of those doves, and listening to their voices. The soft, gentle, peaceful tones in which they were cooing, seemed to awaken my conscience. I thought of the quiet, peaceful lives they were living, and of the violence and wrong-doing that marked my own life. While thinking thus, the sense of my sinfulness overwhelmed me. Then I threw myself on the ground, and, bursting into tears, confessed my sins unto God, and asked Him to forgive me, and help me to turn round and lead a different life. Then I determined to take the first opportunity of leaving my wicked companions, and getting back to my family and friends. It was a hard thing to do, but, with the help of God, I succeeded in doing it; and now I am leading an honest, useful, happy life. And I thank God for making use of the gentle, peaceful voice of the dove to bring about this change."'

And this lesson of peacefulness, which the dove teaches, is one that we should all try to learn and practise. Jesus, our blessed Saviour, is called 'the Prince of peace.' The gospel which He preached is 'the gospel of peace.' When the angels sung their song of gladness over the birth of the infant Saviour, at Bethlehem, they taught us that the object of His coming was to bring 'peace on earth, and good will towards men.' And if we want to be true Christians, we must have a peaceful spirit, and speak peaceful words, and do peaceful works, wherever we go. Here are two short illustrations of the good we may do, if we learn and practise this important lesson of peacefulness. The first may be called—

THE PEACE-MAKING BOY.

Two boys, named Willie and Charley, the sons of pious parents, had a violent quarrel one day over a game of marbles, and separated in great anger with each other. But in a little while one of them got somewhat cooler, as he thought of the Bible command, 'Let not the sun go down upon your wrath.' Then, just before sunset, he went to the house of his friend, and knocked at the door. Charley opened the door, and, seeing Willie there, started back in surprise and anger.

'Charley,' said Willie, 'the sun will soon set. The Bible says we mustn't let it go down on our wrath.' And, reaching out his hand cordially to his friend, he said, 'I'm very sorry that I got so angry ; let us make peace, Charley.'

This touched Charley's heart, and, with his eyes full of tears, he took hold of his friend's hand, and shook it warmly, as he said, 'I thank you, Willie dear, with all my heart, for this visit.'

And so their anger was put away, and peace was restored between them, and they became warmer friends than they had ever been before.

The other story may be called—

A PEACEFUL SPIRIT DOING GOOD AND GETTING GOOD.

A poor crippled beggar, in the street of a large city, was trying to pick up some old clothes that had been thrown to him from a window, when a crowd of rude boys gathered round him. They mocked his awkward motions, and made fun of him, in his rags and helplessness.

Presently a noble little fellow came up, who had a real peaceful spirit, and, pushing aside the crowd, he helped the poor crippled man to pick up his gifts, and bound them in a bundle. And then, placing a piece of silver in the poor man's hand, he was hastening away, when a voice from an upper window was heard, saying, 'Little boy with a straw hat, look up.'

He did so, and the lady, leaning out from an open window, said earnestly, 'God bless you, my little fellow; and I am sure that He will bless you for your kindness to that poor man.'

Then she asked his name, and wrote it down, with his residence. This lady was the wife of a very distinguished man, and any boy would have felt proud to have her speak so favourably of him. And when that kind-hearted boy thought of the poor beggar's grateful look, then of the lady's smile, and her words of kind approval, and especially when he remembered the passages in the Bible in which God says, 'Inasmuch as ye have done it to one of the least of these my servants, ye have done it unto me,' and 'Blessed are the merciful: for they shall obtain mercy,' we can imagine how glad and happy he had made his own heart by the good which he had done to another.

Not long after this, the lady just spoken of heard that this kind-hearted boy had applied for a situation to a merchant who was a particular friend of hers. She went immediately to see him, and spoke of the boy in such warm, strong language, that he at once obtained the situation which he desired, and that was the beginning of a successful business life to him.

And when we think of the good which this boy did to another by his kindness, and of the blessing which it brought upon himself, we may well speak of him as illustrating the usefulness of each of the three lessons that we learn from the dove,—the lesson of gentleness, of faithfulness, and of peacefulness.

Where is our text to-day? Matthew x. 16. What are the words of the text? 'Be ye harmless as doves.' What is the sermon about? The lessons taught us by the dove. How many lessons did we learn from the dove? Three. What was the first? *The lesson of gentleness or kindness.* What was the second. *The lesson of faithfulness.* And what was the third? *The lesson of peacefulness.*

Let us all ask God to give us grace to learn and practise the three important lessons of which we have been speaking, and then we shall be useful and happy wherever we may be.

XV.

THE MONKEY.

'Bringing gold, and silver, ivory, and apes.'—1 KINGS x. 22.

WE come to-day to the most curious and interesting and amusing of all the creatures in the animal world. There is nothing in the animal world so funny as the monkey. He looks like an old man, and seems to know a great deal. The monkey cage at the Zoological Gardens is always the one where the children congregate most. The monkey is scarcely a Bible animal. Monkeys, as such, are not mentioned in the Old or New Testament.

But in the first book of Kings, and second book of Chronicles, the historian gives an account of the cargoes which were brought by King Solomon's fleet to Tarshish, the articles found in the ships being 'gold and ivory, peacocks and apes.' King Solomon must have had some great Zoological Garden, for which he was always collecting new material. He was continually bringing from the East, from India, and the Mediterranean ports, all sorts of curious and interesting objects, for his great city of Jerusalem, so that very probably the elephants and peacocks and monkeys which came to King Solomon's garden in Jerusalem, came from India or the large island of Ceylon.

It would be much easier to write five or six sermons about this animal, than to condense all that we can find about him into one discourse ; but we will try in this sermon to find out something about the monkey, and then—hard as it may seem— we will try to find the lessons which this curious teacher gives us. Of all the lower animals, the monkey race approaches nearest to the structure of man. Monkeys also possess a very large share of sagacity : they will act in concert with each other, and seem by nature devoted to mischief, apparently merely from the love of mischief itself. When they perform their tricks on people, they seem to enjoy the fun to the utmost.

I had a monkey once, which I kept in a large room in my house called the play-room. This monkey used to sit in the window and look at the people passing along the street. He would try to catch their glances, and would bow and make grimaces at them, as if he wanted above all things to make them laugh. Then he would hide thimbles, scissors, needles, prayer-books, Bibles, and everything he could get. When alone in the room, he would put these things in nooks and corners, where he thought no one would be able to find them ; and then, when any one would come into the room, he would sit upon his box, and look at the visitors as if waiting to see if they were not surprised at losing their valuables. My monkey's name was Jocko. We had a parrot in the same room, and Jocko tried the old story of pulling out the parrot's feathers, and in every way he seemed to think that the chief end of life was to make fun.

The word 'monkey' is derived from the word 'monakin,' meaning a little old man. The first person who ever described a monkey in the English language, called it a 'monakin,' because it was so much like a little old man. The word 'monkey' has come to stand in a great many ways for the thought of a little imitation of a larger thing. A monkey boat is a little boat; a monkey jacket is a little jacket; monkey bread is a little piece of bread; a monkey block is a small block used on shipboard; a monkey wrench is a little wrench, which is made in imitation of a larger one. So that the words 'to monkey' have come to mean 'to imitate,' and this is because one peculiarity of the monkey is his power of imitation.

The expression 'to pluck a crow' has come from the story of a monkey, who used to put a part of his food at the foot of a pole for the crows to collect; then the monkey would hide behind the pole, and would suddenly stretch out his arm, and seize one of the crows about the neck, and would deliberately climb up the pole again to his accustomed seat; there the monkey would slowly pick the feathers off the bird, one by one, until there were none left, and after this would throw the bird away. Of course, ever after, the other crows would avoid the plucked crow; and from this habit of the monkey the expression 'to pluck a crow' has originated.

Another expression which has its origin with the monkey, is the expression 'to make use of the cat's paw.' This story originated as follows : A monkey was left alone in a room where there were some chestnuts roasting on the stove. The monkey wanted to get them out of the frying-pan, but was afraid to put his soft paw into the steaming dish; so presently he got hold of the cat, and with her paw knocked the chestnuts out of the frying-pan.

And from this story has originated the expression 'to be made a cat's paw of,' by which is meant the habit of making use of another person to do an unpleasant piece of work for us.

The monkey is a great reader of human character, and can read the half-expressed emotions in the human face. An angry look at once puts a monkey on his guard. They are most unmistakeably the clowns of the animal world. Monkeys do not know how to fight, but they do know how to bully their fellow-beings by intimidating gestures.

Monkeys are great hands for quarrelling, and always talk

back, and keep on talking to the last. Their one idea of getting out of trouble is by running away. They are good hands to conduct a retreat.

They all steal, and delight in stealing. They are light-fingered gentry, and are first-class pickpockets. They get into no end of trouble by their curious habits of investigation. They are martyrs to free inquiry, as I once found out when I saw three monkeys in a cage, running around with a lobster's claw attached to their tails. They had been playing with the lobsters, and the lobsters had nipped them.

Monkeys have a wonderful power of simulating great passions and tender feelings.

A gentleman who knows a great deal about monkeys, says : 'Two years ago, I took temporary charge of a young chimpanzee who was awaiting shipment to the Pacific coast His former landlord seemed to have indulged him in his habit of rummaging boxes and coffers ; for when I attempted to circumscribe the limits of that pastime, my boarder tried to " bring down the house,"—metaphorically and literally,—by throwing himself upon the floor, and tugging violently at the curtain and bell-ropes. If that failed to soften my heart, Pansy became sick. With groans and sobs he would lie down in a corner, preparing to shed the mortal coil, adjusting the pathos of the closing scene to the degree of my obstinacy.

'One day he had set his heart upon exploring the lettter department of my chest of drawers, and, after driving him off several times, I locked the door and pocketed the key. Pansy did not suspect the full meaning of my act until he had pulled at the knobs and squinted through the keyhole. But when he realized the truth, life was not worth living ! He collapsed at once, and had hardly strength enough left to drag himself to the stove. There he lay, bemoaning his untimely fate, and stretching his legs as if the *rigor mortis* (stiffness of death) had already overcome his lower extremities. Ten minutes later his supper was brought in, and I directed the boy to leave the basket behind the stove, in full sight of my guest ; but Pansy's eyes assumed a far-off expression,—life had lost its charms ! The inhumanity of man to man had made him sick of this " vale of tears." Meaning to try him, I accompanied the boy to the staircase, and the victim of my cruelty gave me a parting look of intensest reproach as I left the room ; but, stealing back on tiptoe, we managed to come upon him unawares, and Pansy looked rather sheepish when we caught him in the act of enjoying an excellent meal.'

The monkey belongs to what is known as the 'Quadrumana,' or the monkey tribe. The quadrumanas, or four-handed animals, are familiarly known by the title of apes, baboons, and monkeys.

Although these animals can stand erect, their general attitude
is on all-fours, like other animals. The most accomplished ape
is but a bad walker when it discards the use of the two upper
limbs, and trusts to the support of the hinder legs only. However carefully a monkey may be educated, it never can stand
erect like a man. He imitates man, but he cannot do what
man does ; hence the very word which describes the monkey
class is the 'ape.'

There are many different species of the quadrumana, or the
monkey tribe. The Gorilla, the great big monkey that imitates
man ; the small black ape known as the Chimpanzee ; the
awkward, huge Orang-outang ; the dull, stupid Simang ; the
whiskered Gibbons ; the frowsy Budeng ; the Hoonuman ; the
Entellis ; the proboscis monkey, or Kahan ; the Colobas ; the
Grivet ; the Gueresa ; the Vervet ; the Patas, or red monkey ; the
Dianas, or hunting monkey ; the Maugabey, or dog-like monkey
called the Macaque ; the curious tailed Rhesus, or Bhunder
monkey ; the Maggot, or Barbary ape ; the whiskered Wanderoo ;
the dull Gelad ; the fierce Chacma ; the ugly Mandril ; the
trapeze-like jumping Chamech ; the Corta ; the dull Eniriki ; and
the melancholy, howling monkey ; the Sai ; the Teetee ; the
black Yarke ; the Night monkey, or Dour Ouclei ; the Marmezet ;
the Narakeena ; the Pinchai ; the rough Lemur ; the Loris ; the
owl-like Terziar ; the rabbit-like Galago ; the wolf-like Aye-aye ;
the squirrel-like Cayago ; and the monk-like Capuchin monkey,
—are some of the many varieties of the quadrumana, or the
monkey tribe. Monkey life, monkey nature, and monkey
habits, would form a book by itself.

I can but try in this discourse to give you some little account
of the habits of this most interesting animal.

Let us now leave the monkey, and try and find out some of
the lessons which this clown among animals teaches us.

The first lesson we learn from the monkey is—THE LESSON OF
IMITATING OUR SUPERIORS.

The monkey, as we have seen, is a great mimic. The hunters
of Brazil know what a propensity the monkey has for imitating,
and so take advantage of this habit to catch them. They have
lots of little boots made, about large enough to fit a monkey's
foot, and fill the bottom of each boot, on the inside, with soft
pitch. Provided with these, they set out into the woods, among
the trees where the merry little creatures have their head-
quarters, and are found leaping and swinging by their tails, and
chattering and making observations about everything that is
going on. The hunters are wise enough to know that they
might as well try to catch a bird on the wing, as to lay hands
on one of these active animals, so they sit down under the

trees—where all the monkeys can see them—and set the boots along in a row. The monkeys gather overhead to watch what they are doing; then the hunters pull off their boots, and place them beside the little boots. After letting them remain a while, they take them up, and, having carefully looked at them—while the monkeys in the trees are watching every proceeding—they slowly draw their own boots upon their feet, and hurry away into the thickets, where they cannot be seen, leaving the little boots standing in rows under the trees.

As soon as the hunters are out of sight, down come the monkeys. They look sharply at the little boots, then they take them up and feel them, then they smell them, and eye them over again; until finally they sit down—as the hunters did—and draw them on their feet. As soon as the boots are fairly on, the hunters rush out from their hiding-place. The monkeys take to the trees, but they find they cannot climb. They try to pull off the boots—as the men did—but they are stuck fast to their feet. So they fall easy captives to the cunning hunters, who bear them off in triumph.

One of the old doctors—an old Schoolman, as he was called—of the twelfth century, called Satan the 'ape of God.' He meant by this that Satan was continually imitating for evil purposes the works of the Creator.

Monkeys have learned a great deal by imitating man.

Two boys were once talking about the habits of the monkey, and this was their conversation:—

'I never saw anything so funny as a monkey,' said Arthur Blaine. 'He looks just like an old man, and seems to know so much.'

'Pedro is knowing enough, I tell you,' said Frank. 'He belongs to the organ-grinder, and dances, and goes about collecting pennies, and does ever so many queer tricks. I wonder where monkeys come from?'

'From Africa, and South America, and the East Indies. Sailors often bring them home.'

'I have the queerest stories about monkeys. They are full of mischief.'

'I heard a missionary once in Sunday school tell a real good monkey-story. He said a boa-constrictor—you know that is the largest serpent in the world—caught a monkey, and crushed him, and ate him. The poor monkey cried fearfully, and all the monkeys came to see what was the matter. They scolded and chatted, and flew around as if to see what they could do. Presently they all began to push at a great rock that hung over the place where the serpent was. Ever so many came to help, and they pushed and pushed until at last they started the rock, and down it came, crushing the great serpent beneath it.

'The missionary said the story had a meaning in it for us. One monkey could not have moved that rock, but the wise little creatures knew if they all pushed together they might. He said we had a great enemy, the great serpent, to destroy. One alone cannot move the rock that will crush it; but if we all work together, it can be done. God will help us. He will make us strong, and by and by the rock will move and fall, and this terrible enemy will be crushed.'

Here is another story, which we may call—

A MONKEY HERO.

A nobleman had a favourite monkey, a large orang-outang, which, you know, is the largest species of monkey, except the gorilla. This monkey was very much attached to his master, and to the baby boy, who was the pet of the whole family. One day a fire suddenly broke out in the house, and everybody was running here and there to put it out, while the little boy in his nursery was almost forgotten, and when they thought of him, the staircase was all in flames. What could be done?

As they were looking up and wondering, a large hairy hand and arm opened the window, and presently the monkey appeared with the baby in his arms, and carefully climbed down over the porch, and brought the child safely to his nurse. Nobody else could have done it, for a man cannot climb like a monkey, and is not nearly so strong.

You may imagine how the faithful creature was praised and petted after that. This is a true story, and the child who was saved was the young Marquis of Kildare.

It brings great power into our life to imitate the good, the true, and the brave. You remember it is the poet Longfellow who says in his 'Psalm of Life,'—

> Lives of great men all remind us
> We can make our lives sublime,
> And, departing, leave behind us
> Footprints on the sands of time.
>
> Footprints that perhaps another,
> Sailing o'er life's solemn main,
> A forlorn and shipwrecked brother,
> Seeing, shall take heart again.

We are always tempted to imitate those about us. Let us be careful whom we imitate. Let us learn to imitate only those who are worthy of our imitation.

The first lesson this mischievous animal the monkey teaches us is—the lesson of imitating our superiors.

The second lesson we learn from the monkey is—THE LESSON OF MAKING THE BEST OF OUR SURROUNDINGS.

In the New York Zoological Gardens there is a famous monkey, known as Mr. Crowley.[1] Why he is named Mr. Crowley I do not know, but this monkey is a most wonderful specimen of his race. He sits up at the table, and eats with knife and fork and a spoon, and drinks out of a tumbler; he uses a napkin also, and has a variety of accomplishments. Monkeys have a great deal of etiquette among themselves. They do not possess visiting cards, to be sure, but the correct mode in which your monkey announces his presence to the human visitor, is by dropping a piece of stick upon him. Perhaps he might consider the stick to be only a twig, falling in the course of nature, and so take no notice of it. Down comes another stick; and if that does not cause him to look up, several more are let fall upon him, until his attention is drawn to the assembly in the branches.

The monkey loves to be in his native forest, where he can swing from limb to limb, and climb from tree to tree; but when he is captured and made a prisoner, he learns to make the best of his surroundings, and teaches us, in this way, a lesson of accommodating ourselves to our lot. He very soon acquires an artificial taste for civilisation, and after a while prefers drinking tea and coffee and beer, to water. Indeed, the monkey, if let alone, will become a great toper, and is particularly fond of brandy.

There is something very kind and tender about the monkey, for all his mischief. I was reading, the other day, a story of a monkey, who made himself very much beloved on shipboard. He was petted a great deal by the sailors, and did not seem to have those bad traits which some monkeys have. His name, of course, was Jocko; all monkeys are named Jocko, as all the kings of Egypt were named Pharaoh, and the emperors of Rome named Cæsar.

The sailors liked him so much, they never treated him roughly; and he repaid them with love in return.

On board of the ship was a spaniel with her four young puppies. At first she did not like Jocko at all, and would not let him come near the place where she and her young ones were kept. She would show so much anger, that Jocko would keep away, and go to his friends the sailors.

But Jocko had as much desire to see and pet the pups as some little girls have to play with the babies. So one day, when the mother-spaniel was not present, Jocko went down to the place where the pups were cuddled together. Then, taking them up in his arms, he held them and petted them, just as if they were his own children.

[1] Mr. Crowley has unfortunately died since this was written.

While he was thus engaged, the spaniel came in, and, to her great surprise, saw her children in the arms of their nurse. Instead of being angry, she was so much pleased, that from that time forth she treated Jocko with great fondness. Often she would leave him to take care of her pups while she went off to walk about the ship.

This is a true story ; and it shows how, even among the lower animals, love will win love. Jocko loved the little pups, and the mother-dog loved him for loving her young.

It it a great thing in life to learn the lesson of contentment, and learn to accommodate ourselves to our surroundings.

Here is a fable which shows us the truth of this principle. It is called—

A CHEERFUL VIEW OF THINGS.

'How dismal you look !' said a bucket to his companion, as they were going to the well.

'Arrah !' replied the other bucket, 'I was reflecting on the uselessness of our being filled ; for let us go away ever so full, we always come back empty.'

'Dear me !' said bucket number one, 'how strange to look at it in that way ! Now *I* enjoy the thought that, however empty we come, we always go away full. Only look at in that light, and you will be as cheerful as I am.'

The second lesson we learn from the monkey is—the important lesson of taking a cheerful view of things, and making the best of our surroundings.

Even the monkey, after a while, becomes accustomed to his red and blue monkey jacket.

Let us learn to fit ourselves into our place in life, whatever it may be.

The third and last lesson which we learn from the monkey is— THE LESSON OF MAKING PLEASURE FOR OUR FRIENDS.

The monkeys certainly make it very lively for children at the Zoological Gardens and menageries. They believe in having as good a time as they know how. It does us good to see the monkeys make fun for us. We have reason to believe that God put that sense of fun in the monkey's nature, and that He has put that same sense of fun in us.

> 'God wants the merry, merry boys,
>   The noisy boys,
>   The funny boys,
>   The thoughtless boys—
> God wants the boys with all their joys—

That He as gold
May make them pure,
And teach them hardness
To endure ;
His heroes brave
He'll have them be,
Fighting for truth
And purity.
God wants the boys.

In a social gathering, in a certain town not long ago, the conversation turned to the prevailing tendency among men and women to fret over evils, whether imaginary or real.

A minister who was present related an incident in his own experience, the moral of which is too valuable to be lost.

At a celebrated watering-place he met a lady who seemed hovering on the brink of the grave ; her cheeks were hollow and worn, her manner listless, her step languid, and her brow wearing the severe contraction so indicative of both mental and physical sufferings, so that she was to all observers an object of sincerest pity. Some years afterward, he encountered this same lady, who was bright and fresh and youthful, so full of healthful buoyancy, and so joyous in expression, that he questioned himself if he hadn't deceived himself with regard to her identity.

'Is it possible,' said he, 'that I see before me Mrs. B——, who presented such a doleful appearance at the —— Springs several years ago ?'

'The very same.'

'And pray tell me, madam, the secret of your cure,—what means did you use, to attain to such vigour of mind and body, to such cheerfulness and rejuvenation ?'

'The most simple remedy,' returned she, with beaming face. 'I stopped worrying and began to live ; that was all.'

Many a time since that evening has this sentence recurred to me, when dejected, complaining spirits have passed before me. I wish that all the peevish world could take to itself this specific for its baneful diseases. It is so common for us to turn God's serene sky into blackness. So common to stand under all the bright, beautiful heavens, and, instead of looking straight up to the celestial blue, to interpose a sombre cloud, that our souls weave out of their own morbid tissues.

If fretting and worrying were a mitigation of our troubles, instead of an aggravation, there would be some shadow of excuse.

Our domestic wires are entangled ; the children are cross, the servants careless, everything seems to go wrong. A calm, unruffled temperament is potent to smooth and settle all these difficulties ; a perturbed spirit but adds to the confusion and

M

evil. We have incurred some pecuniary obligation to our neighbour, which we find it impossible to cancel at the promised moment. A depressed soul unfits us for labour, and puts the day of our freedom farther and farther off. A consciousness of our own integrity, a trust in God's blessing, a cheerful, earnest effort, will, in good time, unrivet our fetters, and bring us a grateful liberty.

The world slights us, and confers its favours upon our companions. A morose, irritable, and complaining temper sinks us still further into obscurity. An affable, kindly, and philanthropic character draws all men within the circle of its happy nature. The sadness that comes upon us through great trials is not easily set aside, but the cultivation of a cheerful spirit, even amid life's sorest troubles, is a Christian duty.

The monkey certainly teaches us a lesson of making it pleasant for our friends. Here are two stories which show us this.

A naturalist tells a curious story of a Londoner, occupying an elegant house with ample grounds, who bought a lively monkey, and brought him home dressed in hat, coat, and breeches. A terrier dog, belonging to the establishment, saw the monkey sitting on a terrace in the yard, and started for him. When he got within a few feet, the monkey sat so still and unconcerned that the dog was frightened. He also sat down, and for a minute or two they glared at each other. The dog was thinking of renewing the attack, when the monkey lifted his hat and bowed politely to him. This was too much for the dog, and he took refuge under the porch; as soon as he was gone, the monkey, who was really as much frightened as the dog, made lightning tracks up a tree.

The other story of the monkey is as follows:—

The servant of a medical gentleman, who was some time in India, caught a young monkey and brought it to his tent, where every care was taken of it; but the mother was so greatly distressed with the loss of her baby, that she never ceased uttering a piteous cry, night and day, in the immediate vicinity of the tent. The doctor, at length tired out with the constant howling, desired the servant to restore the young one to its mother, which he did, when the poor animal happily retired, and sped its way to the community to which it belonged. Here, however, she found she could not be received. She and her baby had lost caste, and, like the hunted deer, were beaten and rejected by the flock.

A few days after, our medical friend was astonished to see the monkey return to his tent, bringing the young one along with her. She entered the tent of her own accord, apparently very much exhausted, and, having deposited her young one, she then retired a few yards from the tent, and there laid herself down and died.

The body of the poor animal was found in a most emaciated state, starved, wounded, and scratched all over, so that there can be no doubt that she had been terribly maltreated by her comrades, and, finding no safety for herself or her offspring, returned the little one into the care of those who were the cause of her misfortunes.

My dear children, let us learn from the poor captive monkey, the lesson of making life pleasant for our friends and companions. The monkey, instead of regretting his loss of freedom, and sulking and moping in captivity, tries to do the best that he can to make his companions and friends who are around him happy, and in this way teaches us all a lesson in life.

These, then, I think, are the three lessons which we learn from the mischief-loving monkey.

First, we learn *a lesson of imitating our superiors.*

Second, we learn *a lesson of making the best of our surroundings.*

And third, we learn *a lesson of making things pleasant for our friends.*

The Apostle Paul says in one place, ' Be ye followers or imitators of God, as true children.'

Let the monkey stand in our minds as the model of the best imitators we find among our friends in the animal world. If we can imitate our Lord Jesus Christ, with but half the power with which the monkey imitates man, we will have learned the great lesson of the Christian life.

XVI.

THE DOG.

' Deliver my soul from the sword, my darling from the power of the dog.'—PSALM xxii. 20.

IN going on with our study of Bible Natural History, the last animal that we can consider is the dog.

In the Eastern countries, and in the days when the Bible was written, dogs were not much thought of. They were never properly treated by the people of those countries. The different variety of dogs that we are familiar with were not found in that part of the world. The little lap-dog, the terrier, the greyhound, the mastiff, the bull-dog, and the noble Newfoundland, were all unknown there. The dogs they had were of but one kind, and they were all hungry, half-starved, savage, and cowardly, and were more like wolves than dogs.

The Eastern people used to have a very poor opinion of dogs, and so, when the Prophet Elisha spoke to Hazael, who was soon to be made king of Syria, about the mean and cruel things thas he would be sure to do, he said to him, 'Is thy servant a dog, that he should do these things?'

But with us the dog is a very useful animal, and when properly treated he exhibits some of the noblest qualities that any animal can possess. Our sermon to-day is about the dog and the lessons we may learn from it. And there are four important practical lessons of which we find good illustrations in the habits and character of the dog.

In the first place, we may learn from the dog—THE LESSON OF COURAGE.

This is a very important lesson for us to learn. And God expects us to learn it. His command to all His people is, 'Be ye strong, and of a good courage' (Deut. xxxi. 6). And this command is repeated many times in the Bible. We cannot properly honour God, and do our duty, unless we learn to have a good courage. And the dog sets us a good example in regard to this matter.

The first story we have here may be called—

A BRAVE DOG.

The incident here referred to took place in the town of New Brunswick, New Jersey. A horse attached to a waggon, in one of the streets, became frightened, and started off in a run. The owner of the waggon was thrown from his seat, as the horse started, and was left lying on the street. The horse went galloping along, increasing his speed every moment, till he reached the corner of the next street. There a large Newfoundland dog made his appearance. He looked at the horse for a moment, and then sprang out into the street, and rushed towards the horse's head. The dog made repeated efforts by springing up to grasp the bridle firmly with his teeth. But he failed each time, and fell to the ground, narrowly escaping injury from the horse's feet. But the brave dog kept on trying, and at last, making an extraordinary spring into the air, he grasped the bridle firmly in his teeth, and, pulling down the horse's head, put a stop to his running away. As soon as this was done, the dog turned round quietly and walked away. But the people standing by, who had witnessed the dog's noble action, when they thought of the injury which might have been done by the runaway horse, felt disposed to praise very highly the conduct of the dog, for the greatest act of courage they had ever seen a dumb animal perform.

Our next story may be called—

HOW CARLO DIED.

Carlo was a very brave dog, belonging to one of the leading citizens in a New England town. He was very much thought of both by his master and all who knew him. An intimate friend of his master gives this account of him :—

'Carlo was in the habit of attending all the fires in the town. He could mount a ladder like a fireman, and I remember his adventures with very great interest.

'Once, on a public holiday, there were but few people about, as most of the citizens were absent on a popular excursion. Towards the close of that day the bells of the churches began to ring very loudly, as they always did when there was a fire. Carlo had been guarding the house and sleeping lazily. As soon as he heard the bells ringing, he knew that there was a fire. Starting suddenly up, he gave two or three loud barks to summon his master, and then started off as fast as he could run for the fire. On arriving there, he went to work at once, and busied himself very usefully all the time, dragging down-stairs, with great speed and care, articles of every description.

'As the last house in the row was burning, the cry of a child was heard in the upper storey. It was impossible for any one to make his way up the stairs, and expect to get back. Carlo had heard the child's cry, and seemed to take in the situation at a glance. Knowing in his dog's mind that the lower storeys were all in a blaze, he rushed to the ladder, climbed hastily up till he reached the third storey, and then jumped in through the window. The fire and smoke soon drove him back to the ladder. His master saw him at that moment, and shouted to him to try again, and the people cheered him loudly. He evidently understood what his master had said, for he entered the window again, and disappeared for some time. Then the anxious people began to give up all hope for Carlo or the child. But finally a loud shout announced his appearance again, bringing the child with him. He managed to get on the ladder. He was terribly burned. Before reaching the ground he fell, still holding on with wonderful firmness to the little child.

'The child was not much hurt, but poor Carlo's injuries were fatal. Every possible care was bestowed on the brave dog, but he died the next day.'

Here was a noble example of courage in that dog by which he saved the life of a dear child.

I have one other story for this part of our subject. It is about a brave young girl, and the great good which she did by her courage.

We may call it—

THE BRAVE KATE SHELLEY.

Kate lived in the town of Boone, in Iowa, near a railway bridge over a creek called Honey Creek. She was about sixteen years old when the event took place which called forth her courage.

It was the evening of the 6th of July 1881, when, just after dark, the severest storm of wind and rain ever known in that part of the country took place. In an hour's time the Des Moines river had risen six feet, and the creeks running into it were overflowing their banks. Looking through her window, which in the daytime commanded a view of the Honey Creek and the railroad bridge which went over it, she saw through the storm and darkness the headlight of a locomotive. In a moment it disappeared. She could not hear the crash which its fall must have occasioned on account of the terrible noise of the storm. But she knew at once that the bridge had broken, and that the locomotive with the train attached to it had plunged into the chasm below. Then she thought how surely the people on that wrecked train would perish unless help reached them speedily. And she knew that an express train would soon be due there, and that unless warned in time of that broken bridge, it would plunge into that deep chasm and be dashed to pieces. Her father was away from home, and there was no one to help her. If anything was to be done, she must do it herself.

So filling and lighting an old lantern, and putting on a waterproof, she started out in the storm. She got on the track of the railroad, and went towards the bridge, and found part of it still standing. Crawling along on it to the last tie, she swung her lantern over the abyss, and called out at the top of her voice. It was dark as midnight below, but she was answered faintly by the engineer of the wrecked train. He had climbed up on some of the broken timbers, and though injured was safe for the time being. From him the girl learned that it was a goods train which had dashed through the broken bridge, and that he was the only one of the train hands who had escaped. He urged her at once to hasten to the nearest station and get help for him, and have warning of the broken bridge sent to the approaching express train that it might be stopped in time to avoid a wreck.

The girl then went back over the broken bridge, and started to go as fast as she could towards the nearest station, which was about a mile distant. In making this perilous journey, it was necessary for her to cross the trestle bridge over the Des Moines river, which was about five hundred feet long. Just as she tremblingly stepped on this bridge, the storm was beating against her so fearfully that she nearly lost her balance, and in the effort to keep herself from falling her lamp went out, and she was left to make her way in the dark across that high bridge. How few persons would have had courage enough to go forward in the face of such appalling danger! But this was what that brave girl did. Throwing away her useless lantern, and dropping down on her hands and knees, she crawled from tie to tie across that bridge. On reaching the other side, she ran the short distance that remained, and soon reached the station. Then she told the story of the broken bridge, asked that help might be sent to the wounded engineer, and warning to the approaching express train, and then she fainted, and fell insensible on the floor of the station. She was kindly taken care of; help was sent to the engineer, and warning to the coming train.

Pretty soon that train came thundering along, but was stopped in time. And when the passengers heard the story of the broken bridge, and of the noble girl whose courageous conduct had saved them from destruction, their hearts were melted, their eyes moistened, and their purses opened; and they made up a generous offering to her as an expression of their grateful admiration of her noble conduct.

At the next session of the Legislature of Iowa, a gold medal, in memory of her brave conduct, was ordered to be prepared for her, and a committee was appointed to present it to her in the name of that body, and as an expression of their admiration of her conduct.

The courage of that girl saved a train from being wrecked, and scores of lives from being lost. Let us try to learn and practise the first lesson which the dog teaches us—the lesson of courage.

The second lesson we may learn from the dog is—THE LESSON OF INTELLIGENCE.

When told to do anything, the dog has a remarkable readiness for understanding what is said to him, and then for doing it. And this is just what God expects us to do. In the opening verses of the second chapter of Proverbs, He says to each of us: 'My son, if thou wilt receive My words, and hide My commandments with thee; if thou criest after knowledge, and liftest up thy voice for understanding; if thou seekest her as silver, and searchest for her as for hid treasures; then shalt thou understand the fear of the Lord, and find the knowledge of God.'

And the dog sets us a good example in the way of understanding what we are told to do, and of doing it. Here are some good illustrations of this.

The first may be called—

A DOG'S INTELLIGENCE.

A gentleman connected with the Newfoundland fishery had a dog of remarkable intelligence and fidelity. On one occasion a boat's crew in his employ were seen to be in circumstances of great danger. They were near a line of breakers outside of the harbour, over which the waves were dashing and roaring in great fury. The danger of passing those breakers was so great, that the men, brave as they were, did not dare to attempt it. A crowd of people stood watching them on the shore with great anxiety, but could do nothing to help them. Much time had passed, and the danger was increasing every moment.

Among the people on shore was the fishery master's great Newfoundland dog. He seemed to understand what the danger was. Presently he ran to the water, jumped in, and swam towards the boat.

He soon made his way through the surf, and the men in the boat saw him coming near to them. At first they thought he wanted to get into the boat, but it soon became evident that *that* was not his purpose. He did not come near the boat, but kept swimming round it. While doing this, he looked earnestly at the men, and would whine from time to time. The men wondered what he wanted. At last one of them cried out, 'Give him a rope; that's what he wants!' The rope was thrown; the dog seized the end of it with his mouth, and then turned round and swam towards the shore. The men waiting there took hold of it, and began to pull it, and in a short time the boat with its crew was hauled through the dangerous surf, and the men on board of it were landed safely on the shore.

And so the lives of that boat's crew were saved by the intelligence of that noble dog.

Our next story may be called—

A CLEVER DOG.

A young lady living in Shropshire, England, owned a very handsome brown terrier dog, whose name was Minto. He was a great pet with the lady and all her family, and though he was a very gentle creature to all whom he knew, yet to beggars or strangers who ventured on the premises of his mistress, he would be quite fierce.

On one occasion, Minto's mistress was greatly troubled because she had lost a gold locket which she wore, and valued highly, as it had been given to her by a dear departed friend. She remembered having the locket round her neck on the morning of that day, as she walked across a field in her father's grounds, where the grass was very high. After hunting everywhere else for the lost treasure, the thought occurred to her that perhaps she might have dropped it in the long grass, while taking her morning walk. So she set off at once for the field, followed by Minto, her faithful companion. She was in the habit of talking to the dog, just as she would do to any friend who was with her. In her distress she turned round to the dog that was close by her side, and said, 'Minto, can't you find my locket for me?'

Minto looked at her for a moment; then suddenly leaving her side, he ran on in front of her along the narrow path which led through the field, with his nose close to the ground, sniffing.

Presently the dog came to a tuft of coarse grass. He suddenly stopped, thrust his nose in among the grass, and then lifting up his head, gave a long, low howl. At first his mistress did not notice him; but after awhile his strange conduct excited her attention. On going to the spot where Minto stood, he came up to her looking very much pleased, and laid the gold locket at her feet.

Here we see the intelligence of that dog in understanding what his mistress said to him, and then going at once to do it.

I have one other story here, which we may call—

THE INDIAN AND HIS DOG.

A good many years ago, there was a farmer living in the western part of Pennsylvania who had a large family of children. One day the youngest child of the family, a little boy about four years old, whose name was Derrick, went into the woods near their house and was lost. This was a great grief to his father and mother, who were very fond of the child. The father got several neighbours of his to go with him, and then they went into the woods to try and find the lost child.

They spent the rest of the day in seeking for the child, but without success. When night came on, his neighbours went home, but the father refused to go. He got a lantern, and lighted it, and said he would spend the night in hunting for his child. The night passed wearily away, and the morning came, but the child was not found. Then the father went home to get something to eat before starting again on his search.

Just as he was getting ready to go, an Indian who lived in that neighbourhood, and whom they knew very well, called to see the farmer. The Indian had a dog with him that he was very fond of. On finding what the trouble was, the Indian asked the farmer for the shoes and stockings which Derrick had worn last. They were brought and given to the Indian. He held them out to his dog, and said, 'Rover, I want you to smell these, and then go into the woods, and try to find the child who has worn them.'

The dog looked at his master a moment, as if he meant to say, 'I know what you want, and I'll see what I can do to help you.'

Then he took two or three good smells of the shoes and stockings, and started into the woods.

Knowing that they could not keep up with the dog, the farmer and the Indian concluded to remain sitting in the porch till he should return. As they sat there they could hear him barking every little while. And in about an hour from the time he left, he came running back, wagging his tail, and looking very bright and happy.

'There!' said the Indian; 'he has found the child. Let us go with him.'

They went, and soon found the poor child, almost dead with cold and hunger, lying at the foot of a great tree.

What a happy day that was to the farmer and his family! and how much indebted they felt to that intelligent dog for the kindness he had done them!

In the language of one of the beautiful Collects in the Prayer Book, let us pray that God may 'enable us to perceive and know what things we ought to do, and also give us grace and power faithfully to perform the same,' and then we shall be really useful.

The second lesson we learn from the dog is—the lesson of intelligence.

The third lesson which we may learn from the dog is—THE LESSON OF AFFECTION.

Affection, or love, is the feeling which influences God in all that He is doing for our salvation. This is what Jesus taught us when He spoke these beautiful words: 'God so loved the world that He gave His only-begotten Son, that whosoever believeth on Him should not perish, but have everlasting life.' And as God acts on this principle Himself, so He expects us to act on it too, in what we do for Him, or for each other. And this is just what He means when He says to us: 'If ye love me, keep my commandments.' And it is always pleasant to have the lesson of affection, or love, taught us in the way of practical illustration.

We have many examples of this kind brought before us in studying the character and habits of the dog. Here are several incidents which give us good illustrations of this point.

The first may be called—

THE AFFECTION OF A DOG.

The captain of an artillery company of South Carolina was killed in a battle in Virginia during the American Civil War. His body was placed in a coffin, which was put into a strong box and carried to the home of his family in Columbia. It arrived there about a week after his death.

On his arrival, the captain's dog, that he had reared and petted during his life-time, was at the gate, and, approaching the house, began to smell about him with a good deal of excitement. When the coffin was taken from the hearse, he ran under it, and followed it to the house between the pall-bearers. Although a week had passed by since his master's death, and his body was closely fastened up in the coffin, yet, by the sense of smell alone, the dog had found out that it was his master's body which was in that coffin, and this stirred up all his affection for him. When the coffin was put on the table in the parlour, the dog lay down under the table, and remained there till the funeral took place on the next day. Then, after the funeral, the dog took his place on the grave of his old master. They tried to coax him away, but in vain. He would stay there. He refused to eat or drink, but lay moaning there till the third day after the funeral, when he died on his master's grave.

How real and genuine that dog's affection for his master was!

Our next story may be called—

A FRIENDLY DOG.

A lady in Yorkshire went to make a visit to her father's house shortly after her marriage. Her father was a farmer, and had kept three shepherd's dogs, as he had dealt a good deal in sheep. But, after his daughter's marriage, he gave up keeping sheep, and so he parted with all his dogs but one, whose name was Ponto.

This was one that his daughter had been very fond of, and always treated with great kindness. When Ponto saw his old mistress return to her former home, he was greatly delighted. He ran round her, and licked her hand, and jumped about her, and wagged his tail, and gave some gentle barks as if he was trying to say, 'You are welcome home, good mistress, and we are all very glad to see you.'

This pleased his mistress very much.

But the kindly feeling of Ponto led him to do something else on this occasion which was very remarkable. One of the dogs that used to live on the farm with him had grown old, and become blind ; and his master had secured a nice home for him with a friend, who lived about seven miles off. This dog's name was Carlo. Ponto was always very fond of him.

And Ponto felt sure that his old friend Carlo would be glad to meet his mistress once more. So he made up his mind to go over and tell him about it, and invite him to come and welcome their kind mistress back to her old home again. He did this, and Carlo went back with him. And the next morning, when the lady came down-stairs, and went out on the piazza of her father's house, there were the two dogs waiting to greet her. They jumped about, and wagged their tails, and gave gentle barks, to show how glad they were to see their old friend once more. And the lady was greatly delighted with what she saw.

Carlo spent the day with his friend, and in the latter part of the afternoon Ponto led him back to his own home. And in giving this expression of his affection for his mistress and his old friend Carlo, Ponto had to walk twenty-eight miles : That was noble in the dog.

I have one other incident to mention under this part of our subject. We may call it—

A DOG'S AFFECTION FOR A PIG.

A paper published in New Zealand tells this curious story. A farmer had a dog that he was very much attached to. One season this dog had become interested in a young pig that went about the barn-yard. He showed kindness to him, and would jump about him, and bark pleasantly at him, as though he wanted to be his friend.

There was a wide, deep creek that ran through this farm. The dog of which we are speaking had got into the habit of swimming across the creek, and amusing himself on the other side. One day, when he was going over, he got the pig to go with him. But when they came to the creek, what was to be done ? The pig couldn't swim, and there was no bridge to take him over. So the dog waded into the river, then he crouched down and motioned to the pig to get on his back. He did so, and then the dog swam across with him. After this they went over and back again together, in this way, almost every day, and enjoyed it very much.

How kind it was in that dog to treat the poor pig in this way ! These stories all show us the kindness of the dog, and they teach us the lesson of affection. This is the third lesson we learn from the dog.

*The fourth lesson which the dog teaches us is—*THE LESSON OF FAITHFULNESS.

The lesson of faithfulness is a very important one for us all to learn. Whatever other good elements of character we may have, they will all be of little use to us without faithfulness. Suppose we have a beautiful purse to put our money in. But, if there should be a hole in that purse, so that the money put into it would be sure to fall through and be lost, the purse would not be worth much. And, as the hole in that purse would injure its usefulness, so the want of faithfulness will injure our character, whatever other useful elements we may have.

And so it is always a useful and profitable thing to have examples of faithfulness brought before us. And in studying the history and habits of the dog, we find very good illustrations of this important element of its character.

Our first story may be called—

FAITHFUL TO HIS MASTER'S CHILD.

One day the engineer of a train of cars, near Montreal, in Canada, saw a large dog on the track. He was barking furiously, and leaping up and down, as if he wanted to give notice for the train to stop. The engineer blew a loud whistle to frighten the dog off. But he remained on the track, and, crouching down low, the train ran over him, and killed him. The train was stopped, to examine the case. They got down on the track, and there they found the dead dog, and a dead child lying under it. This child belonged to the dog's master. He had been playing on the track, and feeling tired, he lay down there and fell asleep. The dog, as we have seen, tried all he could to stop the train, but finding that he could not do this, he would not leave the child, but stretched himself over it, and they were both killed together. That was a noble dog! Our next story may be called—

FAITHFUL IN THE PANTRY.

After breakfast one morning, the servant who had charge of the pantry of a large farmhouse in England, locked it up for the rest of the day. In doing this, without knowing it, she had locked up in that pantry a great mastiff dog, belonging to the farm. On opening the pantry door at the close of the day, she was frightened when she saw the dog come out. She expected to find that great mischief had been done by the dog. There were pans of milk and loaves of bread and joints of meat there. But the dog knew that he had no right to use these

until they were offered to him.   And so, hungry and thirsty as
he was, he spent the whole day without touching one of those
tempting things.   What a lesson of faithfulness we have here !
Our next story may be called—

FAITHFUL TO AN UNKIND MASTER.

An English farmer had a dog that had been very useful to
him.   But the dog was getting old, and his master had made
up his mind to drown him.   So one day he took the dog with
him, and, getting into a boat, rowed out to a large stream of
water, near his farm.   He had a heavy stone tied to a cord.
He fastened this round the dog's neck, and then threw him into
the water.   The poor dog sank, but the cord broke.   Then he
rose to the surface of the water, and tried to get into the boat
again.   But his master pushed him off with the oar a number
of times.   At last he stood up with the oar in his hands,
intending to strike him a heavy blow, that would make him
sink to the bottom.   But in trying to do this, he lost his
balance, and fell into the water himself.   He could not swim ;
and when the dog saw his master struggling in the water, in
spite of the unkind treatment just received from him, he swam
up to him, caught hold of his clothes, and brought him safe to
land.   How noble this was in that dog !

I have just one other story here, and have kept it to the last,
because it is the best of all.   We may call it—

FAITHFUL IN DEATH.

A French merchant was riding home on horseback one day.
He had a large bag of gold with him, which was tied to the
saddle in front of him, and was accompanied by a faithful dog.
After a long ride, he stopped to rest himself, and eat a lunch
which he had with him.   He alighted from the horse, and sat
down under a shady tree, taking the bag of gold, and laying it
down by his side.   On mounting his horse again, he forgot to
take his bag of gold with him.   The dog saw the mistake his
master had made, and tried to take the bag to him ; but it was
too heavy for him to drag along.   Then he ran after his master,
and tried by barking to remind him of his mistake.   But the
merchant did not understand what the dog meant.   Then the
dog went in front of his master, and kept jumping up before
the horse and barking loudly.   The merchant called to him to
be quiet, and stop that jumping.

But the dog wouldn't stop.   Then his master was alarmed.
He began to think that the dog must be going mad.   And as the
dog went on barking and jumping with increasing violence, the

merchant felt sure he was right. He said to himself, 'He may bite me, or some one else. The only safe thing will be to kill him.'

Then he took a pistol from his pocket, and, pointing it to the dog, fired at him. The poor dog fell weltering in his blood, and his master, unable to bear the sight, put spurs to his horse and went on. 'I am very unfortunate,' he said to himself; 'I would rather have lost my bag of money, than my good dog.' Then he felt for his bag, but it was not there. In a moment he saw what it all meant. The dog had seen that he had left his bag of money behind him, and was trying the best he could to get him to go back for it, when he shot him! How sorry he felt!

Then he turned his horse, and rode back to the place where he had left his money. On reaching the spot he found the dog there. He had crawled back, all bleeding as he was, and had lain down beside his master's money to protect it. This brought the tears into the merchant's eyes. He kneeled down by his dog, petted him, and spoke kindly to him. The dog looked lovingly into his face, licked his hand, and then turned over and died.

The merchant had the body of the dog carried home, and buried in his garden ; and over its grave he had a stone slab set up, and with these words engraved on it :—

'IN MEMORY OF A FAITHFUL DOG.'

Where is our text to-day? Psalm xxii. 20. What are the words of the text? 'The dog.' What is the sermon about? The lessons we may learn from the dog. How many lessons have we learned from it? Four. What was the first? *The lesson of courage.* What was the second? *The lesson of intelligence.* What was the third? *The lesson of affection.* And what was the fourth? *The lesson of faithfulness.* Let us all try and remember these lessons, and ask God to help us to practise them, and then we shall find our study of the dog a profitable study.

And with this sermon on the dog we close this course of sermons on ' Bible Animals.'

OPINIONS of the BRITISH PRESS on DR. NEWTON'S BOOKS

'The bright sermons, studded with anecdote, will gain a loving hear[t] from the little people.'—*British Messenger.*

'A prince of preachers to children, for his sermons are full of illustratio[n] and his style is simple and bright.'—*Sunday School Chronicle.*

'Ministers, Sabbath-school teachers, and those who address childre[n] churches, will find much material to help them in the difficult work of prese[nt]ing religious truth in a form attractive to the young.'—*United Presbyter[ian] Record.*

'Those who have occasion to address the young will find it worth th[e] while to get the books.'—*Presbyterian Messenger.*

'Dr. Newton is well known to have that peculiar power of address[ing] children which, once acquired, seems never to be lost.'—*Scottish Sabba[th] School Teacher.*

'Write on, good Dr. Newton, our children will never grow tired of y[our] emblems and stories. Every teacher should read this book and then repea[t] to his class. Anything for the young by Dr. Richard Newton should within reach of every Sunday-school teacher and scholar.'—*Sword and Tro[wel]*

'Abounding in apt illustrations. Young people for whom they are intend[ed] will delight to read them; and those in search of books for reading to child[ren] would do well to get these.'—*Footsteps of Truth.*

'A delightful series of books for children by one who is almost unrival[led] in the art of entertaining and instructing them.'—*Sheffield Independent.*

'For clearness, simplicity, and vigour of style, together with wealth of illustration, there are no books for the young that "hold the field" w[ith] greater tenacity than those of Rev. Richard Newton, D.D. They are pack[ed] full of entertainment, always mingled with spiritual instruction of the b[est] sort; and the interest is kept up by the breadth of the field from which author gleans his anecdotes.'—*Christian Leader.*

'His books are all characterised by a true religious spirit, a high moral ai[m] a thorough understanding of child nature, and a happy knack of conveyi[ng] religious truths to childish minds.'—*Glasgow Herald.*

'Can scarcely fail to rivet the attention and reach the understanding children.'—*Scottish Leader.*

'The works of Dr. Richard Newton are well known as distinguished illustrative power and a very happy use of a large store of anecdotes. *United Presbyterian Magazine.*

'To Sabbath-school teachers in search of anecdotes to illustrate lesso[ns] these volumes will be of great use.'—*Arbroath Herald.*

'These are perennials of religious literature, and still hold their place the best of sermonettes for children amid all the matter issued for youth[ful] instruction.'—*Literary World.*

'Rich in striking lessons, interesting illustrations, and earnest pleadings. *Freeman.*

'Just the thing to put into the hands of the young folks. Dr. Newton [is] prince among writers to the young.'—*British Weekly.*

'Full of interest, instruction, and stimulus.'—*Christian News.*

'The name of Richard Newton is familiar to us as one of the most fam[ous] writers for young people. . . . Full of anecdotes and homely illustration, a[nd] will be of good service to Sunday-school teachers whether in the class or [at] desk.'—*Primitive Methodist World.*

'Excellently suited for young people.'—*Northern Ensign.*

'These volumes abound in religious instruction suitable to young perso[ns] and are presented in a form excellently calculated to engage attention.'—*T[he] Bookseller.*

OTHER RICHARD NEWTON TITLES

Solid Ground Christian Books are delighted to be able to offer all the following titles by Richard Newton, "the Prince of Preachers to children."

BIBLE PROMISES

BIBLE WARNINGS

THE SAFE COMPASS

RAYS FROM THE SON OF RIGHTEOUSNESS

THE KING'S HIGHWAY

HEROES OF THE EARLY CHURCH

HEROES OF THE REFORMATION

THE LIFE OF JESUS CHRIST FOR THE YOUNG

BIBLE ANIMALS

BIBLE JEWELS

Call us Toll Free at 1-877-666-9469
Send us an e-mail at sgcb@charter.net
Visit us at our web-site at solid-ground-books.com

Printed in the United States
91493LV00002B/241-246/A